AF437263

ANGLO-CATHOLIC CLASSICS

Writings produced, re-published or edited by the Oxford fathers (or their disciples) that underwrite the Anglo-Catholic tradition.

NASHOTAH HOUSE PRESS

Nashotah House Theological Seminary
2777 Mission Road
Nashotah, WI 53058

www.nashotah.edu

Cover design by Ben Jefferies

Printed 2019

THE REAL PRESENCE

OF

THE BODY AND BLOOD

OF

OUR LORD JESUS CHRIST

THE DOCTRINE OF THE ENGLISH CHURCH,

WITH A VINDICATION OF

THE RECEPTION BY THE WICKED

AND OF THE ADORATION,

OF

OUR LORD JESUS CHRIST

TRULY PRESENT.

BY THE

Rev. E. B. PUSEY, D.D.

REGIUS PROFESSOR OF HEBREW, AND CANON OF CHRIST CHURCH.

Third Thousand.

EAT, DRINK; HAVING IN THY HANDS JESUS CHRIST THE SON OF
GOD THE SAVIOUR.

Inscription at Autun in 2nd Century.

SOLD BY JAMES PARKER & CO., OXFORD,
AND 377, STRAND, LONDON;
RIVINGTONS, WATERLOO PLACE, LONDON,
HIGH STREET, OXFORD, AND TRINITY STREET, CAMBRIDGE.
MDCCCLXIX.

CONTENTS.

CHAPTER II.

PREFACE.

IT was my intention, in addition to the chapters here published, to have written three chapters 1) to vindicate the literal interpretation of our Blessed Lord's words, " This is My Body; " 2) to maintain the belief of the Fathers in the Real objective Presence ; 3) to contrast our English Articles on the Sacraments with the Confessions of the Zwinglian or Calvinistic bodies. But the effort, in the midst of my other duties, to complete this vindication of my belief, as a member and a priest of the English Church, before the trial of Archdeacon Denison should be concluded, has involved a strain, under which my health, for the time if it so please God, has so far suffered, that it becomes a duty to desist.

It was not of my own choice, that I vindicated the doctrine which I learnt from the Church of England, as being really contained in her formularies out of which I was taught and learnt it, before I fully vindicated the truth of that doctrine, as contained in Holy Scripture. For Mr. Goode had raised the question, whether others and myself were holding, or teaching " [a] doctrine consistent with our

[a] The Nature of Christ's Presence, p. 56.

position as *professed* members and Ministers of the Church of England." And "this enquiry," he had urged, "must be determined not by an appeal to Holy Scripture, interpreted by the private judgment of individuals, still less—by an appeal to the Fathers, but by an appeal to the authoritative Formularies of our Church."

Certainly, the question whether a person does, or does not teach in a manner consistent with the formularies of the Church, must be determined by an appeal to those formularies; nor can the appeal to Holy Scripture be admitted in such case, except to determine the meaning of phrases taken from Holy Scripture, if not already defined. Yet neither on the other hand, may the meaning of these phrases be " interpreted by the private Judgment of individuals," or by popular prepossessions. If any phrases which occur in our formularies are neither received Theological terms, as Consubstantial, Proceeding, Propitiation, Satisfaction, Regenerate, Everlasting, nor are determined by any authority of the Church, then, if they are Scriptural phrases, the appeal is open to Holy Scripture. They may not be strained by any private judgment or bias to any meaning, other than they have in Holy Scripture. This has been overlooked in the recent controversy as to the terms, both in the heading and body of Article xxix, "partakers of Christ," " eat not the Body of Christ."

Formerly I have not thought it necessary to vindicate the consistency of my belief with the formularies of the Church of England, because it never occurred to me that it needed vindication. I took and do take every letter of our formularies in what

I believed, and do now believe, to be their simple grammatical sense. I declared my belief[b], not many years since, in a formula, drawn up by a living and unsuspected writer in the words of those formularies. On one point only, what the wicked receive, I had not then come to any definite opinion, but had left it as a mystery.

Of the subjects which I am now compelled to delay, the only argument against the literal interpretation of our Lord's words, which seemed to me to require notice, lay, I regret to say, in a passage of Dr Waterland[c]. It too is capable of a ready answer. I will here only notice that he gives up as untenable, the application of "all metaphorical locutions," "when our Lord is styled a door, vine, a star, a sun, a rock, a lion, or the like;" and " the well-known instances of seven kine being seven years, and four great beasts being four kings, and the field being the world, reapers being angels, and the like ; which appertain only to visional or parabolic representations, and come not up to the point in hand."

When any have got thus far, little, I imagine, remains to be done. Our Lord's words will, I believe, carry their own conviction, except where there is a strong contrary prejudice ; and where there is, argument avails little, and God's enlightening grace must do all.

On the other main subject, the belief of the Fathers, Mr Goode's work is chiefly directed against that of the late Archdeacon Wilberforce, and only

[b] Letter to the Bishop of London, 1851, p. 62 sqq.

[c] Quoted by Mr. Goode, p. 67.

incidentally against mine. He heads his section, " review of the statements of those fathers who are chiefly relied upon by the Authors under review for the support of their doctrine," and then considers, more or less, ten of the fathers. In my own work, I had laid no special stress upon any father or fathers, but, extracting what had been said on the Holy Eucharist by ninety-one authorities[d], I rested, not on the authority or weight of any father, however distinguished, but on the consent of all. The simple and incidental testimony of female martyrs, or the striking testimony of the Greek inscription found at Autun[e], were as impressive to me, as the language of S. Chrysostome or S. Ambrose.

Mr. Goode, in his chapter on the fathers, has addressed himself, not so much to the consideration of what the fathers say directly on the Real objective Presence, as to prove that they believe certain other things, which he holds to be inconsistent with that belief. These I hope to consider, when it shall please God to give me health.

One argument, however, I will now consider, because it has always been the chief argument of the party which has disbelieved the Real Presence.

Mr Goode states it in two theses;

4) "'They [the Fathers] give us reasons why the

[d] Among these I do not include the strange agreement of Marcus the Gnostic, or Heracleon ; nor Adamantius, Eustathius, Palladius and Prudentius, whose statements I mentioned at their date, but from whom there is no testimony on the Real Presence extant ; nor the Synodical letter of the African Bishops in the works of S. Cyprian, whose doctrine is certain, but is not explicitly stated, so as to constitute a formal proof.

[e] p. 385 and 337. See the conclusion p. 717 sqq.   [f] p. 241.

bread in the Eucharist is called Christ's Body and the wine His Blood, shewing that they did not consider them to be so really, but only representatively." 7) "[g] Hence the Fathers themselves tell us, that it is customary to call the *signs* in the Eucharist, as in other cases, by the names of *the things signified* by them, the consecrated bread and wine being styled the Body and Blood of Christ as figuratively representing them."

Plainly, since the Holy Eucharist consists of two parts, "the earthly and the heavenly," as S. Irenæus says; "the visible and invisible," as S. Augustine speaks; the outward and inward part, as our own Catechism has it; the earthly, visible, and outward part can only improperly be called by the name of the inward, invisible, and heavenly part. But so to call the outward, visible, earthly, part, by the name of the inward, invisible, and heavenly, attests the close connexion between them; it cannot be an argument that there is no inward part. Nor is such the common usage of the Fathers. Rather they call the *whole* both outward and inward, by the name of that which gives the value to the whole, viz. the inward. This is common in Holy Scripture and in ordinary language. Thus, we have learnt from Holy Scripture to speak of men, as " souls." We say, "there are in such a place so many thousand souls." Holy Scripture forbids to "[h]steal souls," meaning " men." It says, "[i]give me the souls, and take the goods to thyself;" [k]all the souls which came

[g] p. 247.

[h] Deut. xxiv. 7. Heb. " If a man be found, stealing a soul of his brethren.'

[i] Gen. xiv. 21. E. M.

[k] Ex. i. 5.

b

out of the loins of Jacob were seventy souls," whereas what is derived from the parents is rather the rudiment of the body, into which God infuses the soul; "[l]these she bare unto Jacob, sixteen souls;" "[m]an omer for every man, according to the number of your souls," although the manna was food for the body. Nay, this idiom, by which "the soul" stands for the person, is extended so far in the O. T., that "the soul" is used of the "[n]dead body" from which the soul is separated, but to which it is one day to be rejoined. Further, in consequence of the close union of soul and body, what are affections of the body are said of the soul. The soul is said to be "empty," "have appetite[o]," "[p]be dried away," "[q]hungry," "[r]thirsty," "[s]fast," "[t]be satisfied," "[u]full:" and the soul is said to "[v]die," be "[w]slain," in places where clearly the death of the body alone is spoken of. Contrariwise, but on the same principle, the bones are said to "[x]rejoice;" [y]to speak unto God; the prayer, to return to a man's own bosom[z]; our Lord is said to "[a]bear in His bosom the reproach of all the mighty people."

The "flesh" is so taken for the whole man, that of the Incarnation of our Lord it is said that, "the Word was made Flesh[b];" and of us it is said; "by

[l] Gen. xlvi. 18. add 27.   [m] Ex. xvi. 16.

[n] Lev. xxi. 1; xxii. 4; Num. v. 2; vi. 6; ix. 6, 7, 10; xix. 13; Hagg. ii. 13.   [o] Is. xxix. 8.   [p] Num. xi. 6.

[q] Prov. x. 3; xxvii. 7.   [r] Ib. xxv. 25.   [s] Ps. lxix. 11. Heb.
[t] Prov. vi. 30.   [u] Ib. xxv. 7.

[v] Num. xxiii. 10; Jud. xvi. 30; Job xxxvi. 14; Jon. iv. 8.
[w] Jos. xx. 3. "That the slayer that killeth any soul." Heb.
[x] Ps. li. 8.   [y] Ib. xxxv. 10.   [z] ver. 13.
[a] Ib. xxxix. 50; lxxix. 12   [b] John i. 14.

the works of the law shall no *flesh*[c] be justified,"
"[d]that no flesh should glory in His presence." The
"heart" is, in all languages, used for the soul, in
regard to its affections.

The "communicatio idiomatum" rests on the same
principle, in that, "on account of the union of the
Godhead and Manhood of our Lord in One Person,
what belongs to His Godhead may be said of Him
as Man, what belongs to His Manhood may be said
of Him, as God[e]."

The character of the union in these cases is different, the principle is the same. In our Blessed
Lord, two perfect Natures are united in One Person; in ourselves, the two parts of one and the
same nature are united, in the one person of each
of us; in the Holy Eucharist, the Body and Blood
of Christ do not (as Mr. Goode often represents us
as teaching) form One whole, except sacramentally.
There is no physical union of the Body and Blood
of Christ with the bread and wine. Yet where the
consecrated bread is, there, sacramentally, is the
Body of Christ; where the consecrated wine is,
there sacramentally, is the Blood of Christ. And
so not the Fathers only, but the whole Christian
people of old as I said, called the whole by the
name of the inward part, which makes it what it is.

For it is not by chance or without meaning, that
all these titles are exchanged. Man is called "soul"
or "flesh," i. e. by his higher or lower part, as the
occasion suggests to speak of him, according to that
which is the noblest or that which is weakest in
him. The soul is said to be "empty" &c. in order to

[c] Rom. iii. 20.   [d] 1 Cor. i. 29.   [e] See below, p. 113.

b 2

express how the sufferings of the body extend even to the inmost self, the soul. Our Lord's Human sufferings are spoken of Him as God, in order to express the greatness of His condescension; His Divine attributes are spoken of the Man Christ Jesus ("the Son of Man Who *is* in Heaven"), in order to inculcate the greatness of the elevation of this our poor human nature in His Divine Person. So also as to the Holy Eucharist; the outward part or the whole Sacrament is named by the title of the inward, the Body and Blood of Christ, because in this is manifest the exceeding "love of God," that "He has given His Son, not only to die for us, but also to be our spiritual Food and sustenance in that Holy Sacrament."

"Almost all," says S. Augustine [f], "call the Sacrament His Body." True! but he does not say, that they call it so untruly. So again Theodoret repeatedly says that our Saviour "gave to the *symbol* the name of the Body." But the whole argument of Theodoret shows that he regarded these names, as belonging to two distinct substances, truly present in the Holy Eucharist. The heretic [g], in illustration of his heresy that our Lord's Human Nature was absorbed in His Divine, used an argument from the change of the consecrated elements. He argued that the elements were bread and wine before consecration, and after it, were changed and became other, since *then* they were no longer called bread and wine, but the Body and Blood of Christ. So, he contended, "the Body of the Lord was, after the

---

[f] Serm. 354, quoted Real Presence, p. 531. Mr. Goode, p. 247.
[g] See in Real Presence, p. 85.

Ascension, absorded into the Divine Substance." One who believed like Mr. Goode, would have answered this by denying the fact. He must have said, as he does say, that they were so called, as being such, " not really, but representatively." This would have equally met the argument of the heretic. But Theodoret's belief being different, he met the argument differently. He says, that the elements "[h] remain in their former substance," though they are also what they are believed. In another place, he says, that our Lord "[i] does not change the nature of the elements, but adds grace to the nature." In yet others[k], he says that our Lord said of the symbol "This is My Body."

As then we should not allow any inference which a materialist might draw from the passages which ascribe to the soul attributes which belong to the body; as we should not believe, on the ground of such idioms, that the O. T. taught that the soul dies; as we do not believe that Godhead is material, on the ground that Scripture speaks of the Blood of God, or that our Lord's Human Body was in heaven, while He was on earth, on the ground of His words, " the Son of Man Which is in Heaven;" so neither have we any ground to think that the Fathers disbelieved the Real Presence of His Blessed Body and Blood in the Holy Eucharist, on the ground that they, and the people generally, called the outward part by the name of the Inward. Rather, it is a proof the more of their conviction of that Presence, that they no longer thought of the outward elements, but called the whole by the name of that

[h] Ib. p. 86.   [i] Ib. p. 87, 8.   [k] Ib. p. 113. 675.

which was to them precious above all price, the
Body and Blood of their Redeemer. In ordinary
life we should think it pedantic, if any one were to
speak of "stirring the *red-hot coals*," or "the *coals
on* fire;" or of "going near to the *coals on* fire, in
order to be warmed." We drop the mention of the
outward part which contains the fire, and without
which the fire could not be, because it is from the
fire contained in them, that we gain warmth.
Why then should it be thought a strange thing that
loving faith ceased to speak of the outward elements, and only spoke of That through which
Christ dwelt in them and they in Christ?

Hence, in giving the Holy Eucharist to individuals, the words of old prescribed were, "the Body
of Christ[1]." S. Gregory of Nyssa in the East, and
S. Ambrose in the West, attest that, before the consecration, the elements are called by their natural
names; afterwards they are called what they "become," the Body and Blood of Christ[m]. And the
Fathers, apart from Communion, speak of the consecrated elements, as the Body and Blood of Christ,
because where they are, *there* are also, by virtue of
our Lord's consecrating words, His Body and Blood.
So far from this being a proof against the Real objective Presence[n], it is an evidence that the minds of

[1] See below, p. 174 sqq.

[m] See in Real Presence, p. 238, 293. The genuineness of the de
mysteriis was admitted unhesitatingly, by even Albertinus, p. 498;
nor am I aware that any one now doubts it, except Mr. Goode.

[n] Mr. Goode's 5th head of objections is made up of these
cases, in which Fathers speaking chiefly of the visible part of the
Sacrament, speak of it as the Body and Blood of Christ. See the
passage of Origen in the "Real Presence," p. 341; S. Ambrose, Ib.

those who so spake, were fixed solely on that unseen Presence. So in earthly things. If any one, without opening a casket, had said, " this is the Pitt diamond," no one would question his accuracy, because the visible thing to which he pointed, was the casket. So, as to all things of price, laid up in other things, we say, without fear of being misunderstood, " This is that costly wine," and the like, disregarding the vessel whose only office is, to contain it. S. John Baptist, when he pointed to our Lord, as the Lamb of God, was not hindered by the garb which enveloped Him. The Body and Blood of Christ are not present there, after the manner of a body. Yet it would not be true to say, " This is *mere* bread ;" for this would be to deny the Real Presence ; and so the Fathers deny, that it is any longer "°*mere* bread." But it is true to say, " This is the Body of Christ." For this does not deny that it is bread as to its earthly substance ; but speaks of it, as to its heavenly. Mr. Goode, however, further says,

" *They* [the Fathers] give us reasons why the bread in the Eucharist is called Christ's Body and the Wine His Blood, shewing that they did not consider them to be so really, but only representatively."

Certainly, no one ever did, or could call the outward and visible part of the Sacrament, by the name of the inward and invisible, meaning that it was identical with the invisible. No one could " call the bread in the Eucharist Christ's Body and the

p. 466 ; S. Jerome, p. 476 ; S. Augustine, p. 502 ; S. Chrysostome, p. 561 ; Afric. Auth. ap. S. Prosper, Ib. 711. They might be readily multiplied. ° Real Pres. 91-3.

wine His Blood, considering *them*," the outward elements, to be *themselves* " really His Body and Blood."

The question turns, not on the relation of the outward part to the inward, but on this; whether the inward part be believed to be present, as the Ancient Church believed, or absent, as the School of Calvin thought; whether we receive, under the elements, the Body and Blood of Christ, present in a real, although "heavenly and spiritual manner," or whether, as the Calvinists held, there be, contemporaneously, some effect produced by God the Holy Ghost on the soul, *then*, as in the reading of the Word or any exercise of faith. And on this question the passage of the four writers cited do not the least bear.

S. Augustine simply points out the relation between the outward and the inward part of the Sacraments. " [p] If the Sacraments " [i. e. the outward visible part] " had not a certain resemblance to that whereof they are sacraments" [i. e. the inward] "they would not be Sacraments at all." Our own Catechism points out such a relation between the strengthening and refreshing of the body by the bread and wine, and of the soul by the Body and Blood of Christ. " But from this resemblance," S. Augustine proceeds, " they" [the outward part] " receive, for the most part, the names of the things themselves" [the inward]. " As therefore *after a certain manner*, the *Sacrament* of the Body of Christ [i. e. the visible symbol] is the Body of Christ, the Sacrament of the Blood of Christ is the Blood of Christ, so the Sacrament of Faith is Faith."

[p] Ep. ad Bonifac. see more fully in Real Pres. p. 507.

Facundus, who seems to have imitated this passage, explains the word "Sacrament" to be the outward visible sign. I have, in my former work [q], already alleged the passage, as of one who argued against heretics from the natural substances remaining in the Holy Eucharist.

"[q] The Sacrament of adoption may be called adoption, as the Sacrament of His Body and Blood, which is *in* the consecrated Bread and Cup, we call His Body and Blood, not that the Bread is properly His Body, or the Cup His Blood, but because they contain *in* them the mystery of His Body and Blood."

Facundus says (what none can doubt) that "the Bread" [i. e. the outward part] "is not *properly* the Body of Christ;" but he attests at the same time, his belief in the Real objective Presence; "they" [the Bread and the Cup] "contain *in* them the mystery of His Body and Blood."

The two other passages, those of Primasius and Isidore of Seville, do not bear upon this subject. That of Primasius is, "[r] God our Saviour gave an example, that as often as we do this, we should bear in mind that Christ died for us all. Therefore *it is said to us* [s]" [i. e. when It is given to us communicating] "'The Body of Christ,' that when we remember this, we may not be ungrateful to His grace."

Primasius, who has so closely followed S. Augus-

---

[q] Real Pres. p. 89.   [r] Ep. ad 1 Cor. xi. Bibl. Patr. x. 189.

[s] "1 deo nobis dicitur." Mr. Goode (p. 242) translates "Therefore it is *called by* us." This would have been ",a nobis." Primasius uses shortly afterwards the corresponding expression on the words, "Ye do shew the Lord's Death till He come." "In your hearts, when ye *hear*, 'the Body of Christ.'"

tine, is arguing as to our duties, from the words addressed to Communicants at the time of Communion. In this same context, Primasius asserts, that the wicked also receive the Body of Christ.

" So then, 'whosoever eateth this Bread or drinketh this Cup of the Lord unworthily.' Every one that is pure will eat the Flesh, and the soul which eateth, being impure, shall be rooted out. 'Shall be guilty of the Body and Blood of the Lord.' As though he himself slew Him, in that he despises Him, and accounts of no worth His Body, as did the Jews."

Primasius does not use the expression, which Mr. Goode by mistake has quoted from him.

Isidore is only accounting for the fact that our Lord chose bread, as the symbol of His Body, wine as the symbol of His Blood. I will subjoin the whole passage [t].

" The sacrifice which is offered to God by Christians, Christ our Lord and Master first instituted, when He commended to the Apostles His Body and Blood, before He was betrayed, as is read in the Gospel; 'Jesus took bread and the Cup, and blessed and gave to them.' This Sacrament Melchisedech king of Salem first offered representatively for a type of the Body and Blood of Christ, and he first imaged the Mystery of so great a Sacrifice, bearing the similitude of our Lord and Saviour Jesus Christ, the eternal Priest, to Whom it is said, 'Thou art a Priest for ever after the order of Melchisedech.'

" This sacrifice then Christians were commanded to celebrate; those Jewish victims being abandoned and ended, which were commanded to be celebrated during the bondage of the old people. This then we do, which our Lord Himself did for us, '[u]which He offered, not in the morning

---

[t] De Off. i. 18. T. vi. p. 382.   [u] Taken from S. Cyprian Ep. 63. ad Cæcil. § 13. p. 192, 3. O. T.

but in the evening after supper. For so it behoved Christ to fulfil it at eventide, that the very hour of sacrifice might point out the evening of the world.' Hence therefore the Apostles did not communicate fasting, because it was necessary that the typical Passover should be first fulfilled, and that so they should pass to the true Sacrament of the Passover.

"For this took place then, as a Mystery. I mean, that the disciples at first did not receive the Body and Blood of the Lord fasting. But now by the whole Church it is received fasting. For so it pleased the Holy Ghost through the Apostles, '[x]that in honour of so great a Sacrament, the Lord's Body should enter the mouth of a Christian, before any other food, and therefore is that custom kept throughout the whole world.' For the Bread which we break, is the Body of Christ, Who said, 'I am the Living Bread which came down from Heaven.' But the wine is His Blood, and this it is, which is written: 'I am the true vine;' but bread, because it strengthens the body, is therefore called the Body of Christ: but the wine, because it produces blood in the flesh, is therefore referred to the Blood of Christ.

"These then, as being visible, yet sanctified by the Holy Ghost, pass into the Sacrament of the Divine Body."

Mr. Goode frequently excepts against the belief in the oral reception of the Holy Eucharist. Isidore, embodying in his own statement the words of S. Augustine, states it as explicitly as words could express it; "that in honour of so great a Sacrament, the Lord's Body should enter the mouth of a Christian before any other food."

This rule of the ancient Church, of which we have evidence towards the close of the 2nd century [y], was

[x] Taken verbatim from S. Aug. Ep. 54. ad Januar. See Real Pres. p. 505.   [y] See Tert. ad Ux. ii. 5. p. 427, and note z. O. T. (p. 439. ed. 2), and de Cor. 3. p. 164. and n. x.

of the nature of a positive law. Had there been any intrinsic irreverence, in taking food before receiving the Body and Blood of Christ in the Holy Eucharist, our Blessed Lord would not so have instituted it. Old Canons also dispense with its observance in the case of the sickly; and the Latin Church allows the Holy Eucharist to be received after food by the dying. But to those who hold with Calvin, the whole rule is unmeaning. They would, if they spoke their minds (as in ordinary life they do), account it superstitious. If we only ate "mere bread and wine," in remembrance of our Lord's Death, there would be no more reason, for fasting before we received it, than for fasting before we heard in Church the history of His Passion. The theory of the Calvinists being, that Sacramental and non-Sacramental Communion is one and the same, there could be no more reason for fasting before Sacramental, than before non-Sacramental Communion. But then the practice of the primitive Church, "the custom kept throughout the whole world," as S. Augustine says, implies a different belief from that of the school of Calvin.

I will only add now, that had S. Augustine, and three writers of the *sixth* century [z], who imitated that great Father, meant that, for which Mr. Goode alleges them, four Latin writers of this date could not stand for " *the* Fathers;" nor could *obiter dicta* of their's be the rule of interpretation of all Christian language, whether of Fathers, or simple individuals,

---

[z] Facundus A. D. 540. Primasius A. D. 558. Isidore A. D. 596. The passages have been quoted from the time of Albertinus or before.

or liturgies of the Church, in all times and climes throughout the Christian world.

The above, as far I see, are the only grounds of the canon of Mr. Goode and the School of Calvin, which is to "[a]sweep away at once the larger portion of the testimonies" from the Fathers which I adduced. I have, I believe, shewn how little it can discharge that office. But I would only ask any one who loves, and desires to know, the truth, to examine for himself, the passages of the Fathers which I have adduced, and see whether he thinks that the words "bread and wine" could be substituted for their words "the Body and Blood of Christ," and the meaning remain the same. For if that maxim of Albertinus and the School of Calvin were true, that "the signs are called by the names of the things signified," and the inference which alone would make it bear upon this doctrine also true, viz. that when "the Fathers speak of the things signified," "the Body and Blood of Christ," we are entitled to suppose that they meant *only* the "signs," i. e. the bread and wine, then, of course, we might, in every case which is so to be disposed of, substitute the words "bread and wine" for the "Body and Blood of Christ," and the sense receive no damage. Let any one really and earnestly and perseveringly try this, and I feel no doubt, that he would soon be convinced, at least, that Christians of old, learned or unlearned, believed in the Real Presence of "the Body and Blood of Christ under the form of bread and wine."

---

[a] "The fact that the signs are called by the names of the things signified, sweeps away at once the larger portion of Dr. Pusey's testimonies," p. 541. See also pp. 232, 233, 249, 501.

I have in my work "[b] The Doctrine of the Real Presence as contained in the Fathers, from the death of S. John the Evangelist to the fourth General Council" A. D. 451, set down, to the utmost of my knowledge, every passage bearing upon the doctrine of the Holy Eucharist, from which any argument could be drawn. I have set these down, I may say, with such conscientiousness, that Mr. Goode thinks that I have brought forward passages, which tell against my belief, as well as those which attest it. The largest portion of those passages I have simply translated [c], without arguing from them, because I thought that they would best convey their own impression and doctrine, if left to tell their own tale. And that doctrine, they will, I trust, by the mercy of God, convey, if not to controversialists and to pre-occupied minds, yet to simple hearts who only wish to know, what Gift, the Ancient Church believed that their Saviour has in store for them and dispenses to them in the Sacrament of His blessed Body and Blood.

And now, I have only to thank God for His Mercy in allowing me thus far to labour in behalf of His truth; and, now that He has, for the time, by His Providence checked this war of extermination [d], which some have thought it right to carry on against those who hold and teach the ancient truth,

---

[b] I have often referred to this work in the following pages, in order to save repetition. I have marked it as " Doctrine of the Real Pres." or " Real Pr." or " R. P."

[c] Real Presence, p. 315-715.

[d] I have used this strong term on the ground of the language of a Circular, signed by the Earl of Shaftesbury and two other

to pray Him to heal our breaches, and to turn
men's hearts to one another, that so, loving Him
Who is love, we may in Him love one another,
and together seeking him Who is the Truth, we
may, in Him, together, acknowledge His truth. For
while we, who would love Christ, are thus engaged
in attack and defence, infidelity finds its way undis-
puted, the Old Testament is given over to unbelievers, our Redeemer is blasphemed, His Godhead,
His Atonement, or even His Existence are denied.
While those whom He has set to be His shepherds
are at variance, "the wolf cometh and scattereth
the sheep." But thou, O LORD, have mercy upon us!

gentlemen, which was sent to me, urgently soliciting money for
the Prosecution of Archdeacon Denison; and also on the ground
of the appeal of Mr. Goode, Preface, p. ix. 4, together with
p. 20-22.

CHRIST CHURCH,
       Easter, 1857.

"THE REAL PRESENCE,"

&c.

THE chief object of my sermon, "The Real Presence of Christ in the Holy Eucharist," was to maintain clearly and distinctly the doctrine of the Church of England upon one point, viz. "the Real Presence of the Body and Blood of our Saviour Christ under the form of bread and wine." This doctrine I endeavoured to set forth with all the clearness that I could, out of Holy Scripture, and out of the teaching of the Fathers, as the nearest and best interpretation of the mind of God in Holy Scripture. One such subject may well be thought sufficient for a sermon. Indeed the defence of that one doctrine, on both sides, necessarily involved a detail of argument, which I almost feared would be too abstract for the occasion and the place, the instruction of youth in the House of God. I felt this so much, that I should not have made the attempt at all, but that I trusted that the fervid and devout language of the Fathers, with which I closed that sermon, would leave a fragrance behind, and would impress on the souls of the hearers the piety which they breathed.

This one doctrine I guarded on both sides. I maintained (as the Church of England teaches) "[a] that the sacramental bread and wine remain still in their very natural substances, and yet that under these poor outward forms, His 'creatures of bread and wine,' 'the faithful verily and indeed take and receive the Body and Blood of Christ.'"

I framed my teaching in language, adapted or sanctioned by the Church of England. Two years before (1851), in a book[b] of which some thousands were circulated, I had expressed more at length my belief, in words which a living divine [c] had interwoven exclusively from the statements of our formularies; and which had received the approbation of most or all of the Bishops of our Church.

In my sermon, I removed, in the outset, the only imputations, which I imagined that even a careless hearer could attach to my words. I said that our Articles themselves explained what doctrine they condemned under the name "Transubstantiation;" one "repugnant to the plain words of Holy Scripture," i. e. those words in which our Lord and S. Paul speak of the natural substances as remaining, and one "which overthroweth the nature of a Sacrament" in that the outward and visible part is supposed to have no real subsistence. The statement in the Article has marked reference not to the inward "Sacramental, supernatural, mystical, in-

[a] "The Presence of Christ in the Holy Eucharist," p. 14.
[b] Letter to the Bishop of London, p. 62—8. ed. 8vo.
[c] Palmer, Treatise of the Church, i. 7. p. 527.

effable, Presence" of the Body and Blood of our Lord, but to the outward elements. The Articles except against no statement which does not imply that the natural substances cease to be.

I also stated, (what I proved at large in my subsequent volume[d]) that "Consubstantiation" was a mere term of reproach invented against the Lutherans by those who denied any Sacred Presence at all. It is one of those terms which controversialists should never have allowed themselves, because its natural sense contains a lie. "Consubstantiation" does not express "simultaneous presence" or, as I said, Co-existence, but "union into one common substance," which it were blasphemy to affirm, and which was not believed by those to whom it was imputed, but was expressly denied by them.

Having cleared these two points, I did not enter into any further question about the Articles, because I did not imagine how any further question could be raised upon them.

Engaged, as I was, in maintaining what I believed, and do now equally believe, to be a doctrinal statement of the Church of England, I did not set about proving my agreement with the other formularies of our Church, because I did not imagine the possibility of any disagreement. I did not defend, what I did not imagine to be open to attack. I doubted not, that the formularies of the Church of England were (as I had always received them) in harmony with themselves. From these formularies my own faith was, in early youth, derived; from the Church of England and her Divines I learnt the whole faith

[d] Doctrine of the Holy Eucharist, p. 32—37.

which I hold. My belief may have been deepened
by a study of the Fathers, among whom, for these
last twenty years, I have lived as in my home; but
from the Church of England I learnt my faith; in
her formularies my mind was moulded; her Articles
I have ever defended, when slighted unjustly by a
younger generation.

Ordinarily speaking, a book is its own best defence. It tells its own tale with greater clearness
than any subsequent defence can effect. Now,
however, that a war of extermination is apparently
being carried on against those who believe as I
have learnt from the Church of England to believe,
while unbelief in the faith itself or in its chief doctrines, in the Gospel as a whole, or in the Old Testament, is making daily inroads on our people, and
is left undisturbed, I think it a duty to the Church
of which God has made me a Minister, to clear
away the imputations made against my belief.

In the following pages, I hope, i. to maintain the
clear sense of those statements, which I had especially adopted from our formularies; ii. to clear
away any objections which Mr Goode has drawn
from other statements of our formularies; iii. to explain my belief as to That which the wicked receive,
and the worship of our Lord, truly present in the Sacrament; iv. to vindicate my argument from Holy
Scripture; v. to clear away the objections which
Mr Goode raises to my argument from the Fathers.

I. The authors of the first book of Homilies A.D.
1547, gave notice of a second series of Homilies
which they intended to publish, in the following
words; " Hereafter shall follow sermons of fasting,

prayer, almsdeeds; of the Nativity, Passion, Resurrection of our Saviour Christ; of the due receiving of His blessed Body and Blood under the form of bread and wine, &c." The authors of the second book of Homilies recognise distinctly this statement, as an integral part of the first book of Homilies. They entitle their own book, "The second tome of Homilies, of such matters as were promised and entituled in the former part of Homilies." They recognise, not only the "matters" promised in the former book, but the "titles" under which they were mentioned; "such matters as were promised and *entituled* in the former part of Homilies." The first book of Homilies was reprinted A.D. 1560, having (as the title states) been "*e* perused and overseen for the better understanding of the people;" but this advertisement remained unchanged. A.D. 1562, Archbishop Parker says, "*f* it was again revised and finished with a second part, by him and the other Bishops." The notice still remained.

I never doubted that words, so put forth and so sanctioned, might be used by any teacher in the Church of England, with the full authority of the Church itself. They are as formal and definite a statement of doctrine as any contained in the book of Homilies. We do not subscribe any particular statements of the book of Homilies, as we do the Articles, but only generally acknowledge that they "*g* contain a godly and wholesome doctrine." Yet this notice is a distinct dogmatic statement. It is not even like a mere expression, which dropped from the writer, currente calamo. It is the phrase which,

e In Strype's Parker, ii. 3. fin.   *f* Ib. ii. 13.   *g* Art. 35.

out of many which he might have used, the writer deliberately chose, in order to express the doctrine of the Holy Eucharist which he believed. The phrase which he thus selected, I adopted from him, as expressing most simply and compendiously the doctrine which I had learned in the English Church.

Mr Goode admits the phrase to be a dogmatic statement; only, by a sort of paradox, he contends that "[h]The words were intended to express the doctrine of Transubstantiation." To Mr Goode's mind it is no difficulty, that words expressing that doctrine should remain embalmed in the book of Homilies to this day. The carelessness of printers is to him an adequate solution. "This Advertisement, though of course forming no part of the Homilies, was repeated by succeeding *printers* in *their* editions of the Book." Only, the printers are not the Editors!

It cannot but be a startling paradox, that a distinct enunciation of doctrine, still existing within the compass of our Book of Homilies, should, as far as its authority goes, teach the doctrine of Transubstantiation. Mr Goode would prove this; 1. from the use of the words themselves, "under the form of bread and wine," which he alleges to be used to express the doctrine of Transubstantiation only; 2. from the supposed opinions of Cranmer and the English Church at the time.

I must own that, whenever I have quoted those words from the Notice at the end of the first Book of Homilies, I took their meaning for granted. I did not set myself to ascertain in any learned way,

[h] The Nature of Christ's Presence, by Rev. W. Goode, p. 41.

what, in such a place, could be the meaning of those words, "under the form of bread and wine." I had before me a document of our own Church, and (as others [i] had before me) I took it for granted that the words, as used by writers of our Church, commended to us for their "godly and wholesome doctrine," could not be intended to express any other doctrine, than that held by our Church.

There is nothing to limit the word "form" to an unsubstantial appearance. "Form" is the "outward appearance," but not, necessarily nor naturally, a misleading appearance. The corresponding words "species," and "superficies," are freely used by Bertram on the Holy Eucharist, while expressly inculcating the reality of the outward elements.

"[k]The wine, which by the priestly consecration is made the Sacrament of the Blood of Christ, exhibits one thing on the surface [superficie tenus], contains another within. For what else is seen in the surface than the substance of wine?" "Not as to what is seen, is the 'form' [species] of flesh discerned in that bread." "[l]According to the appearance [speciem] of the creature, and, the form [formam] in visible things, both the bread and wine have nothing in them changed. And if they have undergone no change, they are nothing else than they were before." "[m]One and the same thing is, in one respect, the form [species] of bread and wine; in another, is the Body and Blood of Christ. For as far as each may be touched by the body, they are the forms

[i] Mr Palmer, l. c. p. 527. [k] De Corpore et Sang. Dom.
§ 10, add. c. 19. [l] c. 14. [m] c. 16.

[species] of the bodily creature; according to the power that they are made spiritually, they are the mysteries of the Body and Blood of Christ." "[n] According to the substance of the creatures, what they [the elements] were before consecration, that they abide afterwards also. They were bread and wine before, in which form [specie] also they are seen to abide, when now consecrated." "[o]He [S. Ambrose] teaches that it is Flesh, not in the appearance [specie], but in the Sacrament. For in what appears, it is bread; in the Sacrament, it is the true Body of Christ, as the Lord Jesus Himself proclaims, 'This is My Body.'"

In that same sense, ancient Fathers used the word "species[p]" or [q]τὰ φαινόμενα, to designate that which was visible, "the outward and visible part" of the sacrament. When Roman controversialists, in proof of the doctrine of Transubstantiation, have adduced passages from the Fathers in which those words occurred, Calvinist writers have *here* been at pains to shew, that these words did not mean an unsubstantial surface, but a visible substance. "It is plain," says Albertinus[r], " that in all these places, ' species' is taken for substance. For the 'species' of wine and oil can mean nothing else." But, plainly, they must not use both arguments. They must not argue that a word *cannot* have a certain meaning in the fathers, and that its English equivalent *must* have that meaning, when employed by one who uses the language of the fathers.

<hr>

[n] c. 54.   [o] c. 57.   [p] See "Doctrine of the Real Presence," p. 105, and note 7.   [q] Ib. p. 104, and note 4,

[r] De Euchar. p. 518. tit. Gaudentius. add p. 515.

This language of Bertram bears the more upon this question, because his book was in familiar use both by Ridley and Cranmer. It had been published, as bearing upon the controversy, at Cologne 1532, Geneva 1541. Ridley himself translated it, and published it in English in the following year 1548. It was his great instrument in swaying the belief of Cranmer. I doubt not that Bertram really believed the very doctrine impugned, the inward presence of the Body and Blood of Christ under the outward part of the sacrament, or "the form of bread and wine." But here the question is, not as to the inward part, but as to the outward, whether the word "form" may not be as well used of a real, as well as an unreal, appearance. And for this, the language of Bertram, familiar to Ridley and Cranmer, is decisive. I may add (as stated by the Divine[s] already quoted), that the word "form," as equivalent to "part," is used in another authorized formulary of our Church, the Catechism. It is used of the outward part of the Sacrament of Baptism, of whose substantial existence there has, of course, been no doubt. "What is the outward sign or *form* in Baptism?" "Water, &c." The same language was used freely even by Mr Ford, when writing against the doctrine of the real objective Presence. "[t]They might deservedly be accounted mad, who believe that Christ then lay invisibly concealed under those species[u]," &c.

---

[s] Mr Palmer, l. c.   [t] Quoted by Mr Goode, p. 681.

[u] Sub speciebus illis. Mr Goode quotes this and similar language, against those who hold the " co-existence of Christ's Body and Blood in, with, or under the bread and wine."

The word "form," then, having by the fathers, and by Bertram (whom Cranmer is known to have studied), been used of a "visible substance," and by later Roman Catholics of an "unsubstantial appearance," the question simply is, whether the writers of the first book of Homilies, in their "advertisement," meant to use the word in the same sense which they believed, or in the sense which they did not believe. The words "under the form of bread and wine" imply, of course, that "the form" under which the Body and Blood of Christ are received, is something quite distinct from, and does not belong to, that Body and Blood. The "form" is of "bread and wine;" but one class of writers used it of a substantial, the other of an unsubstantial "form." In which then did the writers of the Homilies use it? Surely, in that which they themselves believed, "the form of bread and wine," which "remained in their very natural substances." Cranmer says of himself, in the year after that (1547) in which the first book of Homilies was published; "[v]This I confess of myself, that not long before I wrote the said Catechism [that published in 1548] I was in that error of the real Presence, as *I was, many years past, in divers other errors, as of Transubstantiation, &c.*"

Cranmer says then distinctly that he, at that time, had a belief in the real Presence, which he afterwards accounted an "error"; whereas, *for many years*, he had ceased to believe in Transubstantiation. There remains then, no other belief, which Cranmer could have then held, than that which we

---

[v] Answer to Gardiner quoted by Mr Goode, p. 46.

now hold, that belief which he embodied in this notice in the Book of Homilies, that same belief which I expressed in these words; viz. that "under the" real and true "form of bread and wine" we "receive the Body and Blood of Christ," really present there.   For Cranmer, when he had gone over to the Swiss School, says that he was *then* "in the error of the real Presence."

This belief Cranmer has been shewn to have held nine years before, in 1538.   On August 12, 1538, he wrote to Cromwell about Adam Damplip "[w] that he had ever confessed the very Body and Blood of Christ to be present in the Sacrament of the Altar, and had only confuted the opinion of the Transubstantiation; and therein," Cranmer adds, "I think that he taught but the truth."   This belief he held, together with other Bishops, for about ten years, until 1548, a year after the publication of the Homilies.   Mr Goode's own authorities establish the date of this change.   Traheron writes of it, Sept. 28. 1548, as a matter of thanksgiving, "[x] that Latimer is come over to our opinion respecting the true doctrine of the Eucharist, together with the Archbishop of Canterbury and the other Bishops who heretofore seemed to be Lutherans."

In the conference, about Dec. 14. 1548, he relates to Bullinger that Cranmer,

"[y] contrary to general expectation, most openly, firmly, and learnedly, maintained your opinion upon the subject.

[w] Jenkyns' Pref. to Cranmer's Works, i. lxxv.
[x] Orig. letters in Parker Soc. i. 322. quoted by Mr Goode, p. 46.
[y] Id. Ib.

I perceive that it is all over with Lutheranism, now that those who were considered its principal and almost only supporters have altogether come over to our side."

Mr Goode's only solution of this is,

"[z] As he [Cranmer] did not *long* hold the Lutheran view of the Eucharist, we may reasonably conclude that, at the date of the first edition of the Book of Homilies, he had not given up the old phraseology of his Church on the subject."

Cranmer, *did* use old language of the Church on the subject, language which, about A. D. 840, had been used by Bertram whom Cranmer studied; language, which naturally expressed the belief which he had then held for nine years; which had been used (as we shall see) in the "confession of Augsburg" in its brief Article on that doctrine, and which expressed a belief then shared by the other Bishops "who seemed to be Lutherans." Can any one really think, that he used it to express a belief which he had laid aside nine years before, not that which he then held?

Mr Goode employs two subsidiary evidences that the words "under the form of bread and wine" express the doctrine of Transubstantiation.

"(1)[a] Nay more; the 'Order of the Communion,' issued by 'public' authority about the same time as the Homilies, and in use for some time after their publication, being enforced by the subsequent 'Injunctions' of 1547, and the 'Articles of Visitation' of 1548, requires the Mass, to be still said according to the old form, contenting itself with the sole change of giving the cup to the laity, and adding some appropriate addresses and prayers."

[z] Ib. p. 47.   [a] Ib.

Mr Goode will doubtless withdraw his argument when he remembers (1) that he has himself argued that,

"[b] The 'Canon of the Mass' as it now stands, and which is no doubt, of considerable antiquity, does not bear out the notion, that the Elements themselves become, upon consecration, the real Body and Blood of Christ. There are clear evidences in it of purer doctrine than that which now rules the Church of Rome; evidences which her claim of agreement with the primitive Church forbids her striking out or altering, but which are practically nullified, both by the additions she has made, and by the dominant teaching of the Church. For in the first place, the prayer offered for the elements on their first oblation (which takes place previous to their consecration) is only this—that the oblation 'may be made to us the Body and Blood of the Saviour.'"
"[c] Moreover, the prayers used after the consecration, with reference to God's acceptance of the consecrated substances, are inconsistent with the notion that they are, or contain, the real Body and Blood of Christ. For instance, the following,—'Wherefore we Thy servants, O Lord, and also Thy holy people, mindful as well of the blessed Passion of the same Christ Thy Son our Lord, as also of His Resurrection from the dead, and further of His glorious Ascension into heaven, offer to Thy excellent Majesty of Thy own donations and gifts a pure host, a holy host, an immaculate host, the holy bread of eternal life, and the cup of everlasting salvation. Upon which [offerings] vouchsafe to look with a favourable and serene countenance, and to give them acceptance, as Thou didst vouchsafe to give acceptance to the offerings of Thy child the righteous Abel, and the sacrifice of our patriarch Abraham, and the holy sacrifice, the immaculate host, which Thy high priest Melchisedech offered unto Thee.' Now this prayer is quite inconsistent with the supposition that the consecrated substances have

b Ib. p. 461.   c Ib. p. 464.

actually become the Body and Blood of Christ. For after referring to our Lord's Ascension, it proceeds to speak of the consecrated substances as God's gifts, and still as the bread and the cup, though now after consecration they are justly styled 'the holy bread of eternal life and the cup of everlasting salvation,' and it entreats God to look upon them with favour and accept them, as He accepted the offerings of Abel, Abraham, and Melchisedech.—A prayer which, if they had become in any way the real Body and Blood of Christ, would be monstrous."

The sequel of that prayer (which Mr Goode has not quoted), has presented a difficulty even to Roman Catholic writers, on *their* supposition that the created substances had, upon the consecration ceased to be; "We humbly beseech Thee, Almighty God, command [hæc] these things to be borne by the hands of Thy Angel to Thine Altars above, in the presence of Thy Divine Majesty; that all we who, by partaking of this Altar, shall have received the all-holy Body and Blood of Thy Son, may be filled with all heavenly benediction and graces, through our Lord Jesus Christ."

Writers then, such as Florus[d], Innocent III. and Aquinas, have explained the words "hæc," "these things," of the "prayers of the faithful." "[e] The priest prayeth not, that the Sacramental species be borne to heaven, nor the true Body of Christ, which ceaseth not to be there; but he prayeth this for the mystical body, which is signified in this Sacrament,

---

[d] "Florus, on the Canon of the Mäss, says that these words are very difficult to be understood; and with him agreeth Innocent III, (Myst. Miss. v. 6,) who thus explaineth, 'Command, O Lord, that the prayers of the faithful may be borne,'" &c. Assem. Cod. Lit. iv. 164.   [e] Aq. 3 p. qu. 83. art. 4. ad 9.

that the angel, who is present at the Divine mysteries, may present to God the prayers of the priest and the people." The words, however, "these things" must surely mean those same offerings, upon which, God had just been prayed graciously to look[f]; the memorials of the Death and Passion of our Lord, whereby we plead to God that same Sacrifice on the Cross, which He, our Great High Priest and Intercessor, pleadeth unceasingly in heaven, in that Glorified Body which still bears (in what exceeding Glory!) the marks of His Passion.

I agree then with Mr Goode, that this language in its obvious sense is inconsistent with the doctrine of Transubstantiation; both because the word "bread" is still used after consecration (and that, as "God's own donations and gifts"), and that the offering is compared with the material offerings of the Patriarchs, which would not be natural, if nothing material remained.

But if (as Mr Goode argues, I think, rightly) these words exclude the doctrine of Transubstantiation, then the directions in 1547 that "the Mass be still said according to the old form," plainly cannot imply that the doctrine of Transubstantiation was still held by the English Church. The use of a form which "rather contradicts the doctrine of Transubstantiation" cannot be a proof that they who use that form believed in the doctrine which that form "rather contradicts."

[f] The structure of the prayer involves this: "supra *quæ* respicere digneris et accepta habere. Supplices te rogamus, omnipotens Deus, jube hæc perferri." The neuters *quæ*, hæc, plainly refer to the same subject.

That the Canon of the Mass should, in its natural interpretation, exclude even the belief of a real objective Presence of our Lord's blessed Body and Blood, is another paradox of Mr Goode, which few probably will share. Indeed, he himself rather admits, that "the doctrine of a real Presence *in the consecrated elements*" is the natural interpretation of the words "that they may be unto us the Body and Blood of Thy most dearly-beloved Son Jesus Christ." For he only contends that[g] "no doubt these words *may* be so explained, as *not* to countenance that doctrine;" while he admits that "they are very open to an interpretation of that kind." The part of the prayer in the Roman Canon which I have supplied, will probably to most seem decisive; "we, who, by partaking of *this Altar*, shall have received the all-holy Body and Blood of Thy Son."

In further proof that *Cranmer* used the words, "under the form of bread and wine," as expressing Transubstantiation, Mr Goode says;

"[h] And even when the Prayer Book of 1549 was being prepared, so far was the doctrine of Transubstantiation from having been publicly rejected, that we are told that in the discussions that took place respecting it, 'the Bishops could not of a long time agree among themselves respecting

[g] p. 618. Mr Goode is commenting on the Liturgy of 1549. The words are so far identical with those of the Canon of the Mass; "ut nobis Corpus et Sanguis fiat dilectissimi Filii tui Domini Dei nostri Jesu Christi." Mr Goode's words are "Now, no doubt, these words *may* be so explained as not to countenance the doctrine of a real Presence *in the consecrated elements*, but they are very open to an interpretation of that kind." [h] Ib. p. 47.

the Article of the Lord's Supper' and it was a long and earnest dispute among them whether Transubstantiation should be established or rejected[i]."

But Mr Goode's own authority states (what is obvious) that the dispute lay between the Bishops of the two opposite parties.   Dryander himself says, that Cranmer and Ridley disputed on the one side, Heath Bishop of Worcester on the other.   There can be no doubt that the dispute was the same as that mentioned in the Journal of Edward VI. as having taken place in Parliament.   "[k] A Parliament was called, where an uniform order of prayer was institute, *before* made by a number of Bishops and learned men gathered at Windsor.   Then was granted a subsidy; and there was a notable disputation of the Sacrament in the Parliament-house."

If the "dispute" was not that actually on the third reading of the bill " for the uniformity of service and administration of the Sacraments to be had throughout the realm," it was, of course, between the same Bishops, those of the old, and those of the reformed school.   When the bill was read a third time in the Lords Jan. 15, 1548,[l] *eight* Bishops voted against it, London, Durham, Norwich, Carlisle, Hereford, Worcester, Westminster, Chichester; *twelve* voted for it, the two Archbishops, the Bishops of Ely, Salisbury, Lichfield and Coventry, Bath and Wells, Peterborough, Bristol, Lincoln, Llandaff, S. David's, Rochester.

The opposition of Bonner, Tunstal, Heath, Day,

[i] Dryander's letter to Bullinger, June 5, 1549.   Orig. letters.

[k] In Burnet, B. ii. P. ii. p. 7.   This is noticed by the Editor of the letters.   [l] Lords' Journals, 2 Ed. VI. p. 331.

Skip, Thirlby, to a service compiled by Cranmer, is no evidence, as to the doctrine which *he* believed, or that he used their language.

2. In proof that even the Lutherans did not hold any doctrine of Consubstantiation or Impanation, I had said[m],

"Such doctrines are expressly denied by the Lutherans to whom they are imputed, and are taught in none of their books. The strongest statement of the earliest Confession of Augsburg—'of the Supper of the Lord, it is taught that the very Body and Blood of Christ are verily present in the Lord's Supper under the form of Bread and Wine, and are distributed and taken in it[n],' like that of our Homilies, offers no physical explanation; but simply expresses the real unseen sacramental Presence under the outward visible form."

On this Mr Goode says[o];

"It is almost inconceivable he [I] could be ignorant what the words 'form of bread and wine' meant; namely their visible shape when the substance was gone. He himself refers to the German edition of the Confession, and to Hospinian, Hist. Sacram. Pt. 11. p. 155. sqq. Now the word in the German edition translated 'form' is 'gestalt' or 'outward appearance.'"

"Gestalt," as used of the outward part of the Holy Eucharist, has two meanings, corresponding with the two uses of the Latin word "species," of which it is a translation. The one sense it has, when used in the phrase of receiving the Sacrament "in" or "under both *kinds*." In this sense, it is used for the Latin word "species," not in the sense of "form or appearance," but in that, for which we

---

[m] Sermon, p. 16.   [n] The Article ends, "Therefore also the contrary doctrine is rejected."   [o] p. 42.

with the words "under the form of bread and wine." 19

have in English naturalized the Latin "species,"
i. e. "kind."   Adelung, whose authority is decisive
as to a word in his own language, of which he had
such a solid knowledge, says,

"In theology, the two visible things in the Sacrament
of the Lord's Supper, the bread and the wine, are called
'two kinds;' [Gestalten] a title, which is now indeed ill-
suited; because 'Gestalt' in the sense of 'kind,' 'species,'
is in high German disused; but in the Southern German
it still occurs in that sense, and they speak 'of all sorts of
gestalten' i. e. kinds, species, of beasts."

In this sense, "Gestalt" continually occurs in the
works of Luther.   The following occur among the
titles of his tracts [p];

"That both *kinds* of the Sacrament are to be received."
"Of the Sacrament of both *kinds*, the Flesh and Blood of
Christ."   "A sermon on both *kinds* of the Sacrament."   "An
account of both *kinds* of the Sacrament, on occasion of the
mandate of the Bishop of Meissen."

The following instances of this usage occur in
the space of a few pages of this last tract;

"[q] Of, with, both *kinds;* both *kinds* of the Sacrament
were instituted by Christ; gave the Sacrament in both
kinds to the laity; to use both *kinds* of the Sacrament; to
receive, enjoy both *kinds;* both *kinds* were allowed, given;

[p] Von beyder gestalt des Sacraments zu nemen. A. 1522.   Von
dem Sacrament bayder gestalt, flaish und blut Christi.   1525.
Sermon von bayderlay gestalt des Sacraments.   1523.   Eine bericht von beiderley gestalt des sacraments auf des Bischofs zu
Meissen Mandat. 1558.

[q] "Von beyder Gestalt; mit b. G.; das Sacrament b. G. der
laien reichte; beyder Gestalt des Sacraments ist von Christo ein-
gesetzt; b. G. d. S. gebrauchen; beyder G. geniessen, empfan-

were imparted to all Christians; to forbid, retain the one *kind;* not to give the one *kind* only; under one *kind* to eat and drink both [on the doctrine of concomitance] ; under one *kind* is the soul of Christ."

The corresponding word was used in the Latin Liturgy prepared in the reign of Elizabeth, for the Colleges of the two Universities, and for Winchester and Eton, A. D. 1560.   "[r] Then the priest himself shall first receive the Eucharist under each *species ;* sub utraque specie."

In *this* sense "Gestalt" has nothing to do with "form" at all.   In that other sense of "outward appearance," "Gestalt" does not mean "unreal, unsubstantial, appearance."   I will state the instances, which Adelung gives, of this sense also ;

"The earth has a round; a die, a square, *form"* [Gestalt]. "A man of a good, beautiful, taking, *form."*   "To take on himself a *form."* "The *form* of a dove." "The *form* of the

gen, erlaubt, giebt; aller Christen gereicht ; die eine G. verbieten, behalten ; die einige G. nicht geben; unter einer G. beyde essen und trinken ; unter einer G. die Seele Christi est." Wercke, Th. xix. 615-22. ed. Leipz.   In all these instances of the phrase, the word "kind" is united with the words " one," "both," " either."   And therefore, although the idiom, "under one *kind* (unter einer Gestalt, sub una specie), to eat and drink both," comes very nearly to that other phrase ("unter Gestalt des Brodts und Weins"); I prefer, (with the writers of the notice in the Book of Homilies), to take the word in its more popular sense, "under the form of bread and wine." Still more remarkable is an Edict of the Margrave Elector of Brandenburg (Jul. 26. 1541. Corp. Ref. n. 2338. T. iv. 594). "The Catholic States should also think of ways, that the *Communion of the Body and Blood* of our Lord Jesus Christ *under both kind of bread and wine* (unter beyder Gestalt des Brods und Weins), be henceforth not forbidden to be given and received in their lands and by their subjects."   [r] Liturgical Services in the reign of Q. Elizabeth, p. 396.

body, of the countenance." " To take all sorts of *forms.*"
" To lose or change his *form.*"

Even in this sense, Mr Goode has confused two things; 1. a form being unreal, unsubstantial, and 2. a form, although real, not being the own form of that which is present under it. But the form is not in that case less a real form, having a real substance and being. Our Lord was "in the form of God." Such was the form which belonged to Him in Himself. " He took on Him the form of a servant," by taking into God the Manhood, which before was the form of His creature only, and under which He, while He dwelt among us, lay hid. He appeared to the two disciples " in another form;" whether this relates to His outward dress (as to Magdalene He appeared in the garb of a gardener), or whether it was, that His glorified Body was not at once recognised by the bodily eye.

All these were, in different ways, real forms. His proper Godhead was the own form of God the Son. His Manhood was a true form, which He made His own, by uniting it inseparably with Himself. The " other form," under which He appeared to the two disciples, was still a real form, under which they might have discerned Him. For Scripture says that their [s] " eyes were holden, that they should not know Him."

So far is " Gestalt " from meaning an unsubstantial form, that " a mere form " would be expressed, as in English, by the addition of the word *mere,* " eine blosse [t] Gestalt." The idea of being " unsub-

[s] St. Luke xxiv. 26. comp. St. John xxi. 4.
[t] Adelung explains schein körper, as " a *mere* form " (" eine

stantial, if expressed at all, lies in the word " mere,"
" blosse," not in the word " Gestalt."

So much for the word. As far then as relates to
the word itself, the idiom " under the *form* of bread
and wine " cannot, by the force of the words, possibly
mean a mere outward appearance. Nor can it be
said, that it was already a secondary technical
expression in a sense which the words did not, of
themselves, convey. For the language is Luther's,
who moulded, in fact, the German language, which
was, up to his time, unformed; nor is there any
proof of any such usage. Luther, of course, used the
words in the sense which he himself believed.

" Under the 'form' [Gestalt] of bread and wine " is
equivalent to Luther's other expression, " sub pane et
vino," " under bread and wine." The words express,
what Luther notoriously held, that " the bread and
wine remaining in their natural substances, the
Body and Blood of Christ were present under
them." The word " Gestalt " then has *not*, either
by its own proper force, or by its actual usage,
the meaning which Mr Goode says, " it is almost
inconceivable that I could be ignorant," that it had.

Although it is really superfluous, I will set down
the words of a German writer commenting expressly
on the passage;

" ᵘ In the tenth Article, the real Presence of the Body
and Blood of Christ in the Lord's Supper is taught without

blosse Gestalt ") without bodily parts, in opposition to a true or
organic form ; " corpus parastaticum."
    ᵘ Tittmann die Augsb. Conf. deutsch und. lat. Dresden. 1830, p.
100. See also Walch Introd. i. 3. 32, p. 287.

further explanation; for it did not seem advisable to turn attention to the difference of opinions about the mode of the Presence. This gave occasion not only to blame the article for indefiniteness, but to find the opinion of Transubstantiation lurking in its German words, 'unter Gestalt des Brods' &c. But the word 'Gestalt' designates, not the outward form (or appearance) of the thing, which alone remains after the change of the Substance, but *that which is really visibly present. The Roman Theologians also understood very well, that their opinion was not expressed here.* Hence they found it necessary, in the Confutation, to suggest, that there must be added, ' that, through the Almighty Word in the Consecration, the substance of the bread is changed into the Body of Christ.' That this was not the opinion of our people, they knew very well; for Luther had, both earlier in his de Captivitat. Babylon. and also in his larger Catechism, explained clearly enough the true opinion. The less was it necessary to reject Transubstantiation here."

I shall, please God, shew presently, that the phrase "under the form of bread and wine" came into our Theology in the time of Henry VIII., being ultimately derived from the Confession of Augsburg.

3. But first as to the facts of the Confession of Augsburg. I had quoted that statement on the Holy Eucharist, as occurring "in the earliest Confession of Augsburg." I ought to have said "the original *German* Confession of Augsburg."

Charles V., after the failure of the Diet of Spire 1529, expressly invited "ᵛ the Electors, Princes and States of the German Empire, to commit to writing *in German and Latin*, each his own opinion on the errors, divisions and abuses, and to deliver it to him,

ᵛ In Cœlest. in Hist. Concil. Aug. i. f. 116.

that this error and division might be the better
understood and weighed, and things be brought
back the sooner to a Christian state." This was to
be done in the ensuing diet at Augsburg April 8,
1530. Upon this, the Elector of Saxony wrote
from Torgau to the Wittenberg divines, Luther,
Jonas, Bugenhagen, and Melanchthon, begging
them to consider, between that time and March 20.
following, in what way matters of faith or ritual
should be brought before the Emperor[w]. Luther,
Melanchthon, and Bugenhagen were employed in
the task March 14, 1530, in the absence of Jonas[x].
The time being so short, they laid as the ground-
work, partly seventeen Articles[y] which Luther and
others[z] had drawn up for the Convention at Schwa-
bach Oct. 16, 1529, in part embodying their belief as
distinct from Zwinglianism[a]. The very language of
these Articles enters into the Confession of Augsburg. The materials for the latter part on the
" abuses, changed," were prepared at Torgau[b]. Luther being, for security[c], left at Coburg, where he
might be consulted, Melanchthon shaped the mate-

[w] Elect. ad Theol. Vit. in Bretschneider Corp. Reformat. ii. n. 671.

[x] Luth. Ep. ad Jon. 1192. ed. de W. and Melanchth. Ep. 672.
in C. R. The Elector summoned them hurriedly, bringing their
books too, if need be, March 21, in a letter from Torgau. Ib. 675.

[y] Printed against Luther's will under the title Die Bekenntnus
M. Luther's auff d. itzigen angestellten Reichstag zu Augspurgk
eynzulegen Cob. 1530. reprinted by himself, Auff das schreien
etlicher Papisten ub. d. 17. Art. (Bodl. Cat. ii. 603.)

[z] Ib. Præf. Luth.   [a] See Seckend. ii. xcvii, viii. add.

[b] In Foerstemann Urkundenbuch z. d. Gesch. d. Reichstages z.
Augsb. i. 41. 66. sqq. also in the Corp. Ref. T. iv. n. 675.[b] Suppl.

[c] Ep. 1217. Probst.

rials at Augsburg, yet sent them to Luther to re-view[d]. He however, had nothing to alter[e]. Hither-to the Confession was in the name of Saxony only. On June 15, the legates of Nuremburg, transmitted to the Burgo-master and senate[f], a copy of the German Articles, including the Article on faith and works, which had been wanting in the copy of the Latin Articles which they had before sent, and which indeed was not yet written in Latin, but would be ready, they thought, in about two days. In this copy, Melanchthon, they say, had substi-tuted a general word, which might include all the states, instead of the Electorate of Saxony "(this or that is preached or held in the Electorate of Saxony)" as it had stood in the Latin Articles. He had delayed writing the German Preface and conclusion, with a view to the like change. The legates ask the Senate to consult their preachers and lawyers about the Articles, and to send them their own opinion thereon, and to signify whether they approved of the Preface and conclusion being written in the name of all, in which case they undertook to send the Articles again. The same doubtless was done as to other Imperial cities. "[g] Early on Thursday June 29, the legates of Nu-remburg and Reutlingen were summoned to the [Elector of] Saxony, [the Landgrave of] Hesse, Margrave George [of Brandenburg], and [Ernest Duke of] Luneburg, and there, in their presence, and in that of their Councillors and Theologians

---

[d] Mel. Luth. C. R. 685. El. Luth. 687. [e] Ep. 1213. Elect.
[f] C. R. 723. [g] Leg. Nor. ad Senat. C. R. 738.

(twelve in number, besides the other learned men
and Doctors), the 'Instruction as to the Faith' which
was to be signed was read, heard, and advised to
be delivered and read before His Imperial Majesty,
yesterday[h] afternoon. For although the aforesaid
Elector and Princes had, through their Councillors,
asked the Emperor for an extension of the time
(there being some delay in the transcribing and
placing of the Preface and conclusion), this had
been refused." The Confession was brought to the
afternoon session of the Diet on the twenty-third,
subscribed by the above parties. " Dr Brueck [the
Saxon Chancellor] prayed His Imperial Majesty to
have it read in German, in the presence of the Electors, Princes and other States, offering them to
deliver it in German and Latin to His Majesty, as
he had proposed " [the year before]. After twice
refusing, the Emperor allowed this on the morrow.
They requested that " it should be left in their hands
that night, that they might carefully look over and
correct it, since it had been hurried." The German
copy was already transcribed, for the Legates say,
"When this 'Instruction,' which runs to some fifty
leaves, [i] shall be fully transcribed, we will send you a
correct copy." The Latin copy was delivered in Melanchthon's own hand, [k] there having been no time

---

[h] The letter is dated on " Friday June 25, early."

[i] The Apology, with the preface and conclusion, occupies
thirty-one 8vo. printed pages. The copy of fifty leaves must
have been that intended for the Emperor. The Cassel copy (see
below) contains fifty-one leaves; Ansp. ii. 56 ; Ansp. iii. 27 ; Weimar, ii. 44. The legates promise a copy from this copy.

[k] Lindanus asserts this solemnly. " I William D. Lindanus
[Bishop] of Ruremund have inspected this autograph, and have,

to transcribe it. The legates of Nuremburg assure the Council; "The Instruction, as far as relates to the Articles of faith, is in substance nearly the same, as we have before sent you; only, in some places, it has been improved, and throughout has been made as gentle as possible, without, as far as we can see, the omission of any thing essential."

The Nuremburg legates mention distinctly, that the Confession was signed by those whom they had named as present, "John Duke of Saxony, Elector; George, Margrave of Brandenburg; Ernest, Duke of Luneburg; Philip, Landgrave of Hesse; also by themselves and the legates of Reytlingen." There is a great body of authority[1] for the addition of two other names, John Frederic, Duke of Saxony, son of the Elector; and Francis Duke of Luneburg, the son of Duke Ernest. Wolfgang, Prince of Anhalt, also certainly signed it. All these signed both copies, and, in signing them, accepted them as con-

---

with D. Joachim Hopper, compared it with the edition of 1531; the Rev. D. Vigli Zwichem, who, with me, was summoned A.D. 72. by our holy Lord Pius IV. to the Council of Trent, having kindly communicated it to me out of the Imperial Archives at Brussels." (Conc. Disc. p. 186. ad marg.) "This copy P. Melanchthon wrote out with his own hand, as I could see from other autograph letters of his." Ib. p. 187, 8.

[1] Koellner puts together the evidence: 1. all known MSS. of the Latin confession in Archives; 2. the first Latin edition; 3. all Melanchthon's editions (he must have known who subscribed); 4. the five German MSS. which have any subscription (three have none). The names stood first at the end of the preface, then were removed to the end of all; 5. the six anonymous editions of 1530; 6. Melanchthon's editions of the German original; 7. his edition of 1531 was again signed by Philip of Hesse at Nuremburg 1561, so guaranteeing the former signatures; 8. Jonas (ad Luth. Cœlestin. i. 135)

fessions of their own faith.   The only difficulty had
been   about   the Landgrave.   He was a brave and
impetuous young man of about twenty-eight; had
been called a Zwinglian, and Zwingli "his earthly
idol [m]." Luther, at the desire of Melanchthon [n], had
written to him, and had gained so much from him
that he subscribed the Confession.   Melanchthon
thought that he approved of it [o].   Jonas says, "The
Landgrave subscribed with us ; but he says that on
the Sacrament he is not satisfied by our people [p]."
He subscribed, however, both Confessions, and presented them with the rest, as his own faith and that
of the preachers in his territory.   He was unhappily
a profligate, but of this the Lutherans had at that
time apparently no knowledge.   "[q] Those of Stras-

and 9. Lindanus, who had seen the original copy (Conc. Disc. p.
186-8), mention the younger Prince of Saxony ; 10. Luther (ad
Hausmann. de W. iv. 70) both ; as does 11. Spalatin (Vit. Elect.
Saxon. in Mencken. ii. 1118) ; 12. Reichsabschied v. J. 1530
(Neue Sammlung d. R.) ; 13. Anzeygung u. beschreibung Rom. K.
Einreyten &c.   The contrary grounds have no weight against
these.   See Koellner Symbolik. p. 201-10.

[m] Frumentarius, a Hessian, wrote in 1527 from Marpurg to
Zwingli ; "1 would not have you ignorant, that my prince and
lord is by his equals daily in joke called a Zwinglian, and you his
earthly idol." (Hottinger, H. E. S. 16. T. v. P. ii. p. 604.)

[n] Mel. Ep. ad Vit. C. R. ii. 721. see Ep. ad Luth. 1b. iv. 34.
N. 721. Suppl.

[o] " The Landgrave approved of our Confession and subscribed
it.   You will do much, I trust, if you will confirm him by your
letters."   (Mel. ad Luth. C. R. 736. June 24.) " I thank you for
the letters to the Landgrave, which you extorted at last.   I hope
they will be of use.   He has already subscribed with us the Confession, where there is an Article on the Lord's Supper after the
mind of Luther." (Ib. 742. Vit. ap. Luth. Jun. 26.)

[p] Ib. N. 752.   [q] Id.

burg sought to be admitted, saving the article of the Sacrament; but the princes would not."

On June 25, the Confession was at last read. The[r] two Chancellors of Saxony, Dr Brueck and Dr Bayer, brought with them the Confession in the two languages, Brueck the Latin, Bayer the German. The Emperor wished the Latin copy to be read, probably in order that none but the Theologians might understand it. The Elector, probably with the opposite desire, that *all* might understand it, pressed that the German copy should be read. " Since," he said, " we are on German ground, I hope that your Majesty will allow us to speak German." " The Emperor readily assented." But when "Chancellor Bayer read it so clearly, that his voice could be heard, even in the lower court of the Episcopal palace," the court was, at the Emperor's command, cleared of all except the members of the Diet and their Councillors[s]. "Bayer finished the whole in two hours. The Emperor was attentive[t]." The reading over, Brueck presented both copies to Alexander Schweiss, Secretary to the Emperor. As the Secretary was giving them to the Elector of Maintz, the Emperor took them himself; and gave the German copy to the Elector, to lay up in the Imperial Archives. For, having been read solemnly in a Diet, it, especially, had become a state-document. The Latin copy the Emperor retained[u]; doubtless, for those unacquainted with German

---

[r] Seckendorf, Hist. Luth. ii. sect. 29. § 65, p. 170.

[s] Brueck in Foerstemann's Archiv. p. 55.   [t] Jonas, 1. c.

[u] Spalatin, Kurtzes Verzeichniss, &c. in Luther's Werke, Th. xx. p. 205, ed. Leipz.

whose aid he sought in this matter. Shortly after (July 12) Brenz[v] reports that it *had* been sent to Rome by couriers; and that on that day the messenger returned from Rome, bringing back the judgment of the Pope, " the nature of which," Brenz says, " we, as yet, have not seen." It was then returned, and deposited in the Emperor's Archives at Brussels. For there Archbishop Lindan saw it and collated it[w]. The Duke of Alba asked for it, for Philip II.[x]; but whether it was sent to Spain, is not known.

The German copy was probably taken, with other documents, .to the Council of Trent, and not returned[y]. It has been looked for in the Vatican and not found[z].

The Emperor asked and obtained from the Elector and Princes the promise that they would not publish the Confession[a], without his consent[b]. Pains were taken to keep that promise. The legates of Nuremberg insist upon it in their letter to the Senate; and so does Melanchthon in his[c], to Luther, Ca-

---

[v] Ep. ad Isenm. C. R. 777.   [w] See ab. p. 26.

[x] *Zwichem ab Aytta.* Ep. ad Hopper. p. 145. (quoted by Weber i. 77.)   [y] Weber found at Mainz a MS. mentioning three Collections " in matters of religion, taken to the Council at Trent." The third " Acta Conventus imperialia Augustan. A. D. 1530, " is no longer there. The original Confession was probably among these Acta; otherwise it must have been lost before 1546. i. 157. sqq.   [z] Hase Symbolische Bucher Præf.

[a] " After this, His Imperial Majesty spoke apart to the Elector and Princes, and begged them to retain the Confession which had been read, and not to put it in print, which also they promised His Majesty." Leg. Norimb. Ib. 743.   [b] Brueck, l. c. p. 51.

[c] Ep. 745. Luth. (Jun. 27.) 740. Camerar. (Jun. 25.) 742. Vit. (Jun. 26.)

merar, and Vitus. He even makes it a ground, why it "[d] should not be sent to Wittenberg, that Bugenhagen did not regard this duty." The Senate of Nuremberg, in their answer (Jun. 18,) promised "[e] not to lend the Confession, or allow it to be copied, much less to print it." But the copies were already too multiplied. Different parties whose adherence was hoped for, had already received it without any restriction, and even afterwards, Brenz does not seem to have known of the prohibition. "[f] Our princes," he says July 12, "lately presented to the Emperor a confession of their faith and of the teaching of their preachers, written in German and Latin. The German copy our magistrates sent *before this time* (ante hos dies) to the Senate at Halle by Buchsenhausen; which if the Senate shewed you and consulted you, well. If they kept it back, they did as they are wont. I send you a Latin copy, to be read with the brethren."

Minds were, at that time, strung up to know the results of the eventful day, and the belief of this new and spreading body. "Many," says Spalatin, "[g] desire to have the Confession, and take all pains to obtain it." The Emperor himself, during the diet, "[h] had the Confession translated into Italian and French by Alphonso Waldes and Alexander Schweiss, his secretaries[i]." He sent a copy of the Latin Confession to the Theological faculty of "Louvain, although eighty [four hundred English] miles distant." He directed the French translation

---

[d] ad Vit. l. c.   [e] Ib. Ep. 748. col. 148.
[f] Ep. 777. ad Isenm.   [g] l. c. p. 286.   [h] Jonas, l. c.
[i] Spalatin, in Luth. Werke, Th. xx. p. 208. ed. Leipz.

to be made with the greatest care word for word (it is said) in order that he might himself better understand the Confession. But the translations, made for him, were never published. A contemporary translation from the Latin, made probably for the Landgrave of Hesse, is still extant at Cassel. "Our Confession has been asked for," Spalatin says[k], "to be translated, for the King of England, the King of Portugal, the Duke of Juliers, the Duke of Lorraine, and other great princes. We purpose, if God will, to bring it with us in Latin and German."

The Emperor probably wished to have a refutation ready, before the Confession itself came out. Both the German and Latin copies came out, however, from some unknown hand, without name of place or printer, while the Diet was yet sitting. The German was entitled "[l] Declaration and Confession of faith and doctrine, which the appealing States have delivered to His Imperial Majesty at the *present* Diet at Augsburg." Copies of six anonymous editions of this German Confession were published during the same year, in different dialects or parts of Germany[m]. In the same period only one

---

[k] l. c.   [l] Anzeigung und Bekantnus des Glaubens unnd der lere, so die adpellierenden Stende Key. Maiestet auff yetzigen tag zu Augspurg œberantwurt habend MDXXX. The Bodleian copy of this very rare edition [Luther. Tracts Fasc. 55. n. 31.] has the characteristics of that, from which Weber (i. 258. sqq.) thinks that the other five were derived.

[m] Weber thinks the 1st, in the Swiss-upper-land Dialect, was printed in Switzerland or Upper-Germany, perhaps at Augsburg; 2. the same dialect softened, perhaps at Breslau; 3. the same dialect still more softened, probably in Upper-Germany; 4. the same extremely softened; here and there Lower Saxon Words; pro-

unathorised Latin Confession was published, and that, by one ignorant of Latin[n]. The preponderance of the German copies shews that the chief interest was with the people. The Confession came out anonymously, " the Emperor having," it is said, " at the Diet published an edict forbidding the publication of books without the Imperial approbation, and this edict having, in fact, been directed against the Lutheran books[o]."

These editions were almost of necessity imperfect and full of errata. Melanchthon then himself, before the Diet was closed[p], published correct copies both of the German and Latin Confessions. The first Latin edition was published within two months of the appearance of the unauthorised edition. In the preface to this Edition Melanchthon says, "[q] This Confession was published *two months ago*[r] by some

bably in some Imperial city of Lower Saxony, perhaps Lubeck. 5. Lower Saxon dialect, perhaps at Magdeburg. [Salig] 6. Upper Saxon at Wittenberg.

[n] Weber i. 405. The instances given by Weber are decisive.

[o] Walch. 1. 3. 13. quoting J. J. Müller Historie von d. Evangel. Stænde Protestat. &c. iii. 23. p. 692.

[p] Pistorius, " I have two copies, one Latin and German, of the very first edition at Wittenberg, in 4to. which came to Augsburg, while the Diet was still continuing." A.D. 1561, published in Kuchelbecker Anal. Hass. Coll. 12. p. 441.

[q] Confessio Fidei exhibita invictiss. Imp. Carolo V. in Comiciis Augustæ Anno MDXXX. Addita est Apologia Confessionis. Beide Deudsch und Latinisch. Witebergæ. The Bodleian has two copies of this, the editio princeps. Luth. Tr. Fasc. 56. n. 20. and 4. F. 19. Th. BS.

[r] In the 2nd edit. in 4to Melanchthon altered the date to " six months ago ; " and the preface to the Apology was subsequently re-printed from this.

greedy printer, without the knowledge of the princes who presented it to the Emperor, and it is so printed, that, in many places, it has evidently been depraved on purpose. But since the princes cannot get it out of peoples' hands, if they would, and yet there is danger that the faults of that edition should give birth to new calumnies, it became necessary to re-publish it, revised and amended, because it apper-tains not only to the estimation of the princes, but to religion also, that faulty works of this sort should not be sent abroad under their names. Wherefore now we send out a Confession, faithfully and dili-gently transcribed from an authentic copy."

In speaking of "*this* Confession, published by some greedy printer," Melanchthon probably meant the Latin copy only. 1. He used the singular twice; "*this* Confession;" "*an* authentic copy." 2. The two copies of the Confession (though in substance, they were one and the same Confession) were distinct, and had been presented to the Emperor together, but as two copies. 3. Melanchthon published the two Confessions simultaneously but separately. The Latin, with the Latin Apology were printed so as to make one whole[s]; the German Confession, with the German Apology, probably made a second whole, or volume. The whole might be united together; but the two "Confessions" did not come together (the Latin Apology, in any case, coming between them),

---

[s] The signature of the Latin copy of the Confession, A. &c. is continued on into the Latin Apology; in which, at fol. 91, the signature Aa. begins, and ends at Vv. iii. and then breaks off. The signature of the German Confession is 𝕬𝕬. which admits of being joined on, but does not continue the signature of the Apology.

so that he could hardly say, " *this* Confession," of what was so distinct.   For both copies of the Confession were printed in that year; but the Apology (which if the whole should be united, *must* come between) not until 1531.   When he printed them then, they could not make one whole.   4. The publisher of the Latin was disqualified for his task by ignorance; not so (as far as appears) the publishers of the German.

Notwithstanding its many errors of the press, the wording of the unauthorised copy has in some cases been even preferred to that put forth by Melanchthon[t].   It corresponds remarkably with what was long accounted, even by Sovereigns, the original of the Confession of Augsburg, the copy preserved in the Archives at Maintz[u].   In the Article on the Sacrament however, with which we are concerned, the reading of the unauthorised copies and those of the editions corrected by Melanchthon are exactly the sense except as to one immaterial, but singular, idiom in the German[v].

[t] Walch (i. 3. 13.) quoting as his authority die nochmalige Haupt-vertheidigung des evangelischen Augapfels. c. 23. p. 347.

[u] Weber, 1. 401—4.

[v] The German copy has, "von dem Abentmal des Herren wirt also gelert, das warer leyb und blut Christi warhafftigklich under der gestalt des brots und weyns im Abentmal gegenwertig sey *gegeben*, und da aussgeteylt und genommen werde, derhalb wirt auch die gegenleer verworffen." Tract. Luth. Fasc. 55. n. 31. The word "gegeben" is pleonastic, and found in no subsequent copy.   I had thought that it might be the blending of two different readings; but Prof. Max Müller has kindly informed me, that its meaning would be, that "the true Body and Blood of Christ are truly *given so as to be present* under the form of bread and wine; according to the analogy of the common phrase 'es giebt.'"

The two copies of the Confession, the German and the Latin, were equally original. Both are, in their substance, the joint work of Luther, Melanchthon, Jonas, and Bugenhagen. The Confession is, in a manner, ascribed to Luther or Melanchthon separately; Luther having mainly conceived it, and Melanchthon having chiefly executed it. In his Table-talk Luther counts it with works, which were entirely his own. " [w] The Catechism, the exposition of the ten commandments, and the Confession of Augsburg, are mine, not Creuziger's or Roerer's." Yet Luther himself calls the Confession Melanchthon's [x], in letters to Melanchthon himself and to others. The question, however, is indifferent. Luther and Melanchthon were at this time wholly of one mind. Melanchthon wrote to Luther as " [y] his father," "his very dear father," and professed in all things to follow his counsels. He was as much opposed to the Zwinglians, as Luther himself. However he altered the Confession in words, he made no alteration affecting any doctrine, until ten years later [z]. *Now*, when the Landgrave of Hesse wished the Zwinglians to be admitted into the confederation, he and Brenz answered, that, though pained at

[w] Tischreden, xxxvii. 23. T. xxiv. col. 1552. ed. Halle, 4.

[x] " I re-read yesterday the whole of *your* Apology [the Confession] and it mightily pleases me." Luth. Mel. Ep. 1243. De W. add 1236. Ib. " I have here a copy of *his* confession; but at [the Emperor's] command to be held back." Ep. 1246. Cordat.

[y] Ep. 741. (C. R.) 745. 792. 879.

[z] In the Editio variata of 1540. " In the first ten years from A. 1530, to nearly 1540, there was no real change made in the points which affect the Articles of faith." Hauptvertheidigung des Augapfels, c. 21. p. 336.

the division, they could not with a good conscience call the Zwinglians " brothers," " [a] since it would be held that we approved of their doctrine, which, before God, we cannot support."

And again to Gorlich [b];

" As to the faction of Zwingli, I bid you be of good cheer. I have myself heard the chief of that sect [in the conference of Marburg A. 1529.] and have learned how utterly they are without all Christian doctrine. They only philosophise childishly. So then they cannot last. For every plant which is not of God shall be rooted up. Were they to dispute for six whole centuries, they have but this one sentence, 'The flesh profiteth nothing.' This they now pervert to mean the flesh of Christ."

In this same year, June 3, he mentions a purpose of writing against them, in a tone which evinces his own personal sense of peril from their doctrine. He writes to Lachmann;

" [c] I hear that in your neighbourhood the Zwinglian doctrine is approved by some. I thought that you, being so good and modest a man, ought to be warned, by no means to fall into the doctrine of Zwingli. Not without very great temptations have I learned, how much amiss there is in that doctrine of Zwingli. Believe me, no one who has been tempted will defend it. I have on hand a writing [d] in which I shall soon deliver the testimony of my conscience thereon. Would that they who are now so eager for new doctrines, would teach as diligently what should serve to edifying, on the power and nature of faith, on repentance, and the other parts of Christian doctrine, as they urge

[a] Ep. 720. C. Ib. On his judgment as to the Zwinglians generally see Ib. 670. 797. and Brenz, 777.   [b] Ib. 670.
  [c] Ep. 711.   [d] The de sententiis patrum de S. Cœna, which came out in 1530. (C. R. xxiii. 732. sqq.)

vehemently their opinion on the Lord's Supper, for which they have no solid ground whatever."

Melanchthon dreaded especially, and with good reason, the alliance with the Divines [e] and people of Strasburg.   It is said that the Zwinglians were then more numerous than the Lutherans [f].   The Lutherans were weak; the union with the Zwinglians would (as the Landgrave of Hesse saw) have increased their political strength.   Melanchthon dreaded injury to their belief, more than their weakness.   "[g]They of Strasburg and some other sworn adherents of Zwinglian doctrine desire to make alliance with us and with your city.—Conscience constrains me to write to you hereon.   I beseech you, as much as you can, give diligence that the Zwinglians be not received into any alliance.   For it suiteth not, to defend their impious opinion or to confirm the strength of those who follow that impious doctrine, that the poison spread not further.—The doctrine itself[h] on the Lord's Supper is altogether profane.   I am now writing against the opinion of Zwingli.   For I see that they must be resisted to the uttermost.   Some of our people do not reject

[e] He suspected Bucer, because he tried to make out, that the Lutheran and Zwinglian doctrine was the same. Judic. de Zwinglii doctr. C. R. 798. so also Brenz, Ib. 893.

[f] "There is no need that I should write, how few are on our side, and how many either with the Pope or the Sacramentaries" [Zwinglians]. Fragm. Ep. Spalatini Ib. 753.

[g] "Our side is, in truth, weak.   Greater is the number of the bad." Mel. Luth. Ib. 744.

[h] Ep. 611. Bomgartnero. M. writes to him as one of the Senate of Nuremberg, whose alliance Strasburg desired.   He uses the word, "lest *profaneness* should spread wider," to Camerarius. Ib. 609.

that alliance with those of Strasburg. But do you, I beseech you, effect that such and so foul an association come not together."

And in another letter, soon after, to the same, "[i] I would rather die than that ours should be contaminated with fellowship in the Zwinglian cause."

The circumstances under which the Confession had been composed, had, in some cases, produced slight differences between the German and Latin Articles. Time had pressed. It had been difficult to prepare the two copies, especially at last, against the day of the Diet. Melanchthon was employed now upon the one, now upon the other, and there was no leisure to compare them, or bring them into exact correspondence. Lindanus[k] pointed out the different wording in the German and Latin copies of the eighth Article. The difference lies in the greater fulness of the Latin. Translated literally they stand;

<table>
<tr><td align="center">GERMAN.</td><td align="center">LATIN.</td></tr>
<tr><td>"Although the Christian Church is properly nothing else than the congregation of all faithful and holy persons,

yet since in this life many false Christians and hypocrites and open sinners too remain among the pious, the Sacraments are *alike efficacious,*</td><td>"Although the Church is properly a congregation of saints and true believers,

yet since in this life many hypocrites and evil men are intermixed, we may use the Sacraments which are administered by the evil, according to</td></tr>
</table>

[i] Ib. 618.   [k] Concordia Discors. iii. 3. p. 185.

although the Priests through whom they are administered, are not pious, as Christ points out: 'The Pharisees sit on Moses' seat &c.' Therefore the Donatists and all others are condemned who hold otherwise."

the word of Christ, 'The Scribes and Pharisees sat in Moses' seat.' *And the Sacraments and word are efficacious on account of the institution and commandment of Christ, although they are exhibited by evil men.* They condemn the Donatists and the like who denied that we may use the ministry of the evil in the Church, and held that the ministry of the evil was useless and inefficacious."

In like way, in the ninth Article, the Latin contains a remarkable addition. There is no contradiction between the Articles; but the Latin contains more than the German.

GERMAN.

"Wherefore the Anabaptists are rejected, who teach that Infant Baptism is not right."

LATIN.

"They condemn the Anabaptists, who disapprove Infant Baptism, *and affirm that children without Baptism are saved.*"

And so then as to the tenth Article. All Lutherans have held that the German and Latin copies state the same doctrine. Each is to be interpreted by the other. It would be absurd to suppose that on such a solemn public occasion, the Lutherans presented, as the test of their faith and the ground of toleration being extended to them, two Confessions at variance with one another, and the one with their own belief. The German also was the popular form, for those of their own communion, that, through which the people were taught[1]; the Latin, as the language understood by all the West, was the form adapted for, and considered by, their opponents.

The tenth Article stood thus[m] in the two copies. The German was never varied; the Latin not till 1540.

<table>
<tr><td>GERMAN[n].</td><td>LATIN[o].</td></tr>
</table>

"*Of the Supper of the Lord* is thus taught, *that the* true *Body and Blood of Christ are truly present* under the form of bread and wine *in the Lord's Supper, and are* there *distributed* and received.. Wherefore also the opposed doctrine is rejected."

"*Of the Supper of the Lord* they teach, *that the Body and Blood of Christ are truly present, and are distributed* to communicants *in the Lord's Supper*, and they disapprove those who teach otherwise."

[1] " Have we not seen their Confession published in German to the people before the convention of the Princes at Augsburg was dissolved ? " Cochl. Velit. in Apol. Mel. 1534. Aiiib. v. in Weber ii. 9.

[m] I have put in Italics what is exactly the same in the two copies.

[n] " Von dem Abendmal des Herrn wirt also geleret, das warer leib und blut Christi warhafftiglich unter gestalt des brods und weins in Abendmal gegenwertig sey, und da ausgeteilt und genomen wirt. Derhalben wirt auch die gegenlahr verworffen." From Bodleian copy (Mason F. F. 390). It has all the marks which Weber in his kritische Geschichte der Augspurgischen Confession ii. 17-20, gives of the third class, or the most correct edition.

[o] De cœna Domini docent, quod corpus et sanguis Christi vere adsint et distribuantur vescentibus in cœna Domini et improbant secus docentes.

The Latin word " vescentibus " corresponds to the German " und genommen wirt." The Lutherans had to defend themselves on the ground that in the Latin form there is no mention of the elements whatever, Walch says indeed truly ;

" ᵖ This difference is of no moment. It relates to the words only, not to the thing itself. For although, in the Latin Confession, nothing is said of the bread and wine, yet it is self-evident that their presence is not denied ; because, in the holy Supper, the Body and Blood of Christ are not distributed without the bread and wine. When then our forefathers professed in Latin, that the Body and Blood of Christ are present in the Lord's Supper, that which, in the German copy, is read in express words, is declared by the very fact of the case. The statement in the Apology (Art. x.) that ' in the Supper of the Lord the Body and Blood of Christ are truly and substantially present, and are truly exhibited, together with those things which are seen, the bread and wine, to those who receive the Sacrament,' so far from varying from the Article of the Confession of Augsburg, explains and confirms what is there taught."

This principle that the two copies, the Latin and the German, were to explain one another, was acted upon by Melanchthon himself in the very year in which they were presented. The Latin Article on Original sin had not been carefully framed ; for though its meaning is plain, yet it speaks of actual rather than original sin. " They teach," it says, " that, after the fall of Adam, all men, propagated according to nature, are born with sin, i. e. without fear of God, without confidence towards God, and with concupiscence ; and that this disease, or

ᵖ 1. 3. 33. p. 284.

fault of origin is truly sin[q]." The Roman theologians in their confutation had said;

"The declaration of the Article, that 'original sin is, that men are born without fear of God, without confidence towards God,' is altogether to be rejected, since it is plain to any Christian, that 'to be without fear of God, without confidence towards God,' is rather the actual sin of an adult than the guilt [noxam] of a new born infant, who, as yet, hath not the use of reason, as the Lord said to Moses, 'Thy little ones, who this day know not the difference of good and evil.'" Deut. i. 39.

Melanchthon treats the objection as a cavil, but appeals to the German Confession, as explaining the meaning;

"That all good men may know, that we teach nothing amiss in this matter, we first ask that the German confession be inspected. For there it is thus written; 'Further, it is taught, that after the fall of Adam, all men, born in the way of nature, are conceived and born in sin, i. e. they all, from their mother's womb, are full of evil lusts and inclinations, and can, from nature, have no true fear of God, nor true belief in God.' This passage attests, that we deny to those who are propagated according to carnal nature, not only acts, but the power also, or gift of producing fear, or confidence towards God."

The passage, in the German confession, is, *thus far*, more correct than the Latin.

In speaking of the outward visible part of the Sacrament, Luther did not confine himself to one form of words, but, in one and the same meaning,

---

q Our own Article on Original Sin is throughout exact, which neither the German nor the Latin Confession of Augsburg is. Here it says more correctly, " has the nature of sin."

he used the words "under the form of bread" "under bread" "in bread;" not meaning thereby any local presence (for that he disclaimed), but that by virtue of our Lord's words, "This is My Body," there is, "in" or "under" those outward visible substances, an invisible Sacramental Presence of our Lord's Body and Blood, external to us, in a manner known to God only.

Besides the Confession of Augsburg, the words "under the form of bread and wine " occur in a place where Luther must have inserted them, expressly for the purpose of impressing upon the people the doctrine which he believed. In 1523, Luther nearly retained the old form. " [r] The Body [Leichnam] of our Lord Jesus Christ preserve my" (or "thy ")

[r] Weise, Christliche Messe zu halten, aus d. Lat. ubersetzt durch Paul. Speratum. Wercke, Th. xxii. p. 236. ed. Leipz.   In the Agenda for Brandenburg and Nuremburg 1533, the direction is, " It shall be given him with these words ' Take and eat, That is the Body of Christ which was given for thee,' and for the Cup ' Take and drink, That is My Blood of the New Testament which is shed for thy sins.' "   (Kirchen Ordnung in meiner gnedigen Herrn des Marggraven zu Brandenburg und eins erbern Rats der Stat Nurmberg Oberkeyt und gepieten wie man sich bayde mit der Lere und Ceremomien halten solle f. 41.)   In the kirchen Ordnung put out, 1580, under Augustus Elector of Saxony for his dominions, the Brandenburg form is enlarged.   " In distributing the Body of Christ, let the Minister say emphatically and audibly, ' Take and eat; That is the Body of Christ which is given for thee.   It strengthen and uphold thee in faith to life everlasting.' And in giving the Blood of Christ, ' Take and drink ; that is the Blood of Jesus Christ which was shed for thy sins.   It strengthen and preserve thee in right faith to life everlasting.'" Des—Fursten— Augusten Hertzogen zu Sachsen &c. Ordnung wie es in s. Churf. G. Landen bey den Kirchen mit der lehr u. Ceremonien—gehalten werden sol. Leipz. cum privilegio Elect. Sax. 1580. f. 39, 40.

"[a] soul unto everlasting life; and the Blood of our Saviour &c."

In a "Saxon Missal," drawn up by Luther for Saxony and used in Torgau, in the time of John Frederic, Duke of Saxony, the words prescribed to be used in delivering the Sacrament are; "[t] Receive under the *species* of the bread the true Body of our Lord Jesus Christ &c." "Receive under the *species* of the wine the true Blood of the Lord Jesus Christ."

At the same date at which Luther, in the Augsburg Confession and his liturgy, employed the words "under the form" &c. he used in the same sense the word "in" in the "seventeen Articles."

"[u] Art. 10. The Eucharistia, or sacrament of the altar, consists also of two parts. Namely, there is truly present *in*

[a] Ex Missa Saxonica Joann. Friderici per Lutherum scripta. fol. H. v. quoted by Lindan. Diatr. Analyt. p. 167. He had just quoted Art. x. of the Confession of Augsburg, as printed at Wesel A. 1563, and says of the Missa Saxonica, that it was "appressam hic." Probably he means that it was "joined on to," the copy of the Confession. The Dialect in both is the same Low German, bordering in some words on Dutch. In both places, and in these alone, (as far as I have seen) the word "specie" is substituted for "Gestalt." In this case the "Communion Office" also was printed at Wesel. The words of Art. x. in that edition are, "Von dem Abentmal des Herrn wordt also gelert. Dat warhafftig Lyff und Blut Christi waerachtelich under die specie des Brodts und Weins im Abendtmaehl tegenwordich sey." Vesal. A. lxii. d. xiiii. Februarii apud Hans de Braecker.

[t] "Ontfangt daer onder die specie des Brodts dat waerachtigh Lychaem [Lychnaem] ons Heeren Jesu Christi etcet." Item folio eodem; "Ontfangt daer under die specie des weines dat waerachtige Blutt des Heeren Jesu Christi." l. c. p. 167.

[u] Die bekentnus Martini Luthers auff den itzigen angestelter

bread and *in* wine the true Body and Blood of Christ, according to the word, 'This is My Body,' 'This is My Blood;' and there is not bread and wine only, as the contrary part now gives out. This word requires also and brings faith too: and exercises it in all those who desire this Sacrament, and do not act against it; as Baptism brings faith, if one desires it."

And in the Confession of faith A.D. 1529,

"[v] In like way, I also say and confess of the Sacrament of the Altar, that there truly the Body and Blood is, in bread and wine, orally eaten and drunken; although the priest who gives it, or those who receive it, believed not or otherwise misused it, for it rests not on the belief or unbelief of men, but on God's word and ordinance."

In the visitation-book also, for the Electorate of Saxony, compiled by Melanchthon in Latin 1527, and published in German in 1528, with a preface by Luther, in which he calls it " a witness and confession of *our* faith ; "

"[w] Of the Sacrament of the true Body and Blood of our dear Lord Jesus Christ these three Articles shall be laid before men. First that they believe that *in* the bread is the true Body and Blood of Christ, and *in* the wine the true Blood of Christ. For so teacheth the word of Christ in the Gospels, Matthew, Mark, and Luke. 'That is My Blood of the new Testament, which is shed for many, for forgiveness of sins.'"

In his own directions for celebrating the Sacrament in German A.D. 1526, he says[x];

Reichstag zu Augsburgk eynzulegen. In siebentzehen Artickel verfasset. Im xxx. Jar.   [v] Bekentnis des Glaubens D. M. Luthers ausgangen im 1529 Jare, Wercke, Th. ii. p. 11. ed. Eisleb.
  [w] Das Visitatorn Buchlin, Wercke, ix. 257. ed. Wit.
  [x] Deudsche Messe xxii. 246. ed. Leipz.

" As the Sacrament is lifted up bodily, and yet there-under Christ's Body and Blood are not seen &c."

This same word "under" Luther retained in both his Catechisms, which he published in German in 1529, and which were translated into Latin in the same year. In the lesser he says;

" What is the Sacrament of the Altar?
" The Sacrament of the Altar is the true Body and true Blood of our Lord Jesus Christ, *under* the Bread and wine[y], instituted by Christ Himself for us Christians to eat and to drink."

The answer in the larger Catechism is nearly the same, but adds the word " in."

" It is the true Body and Blood of our Lord Jesus Christ, *in* and *under* [z] the bread and wine, instituted and commanded through the word of Christ for us Christians to eat and to drink."

The two forms then of the Confession of Augsburg, the Latin and the German, really expressed the same belief. For (as was observed) the word " distributed " implies the presence of the consecrated elements, by means of which that Body and Blood are " distributed."
Of these two forms, the German expresses the Lutheran belief most clearly. In the Latin, they had already made an ineffectual concession (probably to Bucer and the people of Strasburg), by omitting, as it seems, the word " substantially," a concession, not of any moment in itself, but only

[y] Unter dem Brodt und Wein. Wercke, xxii. 49.
[z] In und unter dem B. u. W. Ib. 96.

as far as it implied any temper of compromise. Schnepf, who was present at the conference when this was decided, alludes to, but does not state the reason of the omission[a].

" It is known to all who were present at that deliberation at Augsburg A. D. 1530, in which the Confession, then just written, before it should be offered to the Emperor Charles V., was submitted to the censorship of the theologians of the Princes, and to those who were Councillors of our Princes and the deputies of the two cities, on *what ground it was determined at that time* to use only the word 'truly' [present] although ambiguous (as many then contended), whereas, at that time, no one of all those who adhered to the Augsburg Confession and were admitted to this deliberative congress, held with the Zwinglians. For I too was present, and, although by no desert of my own, formed some part of the transactions; that no one may think that I relate what I have heard of others, and so take off from the weight of my testimony."

"But although the Zwinglians may easily delude the incautious through the Article of the Confession, which uses the adverb 'truly' only, as though they [the Zwinglians] taught nothing on the Eucharist at variance with the Confession of Augsburg, yet the Apology, which nobly defends our Confession, and was presented to the Emperor in the same Diet of Augsburg, but rejected, guards the true doctrine on the Lord's Supper, by adding the word 'substantially,' removes scruples, and clears it from all ambiguity."

The word "truly," does, of course, contain every thing; and, accordingly, it was not on this

[a] Schnepf lived to see the partial developement of this spirit of compromise; and as the title of His tract expresses, put out his "Confession" as a witness against it. "Confessio Ech. Schnepfii de Eucharistia, hanc ob causam hoc potissimum tempore edita,

side that the Roman Theologians questioned the Confession. The Emperor had, on whatever ground, placed the Latin copy, not the German, in the hands of the Theologians, [b] to refute. These prepared the Confutation, while the Diet was yet sitting. They saw very clearly that, although the Confession did not in words *reject*, it did not *express*, their belief. They qualified, therefore, their assent, saying, that it did "not offend *in words*" (i. e. as far as it went and expressed) provided only that two other points were added or understood; 1. the doctrine of concomitance; 2. that of Transubstantiation.

The words of the Confutation are;

"[c] The tenth Article in no ways offends *in words;* since they confess that, in the Eucharist, after the Consecration lawfully made, the Body and Blood of Christ are substantially ["præsentially" one MS.] and truly there; *if only they believe,* that Christ is there under *each* kind [species], so that the Blood of Christ should, by concomitance, be no less under the 'kind' of bread, than under the 'kind' of wine, and conversely. Else in the Eucharist the Body

quod certamina vetera de cœna Dominica, novis libellis classicum canentibus, recrudescere inceperint. Jenæ 1556.

[b] Celestine mentions the names of twenty Theologians, employed by the Emperor in refuting the Confession; " Eck, Faber [i. e. Schmidt], Augustin Marius, Bishop of Salon, Wimpina, Cochlæus, Hang, Stofs, Colli, Conraden Tho. Usingen, Mensing, Dietenberger, Burckhard, Speiser, Arnold of Wesel, Medard, Augustin von Cottelin, Redorffer, Montinus, Kretz. l. c. or, " Etliche Historica, so sich auff diesem Reichstag zugetragen," in Luther's Wercke, Th. v. p. 34. ed. Jen.

[c] Confess. Fid. p. 165. ed. Spiek.

of Christ would be dead and bloodless, contrary to S. Paul, that 'Christ, being risen from the dead, death hath no more dominion over Him.'"

"One thing is to be added, as exceedingly necessary to this Article of the Confession, *that they should believe* the Church rather than some who teach amiss, that, by the Almighty word of God in the consecration of the Eucharist the substance of bread is changed into the Body of Christ. For so it was defined by a General Council. [Lat. iv. A. 1215. c. 1.]"

Lindanus [d], when urging upon the Theologians of Wittenberg, that they had forsaken the doctrine with which their teachers had set out, quotes the German copy of this "Confutation," as approving the doctrine of the Confession, to the same extent, and with the reservation of the same two points.

"The tenth [Article] is right; yet so that it be *moreover* taught, that the substance of the bread and wine ceases, and is changed into the true Body and Blood of Christ. So too the Princes know, or ought to know, that the true Body and Blood of Christ is under each kind of the Holy Sacrament; else the Body were without Blood, and so dead; contrary to the saying of Paul, 'Death shall have no more dominion over Him.'"

The Lutheran Theologians were not, at first, allowed to see the "Confutation." It was read at the Diet, and they were required to accept it. Melanchthon says,

"[e] The Princes bade me and some others prepare an

<hr>

[d] l. c. p. 189.   [e] Præf. ad Apol.

Apology for the Confession, wherein it might be explained to the Emperor, why we did not receive the Confutation, and the objections of the adversaries might be removed. For some of our people had, while the Confutation was being read, taken down heads of the topics and arguments. And this Apology they at last presented to the Emperor, that they might know that we were hindered by very good and grave reasons from approving this Confutation. But the Emperor did not receive the writing when presented."

In the first imperfect sketch of the Apology the Lutheran divines took notice of one objection only, that as to the doctrine of concomitance.

"' We do not feign that the dead body of Christ is received in the Sacrament; or that a bloodless Body, or Blood without a Body, is received, but we hold that Christ whole and living is present in each part of the Sacrament."

This Apology being rejected, Melanchthon enlarged it, so as to make it a new work. And this was chiefly his own. He still called it the same work, but on account of his additions, affixed his own name.

"g Although at the beginning, we framed the Apology, taking counsel with others, yet in printing I have added some things. Wherefore I declare my name, that no one may complain that the book was published, without any definite author."

He then laid down a principle, which may explain his defence of the Article on the Holy Eucharist;

" It was always my custom in these controversies, to retain, as much as ever I could, the outward form of doctrine; that so concord may, at last, more readily be restored. Nor

---

f Apol. Conf. Aug. prima delineatio in Chytr. Hist. Aug. Conf. p. 344. ed. Lat.

g Præf. Ib. " Thou hast then, reader, now our Apology."

do I much otherwise now, although I might rightly withdraw those of this day further from the opinions of the adversaries."

In the enlarged Apology, Melanchthon dropped all direct notice of the Confutation, which he had now obtained, and met its objections incidentally, while bringing out more fully his own belief. In form, the Apology was an expansion and explanation of the Lutheran belief, refuting the Zwinglians, and declaring adherence to the Ancient Church. Against the Zwinglians, Melanchthon argues, that unless the Body of Christ was truly present, "the bread" would not be "the communion of the Body of Christ " (as St. Paul says), "but of His Spirit." He lays down, at the beginning and the end, the belief of the Lutherans, and, in it, states distinctly the existence of the Sacramental elements. Having thus guarded himself, he introduces in the middle the authorities of the Greek Canon and Theophylact, who speak of a Sacramental change, and S. Cyril as declaring a bodily Presence ; and accepts the statement upon which the "Confutation " founded the doctrine of concomitance, while silent on the doctrine itself. Having twice declared the Lutheran belief, it was plainly unjust to fasten on particular expressions, and give them a sense contrary to that belief. He sums up, by declaring their belief in the same words with which he had begun [h];

"These things we have recited, (not with a view of entering here into any discussion hereon, for His Imperial

[h] The whole section is translated in " The doctrine of the real Presence," p. 32-4.

Majesty does not disapprove this Article, but) that, whoever reads this may see more clearly that we maintain the doctrine received in the whole Church, that in the Supper of the Lord the Body and Blood of Christ are truly and substantially present and are truly exhibited, together with those things which are seen, the bread and wine; and we speak of the Presence of the living Christ; for we know that ' death shall no more have dominion over Him.'"

The Latin edition of the Apology had not been published five months[i], when Melanchthon (as his way was, continually to alter whatever he wrote) had nearly finished revising Jonas' German translation of it. In this he again dropped the word "substantially," referred simply to the Greek Canon of the Mass, omitted Theophylact whom he had cited as teaching a change, but retained the passage of S. Cyril. The Article stands thus among the German works of Luther[k]:

" The tenth Article the Opponents do not assail, wherein we confess that our Lord Christ's Body and Blood are truly present in the Supper of Christ, and are, with the visible things, Bread and Wine, presented [dargereicht] and received, as has been held up to this time in the Churches, as the Canon of the Greeks shews. And Cyril saith, that Christ is corporally presented [gereicht] and given in the Supper; for he saith thus." [The whole passage of S. Cyril is then inserted, but the re-statement of their own belief is omitted, as being a repetition.] The Article concludes; " And we

[i] Published the end of April, 1531. Ep. ad Camer. 978. On Sept. 20. he says that " the German Apology, was still being printed," and that he had " some trouble in amending it." Ib. 1006.

[k] Luther's Wercke, xx. 73. Later Editions omit the passage from S. Cyril too, and only have, " as the Canon of the Mass among the Greeks attests and there are some other authorities."

speak of the *Presence of the living Body.* For we know that death shall no more have dominion over Him."

These changes did not affect the doctrine which the Lutherans held. The German Confession too was altered in some respects, chiefly with the view of bringing out more the office of faith, in the Lutheran sense, that a man should believe, not only in Christ, as the Object of faith, but that his own sins are forgiven him for Jesus' sake. In 1533, [1] the Confession was expanded, chiefly in order to inculcate the office of this faith, and so, seven Articles were re-moulded or enlarged. iv. "Justification;" v. "Ministry of the Church;" vi. "The new obedience;" xii. "Penitence;" xiii. "Use of the Sacraments;" xv. "Ecclesiastical rites;" xx. "Good works." Of these iv. v. vi. xx. were altered also in the Latin of 1540[m]. These were entirely re-written in the German[n]. Art. iv. and v. were enlarged by, at least, two thirds; Art. vi. and xx. were increased to twice their size. In Art. ii. "on Original Sin" there is an insertion, not made even in the "altered" Latin edition of 1540. It stands thus, "[o] and this disease or fault of origin is truly sin, bringing eternal death to those who are not re-born through Baptism [[p] and faith in Christ, through the Gospel]

---

[1] Weber, ii. 59.   [m] As also xviii. "on Freewill;" xxi. "on Invocation of Saints." Weber ii. 105.

[n] The Wittenberg edition of Luther's German works 1569. T. ix. contains the German "varied" edition, as Weber himself states, and as I have found by comparing it on the one hand with the original edition, and, on the other, with the extracts of the Edit. of 1533. given by Weber.   [o] Luther's Wercke. l. c. f. 305.

[p] This insertion of faith, as a means, between "Baptism" and

and the Holy Ghost." Amid these changes (of which one bears on the Sacrament of Baptism), Art. x. "on the Lord's Supper," was not altered in one word. In the German "varied" Edition, it is, word for word, the same as in the original[q]. Yet the German edition of the Confession was reprinted far more frequently than the Latin[r]. Subsequently to the six early unauthorised editions, which we know of, and apart from the collections in which the Confession was printed, we still know of twenty-three editions of the "Confession," as published with the Apology[s], up to 1564. These are only specimens of many more, of which copies do not happen to have been preserved. The Confession was also reprinted expressly for visitations[t]. "[u] A copy of it was presented to the Emperor by the Evangelic princes and states, at the Colloquy at Worms, and is still in the Imperial Archives." Reprints of the Confession were not always private undertakings. Those ordered for Visitations were printed by the State authorities, and bore the public Arms[v]. The printers of the edition of Nuremburg 1567, state[w] that they had the approbation of a Counsellor of Nuremburg. They state also that the book was "much in demand." The ori-

"the Holy Ghost" is characteristic. Baptism, probably, stands for the outward part of the sacrament.

   [q] Ib. f. 307.   [r] Weber, ii. 34.

   [s] In Feuerlein Biblioth. Symbol.

   [t] The edition of 1555, after the original German title of the Confession, has the addition, "und durch d. H. Augustum Hertzogen zu Sachsen Churfursten &c. von wegen der Visitation itzt wider in Druck gegeben." and again that of 1558.   [u] Ib. ii. 67.

   [v] Weber, ii. 71. 73.   [w] On the reverse of the Title page.

ginal edition of the German Confession and Apology was reprinted in Luther's Works by the Divines of Jena [x]; the enlarged edition by those of Wittenberg [y]. The German " Confession " was early introduced into the different "bodies of doctrine " (as they were called), or collections of symbolical books, whether these were composed chiefly of works of Melanchthon or Luther. The original form was printed in the " bodies of doctrine [z]," put forth by the Dukes of Saxony, Luneburg, Brunswick, Prussia, as also the State Nuremburg. It formed part

[x] Th. vi. f. 361. ed. Jena. 1561. printed among the works of 1536, " because copies of the first edition had till then been wanting." marg. note.

[y] Th. ix. f. 304. v. sqq. ed. Witt. 1569.

[z] The " unvaried " is in the 1. Corpus *Thuringicum;* that " put together by authority of John William, Duke of Saxony and Landgrave of Thuringen (especially a Lutheran collection) Jena. 1570. 1571. and then again and again in German." (Walch, Biblioth. Sel. 3. 2. 22. T. i. 391.) 2. *Wilhelminum,* by William the younger, Duke of Luneburg, Ulzen 1576. Dresd. 1580. Zell. 1621. 3. *Julium,* by Julius, Duke of Brunswick, Heinrichstadt 1576. 1584. Helmstadt 1603. Brunswick 1690. and a later compilation [with reference to Court Preachers], Brunswick 1715. 4. *Prutenicum,* put together by Chemnitz and Moerlin for Albert Duke of Prussia Konigsberg 1570 and subscribed by 80 Theologians. 5. It was also inserted in the Agenda of *Brunswick* 1563, " frequently reprinted in the dialects of both Upper and Lower Germany." Also 6. in the Libri normales *Norimbergenses* by Saubert of Nuremberg 1646. Nur. and Aldorf. 1721. The details of the books of which these " bodies of doctrine " were composed, are given by Walch, l. e. p. 390-6. The "varied" is in the 1. Corpus *Philippicum* or *Misnicum* (in German), Leipz. 1560. 1561. Frankf. 1560. 1569. [in Lower German, Wittemb. 1563.] Wittemb. 1570. Zerbst. [Anhalt] 1588. 2. *Pomeranicum,* Wittemb. 1561. 1564. 1565. and probably 3. *Hassiacum,* Marpurg 1626.

also of the Agenda of Brunswick, frequently reprinted in the dialects of both Upper and Lower Germany. The enlarged form was introduced into 1. the Corpus Philippicum, the collection composed especially of works of Melanchthon, which "was of great authority among the Theologians of Electoral Saxony, and other followers of Melanchthon," and 2. the "Corpus" of Pomerania, in which the Catechisms of Luther were also inserted. The Landgrave of Hesse also doubtless, used the revised form.

The insertion of the Confession in these "bodies of doctrine," involved its having symbolical authority in those countries.

In 1580, the previous texts were mostly laid aside by those who received the Formula Concordiæ, or Concordien-Buch. The objections which Roman Catholic opponents had raised to the variations of the Confession, occasioned Joachim II. Elector of Brandenburg, in 1566, to obtain a collation (as he supposed) of the original from the Archives at Mainz. This constituted what has, by mistake, been called the "Corpus Brandenburgicum." And this text was adopted in the well-known "formula Concordiæ."

But the question as to the original text is, as far as relates to the German Article on the Sacrament, wholly irrelevant. Besides the Edition of Melanchthon, there are still extant 1. a MS. containing the first nineteen Articles, which has been conjectured [a] to be the abstract of the Confession which the Emperor asked to see, previously to the day of the

---

[a] See Forstemann (Urkundenbuch, i. 344), who has printed it; 345. sqq. It is now in the Archives at Anspach.

Diet [b]; 2. a copy brought back from the Diet by George, Margrave of Brandenburg [c]; 3. a copy brought back in like way by the Landgrave of Hesse [d]; 4. another, brought back, as it seems, by Ernest Duke of Brunswick and Lunenberg [e]; 5. a copy, appended to the account of the diet, by Brueck, Chancellor of the Elector of Saxony, who presented the Confession to the Emperor, and formed part of the negotiations [f]; 6. a MS. written by Spalatin, with his own hand, at the Diet [g]; 7. a copy at Nuremberg [h], whither its legates sent a copy from the Diet; 8. a copy in the State-Archives of the king of Bavaria at Munich [i].

Now, in all these MSS. there is not a single variation which affects the sense. The only real variation is a reading in Spalatin's MS. which was finally omitted. "[k] *Further* it is taught *and preached* in our Churches, on *the Sacrament of the Altar and*

[b] Melanchthon says, "Waldes, the Emperor's secretary, saw the Articles before we exhibited them." (Ep. Camerar. C.R. 740.) He had previously engaged to make out a "list of the Articles which the Lutherans wished to have," and to consult about sending it in. (Leg. Nor. Jun. 21. No. 734.)

[c] Also at Anspach. (see Forst. i. 369. sqq.) A third MS. there, collated by Forst. (i. 374. sqq.), seems to be a copy of the first (Weber, i. 179. sqq.)

[d] Now in the State-Archives at Cassel, see Forst. i. 372.

[e] Now in the Royal Archives at Hanover, Web. i. 180.

[f] In the Weimar Archives, Weber i. 168-74. Forst. i. 310. sqq.

[g] Also in the Weimar Archives, Web. i. 168. Forst. i. 310.

[h] Weber, i. 183. sqq. 321. sqq.

[i] Forst. i. 373. Forstemann (i. 370. 440.) mentions two others of inferior value; 9) at Nordlingen, published by Beyschlag (Augsb. 1830), with various readings from 10) the MS. in the library at Augsburg. [k] F. i. 317.

of the true Body of Christ our Lord, that the true Body and Blood of Christ is truly present *in this Sacrament* under the form of the bread and wine, and is there distributed and received. Wherefore moreover the contrary doctrine is rejected."

The variations in the other MSS. in the body of the Article are simply grammatical[1]; in the "rejecting clause" the Munich MS. alone agrees with the Latin in substituting "the opposed teacher" for "the opposed doctrine[m]."

The great alteration made in the Confession of Augsburg, that which gave rise to the distinction between the "unvaried" and the "varied" Confession, was confined to the Latin Edition. Its main object was, probably, at once to secure toleration to the "Reformed," and by making common cause with them, to gain strength to the whole Protestant body. This change Melanchthon made in 1540. Whereas the older Latin form was, "they teach that the Body and Blood of Christ are *truly present and are distributed to* communicants in the Supper of the Lord," he now substituted, "are truly *exhibited* to communicants &c." It was an ambiguous formula, which, by those who had already subscribed the original Confession of Augsburg, could only be honestly taken in the meaning of that Confession. They still remained pledged to their own subscription to the Latin Confession, and to the German Confession which had no ambiguity. Having already expressed their belief that

---

[1] All, except the Munich, add the article *der* before the word, *Gestalt*; read *alda* for *da*, and genommen *werde* for *wirt*, or *wird*.

[m] " Gegenlerer" for gegenler (as it is sometimes written).

" the Body and Blood of Christ were present and distributed to communicants," they could only honestly use the word " exhibeantur " in the sense " presented ; " and (as has been said) the Body and Blood of Christ could not be presented, unless they were present there, to be presented[n]. But the word " exhibeantur " is, in itself, so vague, that the Reformed could honestly receive it in *their* sense, " exhibited to the soul ; " and that, whether any benefit resulting to the soul at the Communion were supposed to be the mere contemplation of Christ at the Right Hand of God and devout remembrance of His Passion, or whether they believed that some virtue was dispensed by our Lord, through the Holy Ghost.

The Lutherans did not need, nor wish it for themselves. On the contrary, in the Convention at Smalkald early in March 1540, in order to prepare for the then approaching Conference, opened at Hagenau June 1540, carried on at Worms Jan. 1541, continued and broken off at Regensburg in the same year, Melanchthon, with the other Divines, expressly declared that no change was to be made in the doctrine expressed in the Confession and Apology.

" [o] Since the doctrine in all Articles of the Confession, as it is understood and taught in our Churches, is truly and properly the certain Christian doctrine of the holy Gospel ; we will not and cannot make or sanction any alteration therein, or depart therefrom.—Therefore our judgment is, not to commit ourselves to make any new, *unclear,* or

[n] Tittmann, Augsb. Conf. p. 102.
[o] Published " from the Acts " in Cyprian Historia der Augspurgischen Confession, c. 13. § 2. p. 171.

uncertain articles, or patchwork; but to hold out to them [the Roman party] that the sum of our doctrines is contained in the Confession and Apology, *from the meaning whereof we purpose not to deviate.*—To set up Articles with them, such as may be interpreted this way or that, and to play with words (which is their way in such great weighty matters) *that* will we not do."

This deliberate and formal judgment, as the basis of their proceedings in a religious conference, was signed[p], " on the behalf of the Elector of Saxony, by Jonas, Bugenhagen, Creutziger, and Melanchthon; by Nicholas von Ambsdorff, for Magdeburg; by Bucer, for Strasburg; for Bremen, by John Amsterdam; and by many others, from other states."

Luther was absent, on leave by the Elector. He was consulted however on all. Melanchthon writes to him, as the summary of the Convention,

" [q] Matters were brought us on which to deliberate. As to these, there was the most complete consent, that those Articles, which we confess in the Confession and Apology, cannot be laid aside; but that agreement on doctrine being settled we ought not to fight invidiously as to things indifferent. Our deliberation which the rest subscribed, appears to have been accurately and learnedly written, as Paul will be able to tell you."

This " judgment " (Bedencken) was drawn up by Melanchthon himself[r]. It is impossible to conceive that Melanchthon or any one of common honesty could have subscribed this declaration, while he had in hand an alteration of the Confession, which in his

[p] Cyprian, Ib. [q] C. R. 1949.

[r] In the letter to Luther he says " the *rest* subscribed," having mentioned previously himself alone.

mind, would be a real deviation from it.   He wrote
it and signed it, moreover, not in his own name only,
but as the representative of the Elector, who, above
all the Protestant Princes, was a rigid Lutheran, and
jealous of any deviation from any characteristic
expression of the original.

The true way of regarding the change in the Latin Confession is, not as a substitution for the original, nor as intended for those who had signed the
original, but as a *third* form, provided for a distinct
class of persons.   In the next year, 1541, that which
followed the change in the *Latin* Confession, the
whole discussion on the Holy Eucharist at Regensburg, presupposed, as the basis of the negotiation,
the *German* Confession, which contained the same
doctrine as the unaltered Latin.   The " Interim,"
there proposed for the acceptance of the Catholics
and Lutherans was (at the instance of the Cardinal de Granvelle, and perhaps of Eustachius the
Chancellor of Hesse) drawn up by Gropper[s], shewn
to Bucer and Capito, perhaps to Sturm, and was sent
to the Landgrave, and to the Margrave Joachim.
The two parties had, at the Colloquy at Worms,
agreed on the doctrine of original sin[t].   In *this*
Conference, they agreed on the article of Justification, as well as those " of the condition of man
before the fall " and " on free will[u]."   Several other
articles were nearly settled.   On the greater part
there was no prospect of conciliation.   Charles V.

[s] Melanchthon's confidential letter to the Elector of Saxony
July, 1541 (C. R. 2334); add letter of April 8, 1543, " Gropper
who wrote the Regensburg book" (C. R. 2880).

[t] Form. Conc. C. R. 2131. Narrat de Colloq. Ib. 2135.

[u] Acta Colloq.

however, was in real earnest to bring about an agreement[v]; and to him, every point settled was an earnest of future union[w]. At the close of the conference, the Electors desired that "the Articles agreed upon should hold, until there should be a free Christian Council in Germany or a national assembly; or, if neither could be had, a Diet[x];" the other Princes and Bishops rejected them, as being the least important, and unsatisfactory in language, while[y] "the most important as on the most venerable Sacrament of the true Body and Blood of Christ, its adoration or reservation, the change of the bread and wine &c." were unsettled; the "common states;" agreed with the Electors[z]; the Protestants accepted the articles for the time, referring the whole question to a General Council or the assembly if held in Germany[a]. They accepted the articles agreed upon, "understanding them," they say[b], "as the same things are delivered in our Confession and Apology." The Emperor referred the points in dispute to the Council or assembly proposed by the Electors, and renewed the truce of Nuremberg[c].

The discussion lasted long; and, for a time, the

[v] So de Granvelle assured Burchard (Burch. Ep. ad Pont. C. R. 2114). The three Roman legates at Regensburg took no part in it. The Electors of Mainz and Bavaria were opposed to it. [Ib.] Melanchthon speaks of the Emperor's great gentleness [Ib. 2173], of his moderation [Ib. 1198], as do the three Collocutors. [2200]. Jonas gives a striking picture of the Emperor at Augsburg. [Ib. 752.] see also Cruciger, [Ib. 2211.] Reibisch. [2219.]

[w] Cæsar ad ordines [Ib. 2305.] Legat. Sax. ad Elect. [2233. v. fin. p. 301.] The declaratio Cæsaris [2232.] is earnest and evidently sincere.　　[x] C. R. 2313.　　[y] Ib. 2314.

[z] Ib. 2318.　　[a] Ib. 2321.　　[b] Ib. 2301. B.

[c] Imp. ad Ord. Ib. 2305. 2336.

Landgrave of Hesse[d] (probably from apprehensions of the Emperor's displeasure on his recent bigamy), and Bucer as in some way bound up with him[e], were the most yielding ; Melanchthon was unhopeful, and prolonged the conference[f], only lest he should seem to break it off untimely.

On the subject of the Holy Eucharist, Eck and Melanchthon disputed for about eight days[g], when the subject was deferred because they could not agree. In the "book," proposed for joint acceptance, the doctrine of the Real Presence had been originally expressed in terms taken from the German Confession, the word "substantially" being inserted from the Apology. But, on the very ground that this statement did not contain the doctrine of Transubstantiation, Cardinal Contarini wrote on the margin, a parenthesis, asserting that doctrine, which was made part of the "book," as finally proposed to the Protestants. Burckhard, the Saxon Chancellor, explains to the Elector[h];

[d] Melanchthon speaks with anxiety of him to Luther [2190]. Camerar. [2204.] Burchard [May 5], " he too is steady " [to Brueck, 2213]. Melanchthon doubtfully [2274]; see also his private letter to the Elector [2334. p. 479, 80].

[e] This is remarked by Chancellor Burchard [2229, and 30, and 42], the Prince of Anhalt, Saxon legate [Ib. 2231], Bomgartner [2321] and by Melanchthon himself often, e. g. to Camerar [2225], Vitus [2274], Brenz [2299]. He says that he himself was less hopeful than his colleagues [2278. p. 414]. Alesius says that Bucer had " overcome suspicions by his steadiness." [2265.]

[f] Mel. de lib. Ratisb. [2278. p. 414.] The Emperor sent to the Landgrave to blame Melanchthon [Mel. Camerar. 2237], who excused himself to the Emperor [2240].

[g] Mel. to the Elect. 2334. p. 583. and Burckhard.

[h] C. R. 2229.

"As for the book, you will have understood from the letter of the Prince of Anhalt and the Councillors, that it is a melange, at times in conformity neither with the Papal nor the Evangelical doctrine; wherefore also the book has often been attacked on both sides. And in some articles, some addition has been written on the margin without, which before did not stand in the said book. Cardinal Contarenus, (as is credibly stated) is alleged to have done this, which also has occasioned this present contention about Transubstantiation, these last eight days."

Pallavicini relates that Contarini altered it in more than twenty places. His account is [i];

" Gropper had been brought by De Granvelle that, by his aid, the legate might more readily run over and consider the volume, which, being in great measure interwoven of sayings of Scripture and the fathers, contained twenty-two Chapters. The Legate and Nuncio read through the book with Gropper, and they easily conjectured from various indications, that the book was Gropper's, of whose docility, unspoiled by any self-opinionativeness, the Roman Legate wrote very honorably. For when Contarini had lighted upon more than twenty places, which he thought to need correction, Gropper corrected them so readily, that self-love did not draw from him the slightest word, either in defence or opposition."

Contarini not being satisfied with his own judgment, the Legate consulted Eck, who " [k] suddenly imagined that Vesal, one most hostile to himself, was the author of the work. At first he disapproved of the book, afterwards gave way to the judgments of others, always however shewing that he was dragged by the authority of others, not led by his own opinion."

[i] Hist. Conc. Trid. 4. 14. 4. [k] Pallav. l. c.

The proposed article on the Sacrament then finally stood thus, the parenthesis in italics having been added by Contarini[1];

"The Sacrament of the Eucharist hath a word[m], which is the Almighty Word [sermo] of Christ, by the virtue whereof this Sacrament is made, and whereby it takes place, that after consecration, the true Body and true Blood of the Lord are truly and substantially present, and are distributed to the faithful under the form of bread and wine; *(these things, i. e. the bread and wine, being transmuted and transubstantiated into the Body and Blood of the Lord;)* which [word] is of this sort, 'Take and eat of this all of you, this is My Body which shall be given for you;' and at the Cup, 'Drink ye all of this; for this is My Blood of the New Testament, which is shed for many for the remission of sins.' The Element is bread and wine, to which when the word[m] is added, it becometh the sacrament. For this Sacrament is made of two things, the visible form of the elements, and the invisible Body and Blood, which we truly and really partake of in this Sacrament. The force of this Sacrament is, that, through the life-giving flesh of our Saviour Jesus Christ, we are joined to Him, not spiritually only but bodily also, and are made bone of His bones and flesh of His flesh; being assured, that in Christ Jesus Himself we have received remission of sins, and in the Sacrament the power of restraining the concupiscence which cleaveth in our members; certainly a most sweet pledge of remission of sins, of life eternal, and of fellowship with God, promised and bestowed upon us in Christ."

To this addition of the doctrine of Transubstantiation, the Protestant Collocutors, Melanchthon,

---

[1] In Goldastus Coll. Instt. Imp. ii. 193. Melanchthon Acta Convent. Ratisb. Art. 14. C. R. 2207. The Acts were translated by Coverdale, and printed 1542.

[m] "Verbum" in allusion to the well known saying of S. Augustine, "accedit verbum ad elementum et fit sacramentum."

Bucer, Pistorius, allude in their memorial[n] to the Elector Palatine and de Granvelle;

"We had hoped that the reverend and most learned men, appointed to this conference, would have been fully satisfied with the Confession of our doctrine and faith on the Lord's Supper, which we lately gave them, and which we held to be serviceable for good understanding and concord. For we have explicitly acknowledged, that we hold and defend the common doctrine of the Catholic Churches, that in the Lord's Supper, when the bread and wine are consecrated, the Body and Blood of Christ are truly and essentially present and are received. We confess too that we do not hold with those who deny that the true Body of Christ is present, and is received; for we abhor exceedingly such opinions as come from human reason apart from God's Word. In the book which was sent through His Imperial Majesty to consider, *nothing* more *was contained* than in our *Confession* just mentioned; but *some words were added, without, on the margin of the same book, as it seems, by another who did not make the book.* Therefore we had reason to wonder, that the afore-mentioned Lord-deputies were not content *with our simple Confession,* since it was not ill-suited for concord. But other articles were proposed to us in addition, which were ill-suited to concord. For since we retain the doctrine that the Body of Christ is present, what need to enquire thus whether the bread is annihilated? which opinion has come up lately in the Churches, and there is much variance therein, and the Schoolmen have not understood it, much less can the people. Therefore we use the clear saying of S. Paul and the ancient fathers, since Paul says, 'the bread which we break, is it not the communion of the Body of Christ?' &c. So we also say, that with the consecrated bread the Body of

[n] Extant in German (Weber ii. 381. and C. R. 2222.) and Latin (Mel. Consil. lat. P. 1. p. 478. and C. R. 2223). The German copy was given to Frederic; the Latin to de Granvelle (Ib. 2224).

Christ is truly present and received. In like way Irenæus too said, that in this Sacrament there are two substances, an earthly and an heavenly; and there is no question that by 'the earthly' he means the bread. To this he adds also 'the Heavenly,' namely 'the Body of Christ[o].' So Cyril, 'The Lord gave morsels of bread,' saying, 'This is My Body.' He doth not say, that he gave the accidents of bread. This is a new speculation which imagines accidents without a subject, &c. Epiphanius, distinguished among the old fathers, who had diligently written on the Articles of Christian doctrine and the Sacraments, speaks thus, '[p] The food which one eateth is bread, but in the same is the life-giving Body of Christ.' Here he says clearly, '*In* the same bread.' For the world hath not yet heard the word 'transubstantiatio.' So also Cyprian saith, '[q] Nor can His Blood, whereby we have been redeemed and quickened, appear to be in the Cup, when the Cup is without that wine, whereby the Blood of Christ is set forth, as is declared by the mystical meaning and testimony of all the Scriptures.' S. Augustine's meaning is also clear and consistent, if he is rightly understood; for he joins both the bread and the Body of Christ. 'What the eyes see,' he says[r], 'is bread; but according to what faith believeth, the bread is the Body of Christ.' So also is it a clear saying of Pope Gelasius; '[s] Certainly the Sacrament which we receive, of the Body and Blood of Christ is a divine thing, wherefore also we are by the Same made partakers of the Divine Nature, and yet the substance and nature of bread and wine ceaseth not to be.' So also the Council of Nice saith; '[t] let us not

---

[o] See "Real Presence," p. 76.

[p] Rather "the Bread indeed is food, but the might *in* it, is for giving of life." See "the Real Presence," p. 149.

[q] Ib. p. 357.   [r] Ib. p. 530.   [s] Ib. p. 88.

[t] The passage is quoted, as from the Council of Nice, by Bellarmine [de Euch. ii. 10.] and Harding "on the Real Presence" in Jewel, ii. 355. ed. Ox. as well as by Œcolampadius and Calvin Instit. iv. 17. 36. It is from Gelasius, Comm. Actt. Conc. Nic. c. 30, which has no authority of its own.

regard the bread and cup set forth on the Divine table, but, lifting up the mind by faith, let us think that on that table lieth the Lamb of God.' He joineth there the bread and the Body of Christ. We know well what the new teachers have invented, that the Substance of the bread ceaseth; and that there are many such teachers, yea the greater number; but we abide by that which S. Paul and the old fathers have spoken thereof; and through this clear opinion many needless and perilous questions are cut off."

There is extant, another statement on the Roman side, adopting the language of the German Confession, but also adding to it the word "transubstantiation," yet deferring all explanation of that word to the end of the Conference, and conceding that the real Presence should be the only doctrine taught to the people. It was sent for the consideration of the Protestant Collocutors[u], and is extant in a copy in Cruciger's hand[v].

"It is agreed as to the real and corporal presence of the Body and Blood of Christ in the Eucharist, with disapproval of Berengarius.

"It is agreed, that in the Almighty Word of Christ there taketh place the divine and most august transmutation of the bread and wine.

"It is agreed that to express this marvellous transformation, the word, transubstantiation, is not inconvenient or improper.

"It is agreed that henceforth it ought to be taught

[u] "The Papists have sent the following Article, on the venerable Sacrament of the Altar, to be compared with our's, the Evangelicals." Spalat. Ann. ap. C. R. 2216.

[v] See Bretschneider in Illgen Zeitschr. f. d. hist. Theol. ii. 1. p. 303. Weber [ii. 375. sqq.] had published it as Melanchthon's. It is in Latin also in the C. R. 2216, and in German in Spalatin, quoted 1b.

that under the 'species' of bread and wine there is ministered the true Body and true Blood of Christ.

"It is agreed, that when the words of Christ have been
uttered, the Body of Christ is, and is so called; and the
bread also, yet not common bread, but supernatural and
supersubstantial.

"Also, since the Eucharist is always preserved in order
to be received, it is agreed that the Eucharist once consecrated, even if kept, remains the Eucharist and the Body
of Christ.

"Also it is agreed, that since in the Eucharist there is
the true Body and true Blood of Christ, in the Eucharist
also Christ Himself is to be adored.

"For the rest, since that mystery of transmutation is
altogether divine, which may be believed but cannot be
investigated, and therefore, not only the ancient Doctors,
but the more recent also, command to abstain from scruti-
nising in what way transubstantiation takes place, it would
seem to be a mean of conciliation, that discussion as to the
proper meaning of the word 'transubstantiation' or the
mode in which it takes place, be deferred to the end of
the Conference, and that to the people there be no dispute
as to the mode of change or conversion and transubstantiation, but it be simply taught that, after consecration,
there is present the true Body and Blood of Christ, as
aforesaid."

The eight days' Conference turned not at all
upon the statement from the German Article, but
on the addition of Contarini, and, therewith, on
"Transubstantiation, reservation, circumgestation,
and adoration," whereof Cruciger [w] adds, "the mention has been introduced by the opponents, since

[w] C. R. 2220. Cruciger had expressed his fear lest the main
strife should be on "the article of the Presence of the Body of
Christ and of the change of the bread." (Ib. 2214.) Burchard
also mentions the three first (Ib. 2213) and Cruciger (2235).

neither the Confession nor the Apology touched upon them." There are two statements extant, as put in by the Protestants. The first is in answer to some articles on the Roman side, with the three first of which on "the real Presence," it expresses agreement "in substance" (de re ipsa); it comments and asks for explanation on the fourth, on Transubstantiation ; the fifth was on the exhibition of the Sacrament for adoration; the last contained a clause on teaching the right use of Sacraments. Thus much appears from the answer, which is;

" [x] It is agreed as to the real Presence of the Body and Blood of Christ in the Lord's Supper, as it is well known that that Presence has been defended by the writings of many in our Churches. Therefore as to the substance itself, we agree in the first, second, and third paragraphs in this article offered to us.

"But in the fourth paragraph, which begins 'recte itaque' we should wish some words to be explained. When it is said here, 'He converts and transforms into the substance of the Body,' we should wish this 'conversion' to be explained. For we affirm that the Body is truly present, but that the bread is converted and changed by a mystical change, i. e. one by which there is a true making the Body to be present after the consecration. And by a 'mystical change' we do not understand one, which is only significant, but such an one, whereby the Body of Christ becometh present. We ask then that the declaration of this topic of transubstantiation be deferred to the end of the Conference. In the last paragraph but one, beginning 'It must be acknowledged, that when there is shewn[y],' it is

[x] C. R. 2217. from MSS. Acta Coll. Ratisbon. The Articles on the Roman side, to which it refers, are plainly distinct from those just quoted.

[y] Agnoscendum est quod cum ostenditur, i. e. as the context shews, for adoration.

known that in our Churches the people receive the Sacrament with the highest reverence, and adore Christ, who giveth Himself to be present, and maketh us His members. Yet since apart from the ordained use, many abuses have come in, and a vain confidence in beholding, as a deed, we do not approve of these abuses, and wish that what is written in the last paragraph should be done, viz. that the people be diligently taught the true use of this so great gift of God."

In the other statement, that which was finally sent in to the Emperor, Melanchthon uses the words of the Apology.

"[z] Christ saith, 'Take, eat, this is My Body,' and then, 'This is My Blood.' Therefore we confess that in the Lord's Supper the Body and Blood of Christ are truly and really present, and are exhibited with the bread and wine to communicants. As Hilary too saith, 'according to the profession of the Lord and our faith, it is truly Flesh and truly Blood; and these, received and drunk, cause that both Christ is in us and we in Christ.'"

"The end is threefold; the first, that, admonished by this reception, we may remember the Passion and Resurrection of Christ, and pious souls may be raised up, acknowledging by faith that the Son of God suffered for us, and that we, by the reception of the Body and Blood of Christ, are made members of Him and have reconciliation for the sake of the Son of God. By this faith grace is applied to us through the Sacrament. Of this end Christ Himself preacheth, saying, 'Do this in remembrance of ME.' For He willeth that we should retain the memory of His Passion and the promised benefit; nor doth He will only that the memory of the history be preserved, but He willeth that we should apply these benefits to us in the use of the Sacrament.

[z] In Melanchthon's Cons. Lat. i. 477. and C. R. 2254. B.

"The second end is, that, in the use of this Sacrament, we should return thanks to God for His boundless mercy towards us, and for His Son, given for us.

"The third end is, that being made members of the one Body of Christ, we may be admonished as to mutual love. Wherefore Paul saith, as there is one Bread, so we, being many, are one body.

"But as to Sacraments the rule is to be held, that they are principally testimonies of the will of God towards us, or of grace. Afterwards, other ends may be added.

"We teach this also, that no one is meet for this Sacrament, who perseveres in sin against conscience, and that they who are guilty of open crimes are not to be admitted. We teach therefore the Apostolic rule, let a man examine himself, and so let him eat of this bread. But as Irenæus saith, that the Eucharist consisteth of two things, an earthly and a heavenly, and Paul saith, 'the bread which we break is the communion of the Body of Christ,' so we teach, that with the bread, the Body of Christ is given to Communicants. Yet we do not teach transubstantiation, as they call it, or that the substance of bread is cast away, and we follow the firm and clear testimonies of many holy fathers."

The old Elector of Saxony looked with anxiety on this Conference. He was distressed, because the Confession of Augsburg was not laid as the basis of negociation. His chief misgiving related to the doctrine of Justification. To his legates he expressed his fear, that

"[a] although in the Article, sent to him in Latin and German, the opposite party seemed to have abated something of their Scholasticism, they wished to take away or obscure the point, that 'faith alone saves;' that that party might be allowed to append all sorts of things, whereby the Article might come to be misunderstood, and it might be said, that,

[a] El. ad leg. suos. Ib. 2226.

in this the main point, much had been conceded to them, and so that on our side much had hitherto been taught and held amiss; which would make no slight scandal."

It appears from the Elector's letter to his Councillors at the Congress at Hagenau (July 2, 1540), that he was chiefly anxious, lest Melanchthon, Brenz and the other Divines might be induced to abandon

"[b] the word 'only' in the Article on Justification, and substitute some other phrase as 'that man did not become righteous before God through any work which preceded or followed faith,' with which change Dr. Martin was not pleased, when he was informed of the negotiation, and said, 'no one should, with his knowledge and will, take from him the word *sola* out of the article of Justification.'"

The Saxon Councillors reported to the Elector,

"[c] The Theologians on this side, will, with God's help, give way in nothing, as has often been pointed out to them, that they should abide by the Confession, and the counsel and decision at Smalkald, whereto they are, of themselves, inclined."

The Landgrave joined in this. On May 19, the legates again assure the Elector that

"[d] Philip and the rest have, throughout, for the meaning of the article on Justification, referred to the Confession and Apology, from which nothing was to be derogated or given up through such Article."

Again the Elector May 10, acknowledged a letter of his legates in which they had informed him, that

[b] Ib. 1977.   [c] May 5. Ib. 2212.   [d] Ib. 2233.

"ᵉthe other party had given in an Article on the Sacrament of the Body and Blood of our Lord, which you have sent to us in German and Latin, intimating that the Divines on this side were not inclined to accept it, or to concede any thing contrary to the said confession and doctrine, which by God's grace, has been preached and taught until now in the Churches on this side, which we have been glad to hear, and we beg you earnestly to exhort the Divines on this side so to do."

Soon after Burchard wrote to Brueck that he *had been* anxious, but

"ᶠMr Philip, by the grace of God, most strongly defends the truth, so that I am persuaded and hope, that our's will approve nothing alien from Scripture. For their simple wish is, that the Confession of Augsburg be inviolate."

It was in accordance with all this, that Melanchthon expressed himself in an answer which, on the Elector's commissionᵍ, he framedʰ for the Elector and the Protestant states to deliver to the Emperor at the close of the diet. The Elector had sent a copy of the "book" to Luther and Bugenhagen, and received an answer written by Luther in the name of bothⁱ. Luther's advice was,

"The best is, that your El. Gr. should hold out the 'Confession,' and abide by it. For against it, was this conference at Hagenau begun, at Worms a little advanced, and at Regensburg intended to be completed."

This declaration is extant in three forms. The

ᵉ Ib. 2226. ᶠ 2239. ᵍ El. ad Theol. s. Jul. 3. Ib. 2290.
ʰ Leg. Sax. ad Elect. Jul. 13. Ib. 2308.
ⁱ Luther, Briefe. 1997. 2000. ed. de W.

first is a sketch of a letter to the Emperor, confined to general expressions as to the points discussed in the Conference. The second and third (the one in Latin, the other in German) enter, at some length, into the points contained in the " book " proposed for their acceptance. These two agree in substance, but neither is translated from the other. In all, the Protestant states assert, that even the articles agreed upon required more explanation, and they deprecate ambiguous formularies. In the first, Melanchthon writes for them [k];

" We so understood those articles, as the same subjects are delivered in our Confession and Apology. But if they were to add another diverse interpretation, we must needs reclaim against it. Nor is our meaning obscure or intricate or perplexed or senseless. For this whole kind of doctrine, which is set forth in our Churches, and which is extant in our Confession and Apology, is doctrine delivered in the Gospel with the consent of the Catholic Church of Christ, and hath the true testimonies of learned fathers; nor do we depart from that Confession. Wherefore if any should transform these brief articles in the book into false opinions which have been censured by us, with these we should have no agreement."

Of the two later statements, the German declares (in addition to what is contained in the Latin) that the state regarded the Apology as an expansion of the Confession.

" [1] And that every one may know what, on all articles,

[k] C. R. 2300-2. A. also in Melanchthon's Ep.
[1] Ib. B. p. 483. C. p. 496. I have translated the German, as being written most naturally. In the point in question, both texts agree verbatim. Bucer (as well as Melanchthon) published the

is held, taught, and believed in our Churches, we again declare, that we hold the Confession, *delivered at Augsburg to His Imperial Majesty,* together with the Apology appended (which we hold for no other than an explanation of the Confession), doubting not moreover that this same doctrine is the unanimous meaning of the Catholic Church of Christ, continued in the writings of the Apostles and Prophets, and has certain testimony of the first Apostolic Churches and the most learned fathers."

A like declaration was called forth, sixteen years afterwards, subsequently to the death of Luther, at the conference of Worms A. D. 1557. The Lutherans were now torn by internal division. Flacius wrote to Christiern, king of Denmark;

"[m]There are almost as many divers opinions in the Colloquy, as there are Collocutors of the Confession of Augsburg. For one advocates, or at least will not condemn, Zwingli, and other Sacramentaries; another, Schwenkfeld; a third, Osiander; a fourth will not pronounce the Pope to be Anti-Christ; a fifth excuses or extenuates the acts relating to the Interim or the adiaphora, or certainly will not condemn them; lastly, another maintains Majorism on the necessity of works to salvation."

The only question however among the Lutherans

Latin (Actt. Coll. Rat. p. 41.) and it gave it the title: "The answer of the Protestant princes and states, whereby they explained to His Imperial Majesty, to his request, their opinion as to the articles, agreed upon and not agreed upon in the Colloquy. The author, Ph. Melanchthon." Melanchthon inscribed his, "The answer of the princes and states, allies to the Confession of Augsburg, on the book exhibited to the Emperor Charles. July 12." Bucer published a copy in German in his Acta Coll. Rat. But it is a translation from Melanchthon's Latin, as Bretschneider has pointed out.   [m] Ib. 6353. T. ix.

at the conference, was whether to condemn generally every doctrine opposed to the Confession of Augsburg, or to condemn by name those of Osiander, Major, Zwingli, Schwenkfeld, and the Interim [n]. Morlin and the Jena Theologians, at first, at the advice of the Council of the Elector and Princes, contented themselves with giving in their condemnations to them [o]. Some report of these dissensions having probably reached the opposite party, Melanchthon began by declaring the adherence of the Lutherans to the Confession, as *delivered at Augsburg.*

In the first answer Sept. 11. to the President, Julius Flugh, now Bishop of Naumburg, he says [p];

"Lest we should seem to wander to and fro in opinions, we attest now too, that, with pious and firm assent, we embrace the prophetic and Apostolic writings, and that, in the meaning comprised in the Apostles', Nicene, and Athanasian Creeds. And that doctrine we affirm to be comprised in the Confession of our Churches, which was given to the Emperor Charles V. in the diet of Augsburg, 1530. This Confession, we all confess that with pious agreement we embrace. And from this we have not departed, nor will we depart. We reject also all errors and sects, old or new, conflicting with that Confession" &c. [they specify the Council of Trent and the Interim].

This declaration Melanchthon repeated word for word in a statement, meant to be a preface to the argument on the Church [q]; and again in answer to a discourse of the Bishop "of Marburg and his Colleagues."

[n] Mel. Hist. Coll. Ib. 6469.
[o] Id. Bericht d. ganz. Coll. zu Worms, Ib. 6468.   [p] Ib. 6339.
[q] Ib. 6345. Opp. iv. 803.

"¹ The third part was a request, that amid such great dissensions, we should shew, whether with common consent we embrace the Confession of Augsburg, and persevere in that judgment?"

Melanchthon answered,

" in the third place our dissensions are objected to us. To this objection we have answered before, that we all in our Churches with pious and firm assent embrace the Confession given to the Emperor Charles in the Diet of Augsburg, 1530. From that Confession we neither have departed, nor are about to depart. And we reject opinions conflicting with it. Nor among us in our Churches is there any disagreement as to the foundation. Although, according to the infirmity of human nature at all times, at times there are some errors even of good men who yet are curable. But of those external to our Churches it is plain that very many fanatics, Servetus, Thammer, Anabaptists, Stenckfeld, and many impostors have been steadily refuted by us, and our youth has been guarded by most sound doctrine, enabling it to judge and execrate those phrenzies."

In the conclusion of that Conference, he asserts the same universally;

" ² They object to us our dissensions and scandals. To this we answer first, that among all of us who have been sent to this Conference, and among the pastors of all His Churches in our regions, there is, through the goodness of God, a pious consent as to the Confession exhibited to the Emperor Charles at Augsburg A. 1530, and that we reject all doctrines at variance with that Confession. But if any dissensions have arisen or now arise, we have judgments, that those in error may be healed. In the Church, in this life, there always have been, are, and will be, weak members. And the Lord commandeth to forgive seventy times seven, those who are curable."

¹ Opp. p. 791, 2.

² Ib. p. 799.

Melanchthon in his "history of the Colloquy" calls this, his "[t] wonted rehearsal," and expressly names the "depravers of the Sacraments" among those whom the associates of the Augsburg Confession rejected.

Finally, the Roman Collocutors took up the objection of the Weimar Divines, and required the Lutherans to

"[u] declare their dissent from the Zwinglians, Osiandrists, Synergists, Adiaphorists, and others, external to the Confession of Augsburg, inasmuch as the Empire had given peace to the associates of the Confession of Augsburg alone, and the Conference was entered upon with them only. These then disagreed. Schnepf, Strigel, Stossel, Theologians of the younger Dukes of Saxony, sons of John Frederic, formerly Elector, and with them, Morlin and Sarcerius, readily offered to Pflug, the president, the declaration required; the seven others, Melanchthon, Brenz, Bullinger, Illyricus, and the Theologians of August, Elector of Saxony, contended that those other sectaries ought not to be condemned, until their cause had been heard."

[t] Ib. 6469. T. ix. 459. "The first disputation was this. Since there must needs be judgment in the Church, that there ought to be a certain, unambiguous rule of judgment. This the Pontificians made, the perpetual consent of the Church. We in answer, first repeated this wonted rehearsal; that we embrace the Prophetic and Apostolic writings, and the Creeds, and hold that that doctrine is contained in our Confession exhibited to the Emperor Charles V. A. 1530, and that we neither do, nor will, depart from that Confession, and that we reject all sects and opinions at variance with that Confession, and by name the Anabaptists, the depravers of the Sacrament, Servetus, Stenckfeld [a name of aversion for Schwenckfeld], and Thammer. That we reject also the decrees of the Synod of Trent and the Interim, and in fine, all corruptions at variance with that Confession."

[u] Spondanus, A. D. 1557. § 15.

Melanchthon explains that the opposition to these condemnations arose, not with himself, but with Brenz, who condemned the doctrine ascribed to Osiander, but thought *him* condemned wrongly.

" [v] I answered modestly, that in these matters there was need of explanation, and that when an explanation had been made on each article, we would take the condemnations in order, because, nakedly, they would be ambiguous. They [the Roman party] rejecting this excuse, cease not to press for condemnations. On this our Colleagues [Schnepf &c.] who had before exhibited condemnations to the legates of our Princes, wish to exhibit the same publicly to the adversaries also. Our party dissuade them. Yet I had written condemnations in which I had expressly comprised all those which those Colleagues wished to be proposed. I had condemned too the Adiaphoristic, as they call them, lest they should say that I hindered, for my own sake, what they who had proposed this, demanded— but Brenz would not have Osiander blamed by name."

Melanchthon hereon again declared [w];

" We have often answered, both that we have been sent by Churches, which embrace the Confession exhibited at Augsburg, and no other kind of doctrine, and that we ourselves embrace that Confession and no other kind of doctrine. We have added also, that we reject opinions at variance with our Confession, and that there are extant refutations which we have published against many errors. Neither our Churches, nor we ourselves, approve of or embrace the doctrine of Zwingli [x], or any opinions at variance with our Confession."

[v] Hist. Colloq. Worm. C. R. 6469. add 6468.

[w] C. R. 6384.   [x] There are two texts here, but both contain the rejection of Zwingli. In Melanchthon's works, Witeb. 1601, the Munich MS. is followed.

This furnished the excuse, rather than the reason, for breaking up the Conference. For, whether such condemnations were premised, or whether the special errors were condemned precisely and distinctly in order, the Lutherans would equally have separated themselves from them. But the Pope objected to Colloquies, judging that matters of faith should be decided only in Councils; and it had been against his wish, that the Emperor had held this Colloquy [y].

Melanchthon uniformly used this language. In 1548 he, Bugenhagen, Cruciger and Major wrote to the Theologians of Strasburg on the Interim [z];

"All the Creeds, Apostolic, Nicene, and Athanasian we retain most faithfully. On [a] Baptism, the Lord's Supper, penitence, faith which receiveth remission of sins, the power of the Church, the civil magistrate, there are extant also our sentiments in the Confession of Augsburg, and many other writings agreeing herewith. And the doctrine which resoundeth in our Churches, these twenty years, and more, we noways change or shall change."

Melanchthon, whatever were his weaknesses or the defects of his belief, was honest. It is plain, then, that neither he nor the Lutheran Theologians needed any change for their own sakes. Indeed his habit of mind appears to have been, to regard the alterations as expansions of the Confession, not as changes in it. And this was true, with the exception of the one change in the Latin Edition of

<hr>

[y] Raynald A. 1557.　　　　[z] C. R. 4319.

[a] I have altered the punctuation; for Melanchthon could hardly have meant to say that the three Creeds had any doctrine, e. g. on the civil magistrate.

the tenth Article, which obscured the original and made it indefinite, but did not contradict it. This was Melanchthon's defence at the Conference of Worms, Jan. 14. 1541. Here (as appears probable from Eck's complaint), not at Hagenau, the Apology, as altered in the previous year, was presented for public use. Eck, in excusing a delay of ten weeks, which had occurred in opening the Conference, ascribed it in part to the alterations of the Confession.

"[b] The delay was partly owing to some long intervening disputes. But this increased it not a little, that the lords of the opposite party offered us a copy of the Confession and Apology, not in conformity with the recess of Hagenau, by the force of which, the very Confession, such as it was exhibited to His Imperial Majesty and the orders of the Princes, ought, nakedly, truly, to have been exhibited to us also. Hence, we have expended no little time and labor in comparing them, so that we should have had very righteous ground for putting off the Conference."

Melanchthon replied [c];

"I answer that the meaning is the same, although in the later edition some things are more mitigated or more developed."

Eck [d];

"In regard to the variety of copies, whereas I could easily break down his answer, and shew by ocular inspection, that the copies presented differ from the Confession of Augsburg, not in words only but in the substance (for unless they differed, there need have been no trouble at Augsburg as to that little word 'merit,' which there they

[b] Colloq. Worm. in C. R. 2132.   [c] Ib. p. 37.   [d] p. 43.

rejected); to be brief, I refer myself to future articles of the Conference, when I will make it quite clear as in the tenth article, &c."

Melanchthon [e];

"To that which, in order to bear us down, the Doctor premised as to copies and edicts, we shall answer more conveniently elsewhere. Let there be some moderation in these upbraidings."

The discussion was deferred then by mutual agreement. But to the tenth Article they never came. For after the settlement of the second, the Conference was adjourned to Regensburg; and *there* the direct consideration of the Confession of Augsburg was not resumed.

Melanchthon, in his history of the Conference, treats the imputation of a change as a calumny.

"[f] As we were in hopes that the Colloquy would begin, the Theologians on the other side, calumniated the Confession and Apology, and would reject it, as not being conformable with that, delivered to His Imperial Majesty at Augsburg, because somewhat was altered in the second Edition."

Melanchthon, however, doubtless had an object in the alteration of the tenth Article, and that, in favor of the "reformed."

The Emperor had invited all to send in statements of their faith to him at the Diet of Augsburg. When then those of Strasburg were not allowed to subscribe the Confession of Augsburg, "reserving the Article on the Holy Eucharist," they joined

[e] p. 47.

[f] Handlung d. Gesprachstags zu Wurms, &c. Ib. 2135. n. 10.

with the other three "Zwinglian cities" to send
in a Confession of their own, which was called the
"Confession of the four cities," "Confessio Tetra-
politana." "[g]The Zwinglian cities" [Strasburg,
Constance, Lindau, and Memingen[h]] have "offered
to the Emperor a Confession of their own," Brenz
relates, July 12; "and Zwingli has sent one of his,
foolish, in the first place, and in the second, alien
from Holy Scripture." "[i]Ulm," it was related at
the time on the spot, "also sent in its own Confession." "[k]Zwingli" too "sent one, already printed."
"You would say," says Melanchthon to Luther,
"that he was simply mad. On original sin, on
the use of the Sacraments, he renews openly the
old errors. Of ceremonies he speaks like a Swiss;
i. e. very barbarously, that he wishes them all
abolished. He urges his own cause on the Holy
Supper. All Bishops he wishes done away with.
I will send a copy, when I can obtain one. That
which I had is being circulated among the Princes."
The Strasburg Councillors write of it[l];

"On the 8th of July Zwingli sent in a manly account
of his faith by a special messenger to the Emperor, and
with what prospect it was received, you may readily perceive, from the excitement among the Papists."

[g] Ep. ad Isenman. C. R. 777. The legates of Nuremberg also
relate, on the authority of the Duke of Bavaria, that it "had been
given to the Emperor." Ib. 785.   [h] Legat. Norimb. Ib. 779.

[i] Ib. 785. and 918. Ulm, Frankfort and Halle seem to have
stood aloof. Ib. 921.

[k] Ib. 781.

[l] In a letter printed in Neue Beytrage von Alten und Neuen
Theol. Sachen, &c. 1756. p. 307. as from "Swiss Theologians."
But they speak of a Confession presented "in the name of *our*

The Confession of the " four cities " was an afterthought, consequent upon their not being admitted to sign the Confession of Augsburg, to the exclusion of the Article on the Holy Eucharist. It was written in great haste. Pappus, in a controversy about seventy years afterwards, states,

"[m] It can be shewn from the original letters of Jacob Sturm and M. Pfarrer, envoys at the Diet of 1530, that they did not bring with them to the Diet any such Confession, framed at Strasburg; nor was any such sent after them. But, when neither the protesting States, nor their Councillors and envoys then present, nor their Theologians would own them, or admit them to a common Confession, they then first in great haste begged that two Theologians should be sent them, when they came at last to Augsburg, in a few days and great haste they framed the Confession of the Cities, so that in a letter, dated June 21, they own that they had not time to send the Confession here [to Strasburg] to be seen and consulted about."

The Confession was written in Latin and German by Bucer[n]. The Article on the Holy Eucharist is framed, so as to seem to teach the Real Presence. It ought to mean this, honestly understood; yet leaves room for evasion.

"[o] Of this venerable Sacrament of the Body and Blood of

Senate which Constance, Memmingen and Lindau had subscribed." " *Our* Senate " must then be the fourth city, Strasburg.

[m] Wahrhaffte und wolgegrundete Widerlegung dess unwahrhafften und falschen berichts, so wider d. Strassb. A. 1598 ausgegangene Kirchen-Ordnung zu Zweybruken A. 1603, getrukt &c. p. 234, quoted in the Analecta ad Hist. Conf. Tetrap. in Schelhorn. Amænit. vi. 349.

[n] Agend. Eccl. Argentorat. p. 24, 27. ap. Schelhorn, p. 370.

[o] c. 18. Conf. Libb. Symbol. Ref. p. 352, 3. ed. Aug.

Christ, ours in truest faith, teach, commend, inculcate, all which the Evangelists, Paul, and the Holy Fathers, left in writing concerning it. . Thence, with special zeal, they ever extol the goodness of Christ to His own, whereby, at this day no less than in that last Supper, to all who have truly given themselves to be His disciples, when they receive this Supper, as He instituted it, He vouchsafes to give through Sacraments His own true Body and His own true Blood for the food and drink of their souls, whereby they are nourished to life eternal, that He may now abide in them and they live and abide in Him, to be raised by Him at the last day to a new and immortal life, according to those words of the Eternal Truth Himself; ' Take, eat, this is My Body;' and ' drink ye all of this, this Cup is My Blood.' But with special diligence do the Preachers withdraw the minds of our people from all contention and curious disquisition to that which alone profiteth, and which alone was regarded by Christ our Saviour, that, fed by Himself, we should live in Him and by Him, a life well-pleasing, holy, and therefore everlasting and happy, and that we should all be among ourselves, one bread, one body, who in the Holy Supper partake of one bread."

They further treat with indignation the imputation, that,

" our people should change and rend with human glosses the words of Christ, and that mere bread and mere wine are administered in our Suppers, and that the Supper itself of the Lord among us is despised and rejected. For ours ever teach and exhort, that each should with simple faith embrace these words of the Lord, rejecting all comments and false glosses of men, and give his mind to their meaning without wavering, receiving, with all the devotion he can, the Sacraments themselves, to the life-giving nourishment of his soul, and for a grateful commemoration of so great a benefit."

This Confession *ought* to be understood of a real,

objective, Presence, in that it speaks of our Lord, giving His true Body and Blood *through* Sacraments; and appeals to His words, " This is My Body," as the proof that His Body is really given in it.

Up to a certain point, this Confession went through the same stages, as that of the Lutheran of Augsburg. It too was delivered to the Emperor in German and Latin; by him it was given to his Theologians, Faber, Eck, Cochlæus, to refute [p]. The Emperor would not give the Envoys a copy of the refutation, but offered to allow them to have it read two or three times [q]. After the Diet, Ehinger, the envoy of Memmingen, obtained a copy of it, and sent it to Strasburg [r], whereupon this Confession too, with the Apology, was published, A. D. 1531, the same year as the Apology of the Confession of Augsburg [s].

Herewith, however, the likeness ceased. The four cities had no political weight by themselves. The Emperor had no special ground to conciliate them. The Zwinglians also, to whom they had originally belonged, were in far worse repute than

[p] Ehinger. MS. in Schelhorn, p. 353.

[q] d. H. Romischen Reichs Abschiede f. 247. quoted Ib.

[r] Ehinger Ib.

[s] In German, under the title Bekandtniss der vier Frey und Reichstätt, Strassburg, Costantz, Memmingen, und Lindaw, in deren sie Keys. Majestat, uff dem Reichstag zu Augspurg, im xxx. Jar gehalten, ihres Glaubens und Furhabens, der Religion halb, rechenschafft gethan haben. Schrifftliche Beschirmung und verthedigung derselber Bekanntnuss, gegen der Confutation und Widerlegung, so den Gesandten der vier Stätten, uff bemeldtem Reichstage offenlich fürgelesen, und hie getrewlich eingebracht ist. In fine, Strassburg, durch Johan Schweintzer uff den xxii. Augusti, Anno M. D. xxxi. 4. In Latin, Argentorati, G. Ulrich Audlons impressore 1531, 4.

the Lutherans, as going much further. The Strasburg Legates wrote;

" ᵗ The Gospel is in ill repute; especially the Sacramentaries, as they call them; and our Christian city.—About the same time threats are brought us from the Emperor's intimate friends, that he will rather lose his life, than allow us to persist in our disobedience. But," they add, " they are threats; for stronger is the Lord's truth."

In his Edict ᵘ the Emperor threatens them with the consequences, alleging

" We, out of their own Confession which they delivered, and from other credible accounts, have learned, that these four cities, belonging to us and the Empire, have severed themselves in faith, not only from the other free and Imperial cities, but from the whole German nation, and Christendom in common, and have been guilty of grievous errors against the venerable Sacrament, and of Imagebreaking, and other things, and have until now set on foot much offensive sectarianism, and circulated it among the lower orders in the German Nation, and that the same is contained in the book, carried about hither and thither; which is befitting neither in them, nor in any other."

The result of this was, that the four cities satisfied the Elector of Saxony as to their belief on the Holy Eucharist, and were admitted A. 1531, into the defensive treaty of Smalkald, Luther having previously advised that none should be admitted, who did not confess the real and substantial presence of the Body and Blood of Christ in the Holy Eucharist; and that these were received by the unworthy as well as the worthy. At the Convention

ᵗ In Schelh. l. c.   ᵘ l. c.

of Schweinfurt A. 1532, they subscribed the Confession and the Apology[v], and earnestly enjoined all their ministers to teach no otherwise than was therein expressed.

A. D. 1536, a convention took place at Wittenberg, with the view of uniting the Lutherans and the Swiss. The Germans who had been Zwinglians acted as mediators. Capito and Bucer came from Strasburg; Frecht, a licentiate, from Ulm; Musculus and Lycosthenes from Augsburg; Otther, a licentiate, from Esslingen; Zwick from Constance; Bernhardi from Frankfort; Schuler from Memmingen; Germanus from Furfeld; Aulbert and Schradin from Reutlingen. Melanchthon wrote that there was a change on their part[w];

" Capito and Bucer are here, and certain others, who indeed are inclining their judgment about the Eucharist, or mystery of the Body and Blood of Christ; but I know not whether by such counsel so great a scandal can be healed. Ours, I think, will make no covenant with them; you can easily divine, why."

Bucer and his companions stated that they held[x],

"that by the institution and doing of the Lord, (as the words of Christ express) His true Body and true Blood are truly exhibited, given, and taken, with the visible signs, the bread and wine—that they believed also that, through the minister of the Church, the Body and Blood of Christ are offered to all receivers, and are received, not only by the worthy, with both heart and mouth, to salvation, but by the unworthy, with the mouth, to their judgment and condemnation."

[v] Ep. Cap. et Buc. ad Luth. Jan. 19. 1537. ap. Schelh. p. 361.
[w] Ad Bomg. C. R. 1427.
[x] Hosp. ii. 243. C. R. 1429. Mel. Cons. Lat. i. 253. sqq.

They explained that they had supposed that Luther

"united the Body of Christ with the bread into one natural substance; and that he taught that the Body of Christ was naturally contained in the bread; and that by the touch or taste of the bread all, pious or impious, became partakers of grace."

Luther, on his side, explained (to use his own language)

"that he did not unite the Body and Blood by any natural bond with the bread and wine; nor did he locally include it in the bread and wine; nor did he ascribe to Sacraments any virtue of their own, whereby they should of themselves bring salvation to those who receive them; but only laid down a sacramental union between the Body and bread of the Lord; that he taught, moreover, that the strengthening of faith, which he ascribed to Sacraments, resulted from a virtue, not inherent in the outward things by themselves, but of Christ, and was dispensed by His Spirit, through words and symbols."

Finally, the two parties agreed in a formula drawn up by Melanchthon;

"We have heard Bucer explaining his own mind, and that of others with him, as to the Sacrament of the Body and Blood of Christ, thus,

"1. They confess according to the words of Irenæus, that the Eucharist consists of two things, an earthly and a heavenly. Therefore they hold and teach, that with the bread and wine there are truly and substantially present, exhibited, and received, the Body and Blood of Christ.

"2. And although they deny that Transubstantiation takes place; nor do they hold that there is any local inclusion in the bread; or any lasting conjunction out of the use of the Sacrament; yet they grant, that by Sacramental union the bread is the Body of Christ; i. e. they hold that, when the bread is offered, the Body of Christ is, at the same time, present and is truly exhibited. For, out of the use, when it is preserved in the pix, or shewn in processions, they hold that the Body of Christ is not present.

"Lastly, they hold that the institution of the Sacrament is of avail in the Church, and does not depend on the worthiness of the minister or the receiver. Wherefore, as Paul saith, the unworthy also eat, so they hold that the Body and Blood are truly presented to the unworthy, and that the unworthy receive them, where the words and institution of Christ are preserved. But such receive to judgment, as Paul saith, because they abuse the Sacrament, using it without repentance and without faith. For the end to which it is offered is, to attest that the benefits of Christ are applied to *those*, and that *they* are washed with the Blood of Christ who do penance and by faith raise themselves up towards Christ."

They conclude,

"But since we who have met are few, and we need on either side to refer this matter to other preachers and superiors, we cannot yet agree as to this Concord, until we have referred it to others.

"But since all profess, that they wish, in all Articles, to hold and teach according to the Confession and Apology of the Princes, we greatly desire, that this Concord be sanctioned and enacted. And we hope that, if the rest, on either side, consent, there will be a solid Concord."

Bucer proposed this formula to the Theologians on his side,

"As to the Article on the Eucharist, we must condemn loudly as an error, the teaching, that nothing but bread and wine is given and received in the holy Supper, when celebrated according to the word of the Lord. Also, we must affirm and teach, that it is the truth of Christ that, in the sacred Supper, the true Body and true Blood of the Lord are given and received, as was said however, not united naturally with the bread, nor included locally in the bread, nor as food for the belly. Lastly [we must affirm and teach] that the truth of this Sacrament, as of the Word of God and all Sacraments, rests on the word and Institution of the Lord, not on the merits of men, either receiving or giving.

"Whoso then owns these things to be true, and hath purposed in good faith, so to teach them, let him subscribe and perform what he had undertaken. If any think otherwise, we offer ourselves to answer in a friendly way to all things, which can hinder him from subscription."

"All answered 'that they had no reason for declining to subscribe, since they all earnestly so believe and hold; and they subscribed, each with his own hand." Their names are still preserved. Capito and Bucer head the list; then the other delegates before mentioned; then "Luther, Jonas, Cruciger, Bugenhagen, Melanchthon, Menius of Eisenach, Myconius, Urbanus Reg., Spalatin, Melander of Cassel and many others."

The German cities, and even the Swiss Zwinglians, accepted the concord, as agreeing with their previous Confessions. On the part of the four cities, this was, probably, a real agreement, since they subsequently accepted the formula Concordiæ, and its rigid Lutheranism. They with their preachers received indeed, and subscribed, the Concord of Wittenberg, as "conformable to our Confession and Apology which have been published," "our Confession given to His Imperial Majesty at Augsburg ʸ." But this was rather to save their consistency. It

ʸ Letter of Council of Strasburg to Memmingen Aug. 28. answer Sept. 7. in Schelh. p. 365.

had been truer to say, we interpret by these articles
our previous Confession. For their previous Confession was ambiguous, capable of being taken in
the same sense as the Confession of Augsburg;
these articles, which they now received, honestly
taken, admitted of no other meaning. And so,
that previous Confession of the four cities, in fact,
died out. When it was reprinted at Strasburg
after about half a century, A. D. 1579, it was in-
stantly suppressed by the Council[z]. The Council
feared lest the other three cities might be offended,
if their common, but obsolete, Confession were reprinted against the will of the rest. They feared
also, that the act might be interpreted by other Lutherans, as implying an intention to go back to their
first Confession, and abandon the Confession of
Augsburg. It was reprinted at Deux-Ponts in 1604
on occasion of some Ecclesiastical Agenda introduced at Strasburg in 1598[a]. After this, it became
mere matter of history.

The Swiss cities accompanied their acceptance of
the Concord with a very long and wordy answer,
repeating all their old theories, which yet did not,
in themselves, absolutely exclude all further belief.
It is remarkable, that even as to the participation
by the wicked, so clearly affirmed in the " Concord,"
they only observe that, such cannot (which of course,
they cannot) be partakers of Christ.

---

[z] Schelhorn § 30. fin.

[a] The title states that it was printed zu fernerer Erklärung d.
Berichts auf d. neuer Strassburgischer Kirchern-Ordnung 1598.
erstlich gedruckt zu Strassburg 1531 jetzt nachgedruckt zu Zwey-
bruck 1604. 4. The title is given in Feuerlin Symbolik.

"[b] Since we perceive that our Confession, framed at Basle, is not weakened or changed by those Articles, nor is the true Humanity of our Lord Jesus Christ and His Bodily ascent into heaven denied (inasmuch as He is no longer carnally in this world but abides in His own heavenly condition), nor do they deny that our Lord Jesus Christ, (when the holy Supper is in the assembly of the Church rightly celebrated and distributed) is really apprehended, partaken of and perceived only by the faithful, we could perceive nothing else, than that we always have before so taught and believed, and in future will so teach."

Luther showed, by his answer, that he saw that the Swiss did not hold the same as himself [c]; but he accepted the subscription, as he elsewhere says, as a step towards the true doctrine [d]. Luther was deceived. The Zwinglians had a strong antagonist system of their own, consistent within itself, and making no demands upon faith. The Concord was signed. A few leading Zwinglian preachers lutheranised for a while. In seven years a more decided re-action took place. The Concord made no more impression upon the Zwinglian system, than the stone, which passes through the waters, and is buried in them, does upon their surface, which it, for the moment, rippled.

[b] Declarat. Helv. Eccl. in Hosp. ii. 263.

[c] "If we have not as yet fully understood one another." Luther's answer in Hosp. ii. 276. and briefe V. 83. ed. de W.

[d] Luther wrote to Albert Duke of Prussia, May 6, 1538, "with the Swiss, who have hitherto been at variance with us on account of the Sacrament, things are on a good road; God help them further. Basle, Strasburg, Augsburg, and Berne, with others, are setting very beautifully towards us. So we too accept it friendlily, that I hope God will make an end of that scandal."— Briefe, 1801. V. 170. ed W.

In Germany, every thing now seemed to be Lutheran. In the following year, 1537, deliberations were held as to Articles to be sent in to the Council, then appointed by Paul III. to be held at Mantua.   Melanchthon relates[e];

" Of those supposed to dissent from ours, no one was present save Blarer and Bucer.   There were two causes of the Theological meeting; the one, that there should be no vain, but an accurate, conference as to doctrine; that dissensions might be removed, and there might be in our Churches a consentient and explicit doctrine.   The other, that we should deliberate, *which* Articles are to be maintained and retained to the last, and to be preferred to the common tranquillity and all human things; *which* should, be conceded to the Pope and Ecclesiastical polity for the sake of peace and in order to restore the general concord of the Church, if matters could be brought to any temperament.   Most honourable was the purpose of both discussions, arising out of our many complaints and discourses.   But neither took place.   For the unlearned and most impetuous would not hear of concessions.   They say that the opinion of our unsteadiness, now at the very crisis, would injure us not only with others but with our own people too; and that, if we gave way, the Emperor would press harder. These things beget manifold suspicions in the good and moderate, and increase anxiety.   Then we were asked in the name [of the Princes] nót to confer on doctrine, lest any controversy should increase discord, and dissolve the alliance.   I saw these dangers impending, before we came, and warned our people; but they were full of hope—We were bidden to run hastily over the articles of the Confession, and hear if any one dissented in any article, or disapproved aught.   And the Princes protested distinctly, that they would maintain the formula of Concord.   There was a brief conversation about the Mysteries.   Bucer spoke

[e] Ep. ad Camerar. C. R. 1534.

plainly and clearly, affirming the Presence of Christ. He satisfied all of our's, even the more rigid. Blarer spoke in generals, that Christ was present. Afterwards, he added some ambiguous things. Osiander urged him somewhat acridly, but since we wished that no vehement contest should be raised, I interrupted him. We parted then, agreement having been established among all the rest, and this one [Blarer] not appearing to dissent."

In a letter to Jonas he adds[g];

" He [Blarer] subscribed the Confession and Apology. Thus the Theological Congress was ended, when, the Agreement having been ascertained, all had subscribed the Apology and Confession."

The " associates of the Confession of Augsburg " were the only parties to whom toleration was extended. Charles V. appears sincerely to have regarded them with an interest, which he did not entertain towards the Zwinglians, who denied the real Presence. With this, coincided the power of their political supporters to gain them consideration, and the Emperor's need of their help against the Turks. In all Conferences with the Roman side, they alone were owned. In 1534, when Ferdinand, King of the Romans, at Cadan, gave to the allies of the Confession of Augsburg, an exemption from fiscal prosecutions, he expressly excluded " the Anabaptists and Sacramentaries, with other like sects." The Landgrave of Hesse wrote to those of Strasburg[h],

" Although there is found therein a little word ' Sacramentaries,' which may perhaps be looked upon as a

g Ib. 1538.　　　h Letter of July 13, in Schelhorn, 1. c. p. 362.

grievance to some, we know that you do not consider yourselves such, but as Christians, and hold much and honourably of the Sacrament and Supper of our dear Lord Jesus Christ; but if any misunderstanding should be made of it, and you should be harassed, ye know beforehand our mind; and as we are disposed to be friendly to one another, so, God willing, we will remain, and not allow ourselves to be moved against you, nor in any righteous matter detach ourselves from you."

In all the negotiations for truce or peace, it was a question how far the toleration should extend. In those which preceded the peace of Nuremberg, July 23, 1532, the Roman party had originally demanded that the Protestant should not help the Zwinglians or Anabaptists[i]. Luther recommended the Elector to accept the terms, confining the pacification to the actual adherents of the Augsburg Confession[k]; and they probably would have obtained no other terms. The treaty of Cadan 1534, has just been mentioned. The peace of Nuremberg, when prolonged after the Colloquy at Worms, was still contracted with the adherents of the Confession of Augsburg. Only, these now included Electoral Brandenburg, the Dukedom of Saxony, Wirtemburg; Barnim and Philip, Dukes of Pomerania; Rupert Palatine of Deux-Ponts, William of Nassau, Princes George and Joachim, of Anhalt. Many more had joined, when the Diet of Spire, A. D. 1544, confirmed the declaration at Worms. The same limitation occurs in the Pacification of Passau, A. D. 1552, and in the peace of Augsburg, A. D. 1555.

[i] Luther, Werke, xvi. 2185. ed. Walch.
[k] Luther to the Elect. iv. p. 382. ed. de W. and to his Son, p. 384.

"The reformed" were recognised for the first time after the thirty years' war, in the peace of West-phalia A. D. 1648.

The presentation of the altered copy of the Confession at the Conference at Worms, increases the probability that the change had a political object, the extension of the toleration attached to the Confession of Augsburg. This toleration was still temporary. The negotiation at Worms was a new one. But the Protestants certainly altered the terms, by passing under the name of the Confession of Augsburg, a form which would admit those whom the Roman party had intended to exclude.

It could not indeed secure to them those benefits, without a fresh act of the Emperor, prolonging the pacification. But it belonged rather to the stratagems of war, than to the negotiations of Divines, to introduce silently a change, involving considerable consequences, and to leave it to the acuteness or watchfulness of the party who was to accept the change, to discover that any such change had been made. It would not have been honour-able in ordinary diplomacy. The truce too did not relate to religious toleration only, but carried in-demnity as to the property of monasteries which the Protestant states had taken possession of. The older Lutheran Theologians directly called this change, "Melanchthon's falsification[1] of the Con-fession of Augsburg;" his apologists allege[m] that it

---

[1] e. g. Cyprian, Hist. d. Augsp. Conf. c. 13. " of Melanchthon's premeditated falsification, &c."

[m] Magdeburg. Bedenken quoted by Semler, Vorrede zu d. Ab-druck d. Torgischen Buchs.

H 2

was done "with the knowledge, good-will, counsel, and participation of Luther," "at the command of the Protestant Princes." The History is unexplained. It seems impossible that the strict Lutheran, the Elector of Saxony, should have knowingly assented to it. But he did not probably understand the niceties of Latin[n]. Then also the alteration which he is known to have disapproved was introduced into both the German and Latin copies, and so changed the Confession as a whole; the change as to the Holy Eucharist was only in the Latin; while the confession of the truth remained untampered with in the German. Even in 1537, the Elector had been troubled at the changes which Melanchthon had made in the Confession, at his supposed disagreement with Luther on justification, in that he made works a "sine qua non;" and at the prospect of innovations after Luther's death[o].

[n] Having received an English proclamation of Henry VIII. in print, he wrote to Melanchthon to get it translated into Latin, by one who knew English, and then into German by Jonas for himself (C. R. 1771. Jan. 21).

[o] C. R. 1573. May 5. The changes, it was supposed, would come from Melanchthon and Cruciger. Cruciger had, in 1536, supported Melanchthon's formula, that good works were not, indeed, an efficient cause of salvation, but yet a cause "sine qua non." On the holy Eucharist the Elector only mentions a report, that when an arbitrary authority would not allow the Protestants to receive in both kinds, Melanchthon had given an opinion that they might receive in one. Some also would not receive the Sacraments from Priests who had not the old orders, or from those who had, but had married a second or third time. Strobel (Apol. Mel. p. 144.) questioned the genuineness of this paper. There can be no doubt of it from internal evidence. Bretschneider says, " No one who ever saw the Acta Vinariensia will doubt it."

This is stated in a remarkable document, notes drawn up by Brueck, Chancellor of the Elector, as to the points upon which he was, at the Elector's desire, to obtain advice of Luther and Bugenhagen touching Melanchthon.

"Mr Philip is said to have taken on himself to alter, soften, and otherwise express, in some points, the Confession of your Elect. Gr. and of the other princes and states, made before H. Imp. Maj. at Augsburg, without the previous knowledge and consent of your El. Grace, and the others; wherefrom, in the judgment of your El. Gr., he ought in justice to have abstained, since the Confession is especially that of your El. Gr. and the other allied States; whence your El. Grace and the other allied States would have to bear this, that you never should be certain of your doctrine, and should be unsettled. Thereat too the people take offence."

The only changes, *then* made, were expansions of the Confession in its real meaning. The Elector expressed himself ready to see his University of Wittenberg, which mainly hung upon Melanchthon, dwindle away, rather than allow an un-Lutheran tone of teaching to spread. Brueck reports Luther's answer, short, full of misgivings, but deprecatory, and dwelling only on Melanchthon's belief as to the Sacrament, and the prospects after his own death [p]. On the changes in the Confession, no answer of his is reported by Brueck.

The twofold character of the changes makes it the more difficult to know what was approved, what disapproved. The expression reported from Rorarius, Luther's secretary, is too characteristic, not to

[p] Ib. 1620.

be true.   Wigand relates [q]; "I have heard from Mr. G. Rorarius, that Luther said to Philip, 'Philip, Philip, you do not well to alter the Confessio Augustana so often; for it is not your's, but the Churches' book.'"   But the expression "so often" must bear upon other changes also; not especially, and perhaps not at all, upon this.

It implies too that Melanchthon did, in some measure, regard the Confession, as "his own book," and that he changed it, without previously consulting Luther.   The only strong ground urged for supposing, that the princes generally knew of the change, is the improbability, that Melanchthon should have ventured upon it without their knowledge [r].   The policy, however, of the Landgrave of Hesse had been, from the first, to include the Reformed under the Confession of Augsburg [s].   Melanchthon may have done it at his instance, trusting that the Elector of Saxony would admit, when done, what he would not have sanctioned beforehand. Melanchthon had vehemently resisted the Landgrave's wish in 1530; his own mind had since undergone a change.

He appears to have been shaken as to the definiteness of his faith by a collection of passages made by Osiander from the fathers, in which they

[q] Vorrede zu d. Augs. Conf. 1579, quoted by Cyprian, Hist. p. 194.

[r] Chytræus says that "it was presented at the Colloquies of Worms and Regenspurg by the Evangelical states," i. e. in their names by the deputies. Hist. d. Augsb. C. p. 56. v.   The Theologians of Hesse on the formula of Concord allege the same fact. ap. Semler l. c.

[s] See above, p. 28. 36—9.

spéak of the Eucharistic "symbols[t]". This was early in 1535, just before the Conference of Wittenberg. He writes to Brenz [u];

"Thou hast written several times about the Sacramentaries, and dissuadest from concord with them, even if they should bind themselves to Luther's judgment—As to concord, nothing is yet done—Only I have brought with me the statements of Bucer. I would that I could speak of this controversy with you, face to face. I do not make myself a judge, and I willingly give way to you who are over the Church, and I affirm the real Presence of Christ in the Supper. I would not be either author or defender of any new doctrine in the Church. But [v] I see that there are many testimonies of ancient writers, who without ambiguity, interpret the mystery of a type and typically; but the opposite testimonies are either more modern or spurious. But you too should consider, whether you defend the ancient opinion. I wish most earnestly that the godly Church should judge this matter, without sophistry or violence.

"Many in France and elsewhere are put to death for this opinion [w]. And many applaud such judgments without good reason, and confirm the fury of the tyrants. To say truth, this troubles me not a little. I beseech you then, settle nothing rashly in this matter, but deliberate with the ancient Church too.

"My great wish would be, that concord should be formed without any sophistry. But I would too, that good men could confer lovingly on so great a matter. So could concord be formed without sophistry—For I doubt not

[t] Osiander's dialogue, quid de Eucharistia veteres tam Græci quam Latini senserint. A. 1530.

[u] C. R. 1241. Jan. 12.

[v] This and the next two sentences are in Greek, as Melanchthon was wont to write what he wished not to be generally understood, in case it should fall into wrong hands.

[w] They had been called "the devil's martyrs."

that the opponents would willingly cast away their whole dogma, if they thought it modern. For you know, that many among them are very good men.

"Now, of themselves, they are bending themselves to Luther. And indeed they are moved by some testimonies of Ecclesiastical writers. What would you have done? that we should hold no conference? For my part, I would that we could often confer on this and many other matters. You see that, in other articles, both they and we explain many things more dexterously, since they have been more discussed among us."

And in 1538 in answer to Veit, who had inadvertently used heretical language on the Presence [x],

"I, not to depart over far from the ancients, have laid down a Sacramental Presence, during the use; and I have said, that the elements being given, Christ is truly present and worketh. This is enough. I have not added inclusion, nor any such conjunction that the Body should be affixed to the bread, or soldered, or mingled. Sacraments are covenants, that the things being taken, somewhat else is present.

"This being so, the worship should not be added; or, if added, it is not to be referred to the bread.

"In what you argue about hypostatic or bodily union, first, you err in the word. Hypostatic is called the Personal union, such as is that union of the Divine and Human Nature in Christ. Such an union of the bread the Papists too do not assert, and it is altogether new, and, without doubt, unholy. I would not then have you use this word in this matter.

"Nor did you mean that there is a hypostatic union of the bread and the Body, but a real one; as of iron and fire in the heated iron (to use such likeness as we may), or as of the vessel and the liquor. I, altho', as I said, I assert a

---

[x] C. R. 1667. April 23.

real union, yet it is not by conclusion or soldering, but Sacramental, i. e. that the signs being there, Christ is present, truly working.

"What requirest thou more? To this you must come at last, unless you maintain what some say, that the Body and Blood are delivered separately. This too is new, and will not please the Papists either. Error is fertile, as the saying is. That physical conjunction begets many questions. Are they given separately? or are they 'included,' when present? or, out of the use? Nothing of this is read among the Ancients.

"I, my Veit, will not introduce these disputations into the Church, and therefore did I speak so sparingly of this matter in the 'Loci,' that I might withdraw the youth from these questions. Thou hast in sum and categorically, what I think. But would that the whole matter could at some time be fully considered, those two most cruel tyrants, passion and sophistry, being set aside for the while!—I think that I too speak of the symbols religiously and reverently, and come nearest to the mind of the Ancients."

Luther spoke anxiously about Melanchthon to Brueck when sent to him by the Elector, and dated his change from the conference with Bucer in 1535.

Brueck reports to the Elector [y],

"Dr Martin owns that he never had thought that Philip still stuck so fast in those 'phantasies' [the Elector's word] whence I understood, that Philip had kept your El. Grace's letter to Dr Jacob [Sturm] hidden from him. He showed at the same time, that he had all sorts of anxiety, and could not make out, how Philip stood as to the Sacraments. For that he called it no otherwise, held it too only for a mere ceremony. For a long time too he [Luther] had not seen him receive the holy supper. He [Melanchthon] too had used arguments, after he had been to Cassel, whence he

[y] C. R. 1620.

[Luther] had perceived that he was almost of Zwinglian opinions. Yet how it stood in his heart, he [L.] knew not. But the secret counsel, ' that under the tyrants one might receive the Sacrament in one kind,' gave him [L.] strange thoughts. But he would lay open his whole heart to Philip, and desired earnestly that Philip, as a man of eminence, might not remove from them and the University here; for he did great work. But if he would hold to the opinion, which he [L.] had observed in his letter to Dr Jacob, the truth of God must take its course. He would pray for him."

In 1539, the Concord of Wittenberg must most have expressed Melancthon's mind; for in his Testament which he then wrote, expecting shortly to die, he says[a], "On the Lord's Supper, I embrace the formula of Concord made here." Then he says generally;

"Nor was it my purpose to propagate any new opinion, but perspicuously and correctly to explain the Catholic doctrine, which is delivered in our Churches, which I judge to have been, by the singular goodness of God, laid open in these last times by D. Martin Luther."

Melanchthon had wished to turn from the study of Theology, when but twenty-five. He wrote in July, 1522, to Spalatin[a];

"Theological matters, which I had begun to lecture in, on the ground of the Baccalaureate, as the custom is, I had rather omit—I see that there is need of many and diligent teachers of classical literature, which are not less neglected in this age, than in that sophistical [scholastic] age."

It is not strange, then, that amid the then limited

---

[a] Cons. Lat. i. 389. C. R. 1873. comp. 1872. fin.
C. R. i. 575.

knowledge of the Fathers, he should have been perplexed by Osiander's collections of passages, in which they speak (as so many do) of the consecrated symbols, as types. His own store of those passages in which the Fathers so strongly affirm the doctrine of the real objective Presence, was very limited. In his Apology, he had quoted Theophylact, of the 12th century, with S. Cyril of Alexandria. His favourite passage for expressing his own belief, is a single saying of S. Hilary. Perhaps too, Luther's mode of stating the doctrine hindered its occurring to him, that these Fathers, when they speak of the Eucharistic elements as types, meant, " types of that which, although invisible, was present, not absent." Passages, which expressed only a belief in the relation of the outward form to the inward Substance, shook his belief in the Real Presence.

A few months before his death, when the Count Palatin referred to him the controversy between Heshus and Klebitz on the Holy Eucharist, he still referred to those same passages [b];

" Heshus denies that he agrees with Origen, who calls the bread and wine 'symbols of the Body and Blood.' He rejects contumeliously Clement of Alexandria. He will pronounce in the same way of Augustine, Ambrose, Prosper, Dionysius, Tertullian, Bede, Basil, Nazianzen [c], who calls it ἀντίτυπον σῶμα, Theodoret, who says of the bread, 'not changing its nature.'"

[b] C. R. 6861. T. ix. p. 963.

[c] He probably means, Orat. viii. 18, ἀντιτύπων τοῦ σώματος. On the passages in which the fathers speak of the consecrated elements as "types, figures, symbols, images," see "The doctrine of the Real Presence," p. 94-118.

It needed not to "reject" these Fathers, but to understand them. But here too he desires that the decision should be with others. His closing words are; "I hope that, at some time, all the controversies of these times will be deliberated upon in a pious Synod."

Melanchthon did not, in some sort, deny a real Presence in the act of communicating. He wished, as he said, that the Church should decide the question for them all. But his own habit of mind was to attach himself exclusively to the words of S. Paul, "the bread which we break, is it not the Communion of the Body of Christ?" "So then," he continues [d],

"these things, the bread and wine, being given in the Supper of the Lord, the Body and Blood of Christ are given [exhibentur] to us. And Christ is truly present to His Sacrament, and is efficacious in us; as Hilary saith, 'which things being taken and drunken by us, cause that Christ should be in us and we in Christ.' Wonderful, truly, and mighty pledge of His exceeding love towards us, of His exceeding mercy, that by this Supper He willeth to attest that He imparteth Himself to us, that He joineth us to Himself as members, that we may know, that we are loved, regarded, saved by Him."

Even here Melanchthon says, that "our Lord *attesteth* that He imparteth," rather than that He there in very deed imparteth Himself to us. Melanchthon's mind however was undogmatic, and, as he grew older, became yet more so. He and Luther each had half of the truth; he, the personal; Luther, the objective. Luther vindicated the simple adherence to our Lord's words, yet had no heart

[d] Loc. Theol. de Cœn. Dom. § 8. ed. 1535.

for the blessedness which they convey. Melanch-thon overlooked the force of our Lord's words altogether; yet to the last, he differed from Zwingli and Calvin, believing, not that the soul fed on Christ, but that Christ fed the soul with His own Body and Blood. The strength of the strict Lutheranism was its adherence to the meaning of our Lord's words, as the Church has ever received them; its weakness was, to make our Lord's Gift of His own Body and Blood, a *mere* testimony to faith, like the bow in the cloud. Zwinglianism was consistent in itself. It was consistent to make mere outward things of this world, bread and wine, mere tokens of the covenant of God's mercy to us in Christ. It was inconsistent to make the greatest of all realities here on earth, the very Gift of Christ Himself, His Body and His Blood, whereby He dwells in us, and we in Him—a *mere* sign of a covenant to assure our faith. Lutheranism then contained in itself the elements of its own decay. Melanchthon almost injured his own belief by what he retained of it. He let go Luther's strong adherence to the words, "This is My Body;" and he retained what undermined the faith, Luther's theory that its very end was to be a sign to faith.

Melanchthon avowed his purpose to withdraw the young from dogmatic statements on the Holy Eucharist. To withdraw minds from dogmatic statements is to declare those statements to be no part of the faith; and so it is to withdraw out of sight the faith itself, as far as it depends upon those expressions of it. The growth of what was called Crypto-Calvinism, at Wittenberg and elsewhere, was the natural result of such teaching. As the pupils of Doddridge, to his surprise, became Socinians, so the pupils of Melanchthon became Calvinists. But they were outwardly Lutherans, and so gained the name of Crypto-Calvinists. The Statutes for the Theological faculty, framed by Melanchthon himself, declared ;

" °As in the Churches of our dominion—so in the University,—we will that the pure doctrine of the Gospel, agreeable to the Confession *which A.* 1530 *was presented to the Emp. Charles*—be piously and faithfully proposed, preserved, and propagated."

The oath for the Doctor of Divinity ran [f];

"I promise to God—that, God helping, I will faithfully serve the Church in teaching the Gospel without any corruptions, and will steadfastly defend the Creeds, the Apostles', Nicene, and Athanasian, and will persevere in consent to the doctrine comprised in the Augsburg Confession, *which was exhibited by this Church to the Emperor A.* 1530."

The varied Latin Confession could not, then, by virtue of their oath, be substituted for the original by the Divines of Wittenberg, except as equivalent to the unvaried.

But apart from the Article on the Holy Eucharist, the varied edition of the Confession was fuller than the original. It had its own recommendations to Lutherans. And so, since the effect of such a change, as that made in this Article, is not readily foreseen, it was natural that in a body which had so little internal union as the Lutheran, the altered

---

° Liber decanorum facultatis theol. Acad. Viteberg. ed. Forstem. quoted by Gieseler K. G. iii. 2. 1. p. 142.   f Ib.

Confession found its way, and became the lecture-book in Lutheran states. The princes and states in the Convention of Nuremberg 1561, even while they subscribe in the first instance the unvaried Confession, in German and Latin, still recognise the varied Latin, on the ground that it was more full, had been presented at religious conferences (as at Worms), and had been introduced "into the Churches and Schools of the Confederates."

"ᵍ We have not neglected again to take in hand and consider the said Confession as it was printed and published in German and Latin at Wittenberg, soon after the Diet, and the services were reformed according to it:

"Then, although afterwards in the years 1540 and 1542, the said Confession was repeated, somewhat more statelily and fully, and was from grounds of Holy Scripture explained and enlarged, and again printed at Wittenberg, and was then, at the Colloquy at that time instituted at Worms, again, by the States, the allies of this Confession, delivered to, and received by, the Imperial President and Collocutors there appointed, and the Colloquy took place thereon;

"Yet we have now on this occasion, taken in hand the aforementioned [i. e. the original] Confession of Augsburg, that your Imp. Maj. and all others may perceive, that our intention is not to defend or spread any other, or any unfounded doctrine.—

"In thus renewing, however, and subscribing the first printed Confession, it is not at all our intention, in the least to depart from the aforementioned Confession, delivered and explained in the year 1540, or to part with it. For since, upon frequent discussions with the opposite party, it has been, therefore, in some Articles, stated the more fully, in order that the Divine truth may come the more to the light,

ᵍ Published from the Royal Archives at Berlin by Weber, ii. 344. sqq.

and the faith and trust in the satisfaction and merits of our only Mediator and Redeemer Jesus Christ, may (setting aside all traditions and commandments of men) remain pure, clear, and unadulterated, and so be transmitted to posterity;—We can as little depart from the same, as from the first Confession delivered by our forefathers, and, in part by ourselves; whereto we are the more induced, since the said explained Confession, printed in 1540, and 1542, is now in use in the Churches and schools of most of us.

"In like way would we herewith give in the Apology (which at the aforesaid Diet of Augsburg was delivered by our forefathers, and in part by us, but was not received), as it was afterwards printed at Wittenberg, and as, at the aforesaid Colloquy at Worms in the year 1540, we gave it in with the aforesaid improved Confession, expressly renewed it, and pledged ourselves to it."

The Duke of Saxe-Weimar refused to sign this, on account of the partial recognition of the altered Confession; the Elector Palatine, on the contrary, signed the unaltered Confession, although he introduced the "reformed" religion into his territory.

But although the altered Confession was admitted only in the sense of the unaltered, the use of it, as being less definite, conspired with the undogmatic character of Melanchthon's teaching. It is better never to have had a clear expression of faith, than to lay it aside. It is laid aside through diminished faith; and the act of laying it aside diminishes faith.

The Wittenberg Divines, after Melanchthon's death, were not honest. The Elector trusted them, and they deceived him. But error was opposed by error; the error of the Sacramentaries was opposed by the error of the Ultra-Lutherans.

These, having neither the authority of the Church to fall back upon, nor the personal influence of Luther, nor being able somehow to take up his ground, that the mode of Christ's Presence in the Holy Eucharist must be left to God's Omnipotency, adopted a heretical defence of that Presence, derived originally from Luther. This was the supposed ubiquity of Christ's Body, by virtue of Its union with His Godhead. This was an error, founded upon a misconception of the Catholic doctrine of the "Communicatio idiomatum." The truth expressed by that term is, that our Lord being, in one Person, Perfect God and Perfect Man, what belongs to His Divine Nature may be said of Him, as Man, and what belongs to His Human Nature may be spoken of Him, as God.' "[h] Because of the perfect union of the flesh which was assumed, and of the Godhead which assumed it, the names are interchanged, so that the human is called from the Divine, and the Divine from the human. Wherefore He who was crucified is called by Paul, Lord of Glory, and He Who is worshipped by all creation, of things in heaven, in earth, and under the earth, is named Jesus." Our Lord Himself so spoke. He saith, "No man hath ascended up into Heaven, but He that came down from Heaven, even the Son of Man which *is* in Heaven." And God the Holy Ghost has taught us to speak of " the Blood of God," since He has said, " the Church of God, which He hath purchased with His own Blood."

[h] S. Greg. Nyss. in Apoll. ii. 697. See other authorities in S. Athanasius against the Arians, p. 443. not. h. add i. k. 244. l. 448. z. 450. b.

And again He says, "they would not have crucified the Lord of Glory." But since our Lord, in His One Person, exists of, and in, two perfect Natures, without confusion, what belongs to the one *Nature,* may not be ascribed to the other. It may be said, "God died" (provided it be not in the sense which some heretics meant, that "the Godhead died"), "God suffered," "the sufferings of Christ our God," "the Infant weeps, but *is* in heaven." But it would be blasphemy to say that "the Godhead suffered." It might not be said that the Manhood, when, for us and for our salvation, our Saviour dwelt among us, was in heaven, or that, now that It has been exalted to God's Right Hand, *that* Manhood, in its natural mode of being, is on earth. Our Lord, Who is God and Man, has promised to be with us, "unto the end of the world;" but He Who is God and Man, is with us as God only, except that, in some way known to Himself, He, while abiding in heaven in His natural mode of being, causes His Body sacramentally to be with us.

Luther, at one time, fully recognised this, and defended on this principle the word Θεοτόκος, "she who bare God." For if our Lord, when she bare Him, had not been God, then she had borne a man only, and God would not have been Incarnate, nor "the Word" have "become flesh." In his controversy with Zwingli, Luther, in answer to Zwingli's argument that "a body could not [after the natural way of being] be in two places at once," fell on the heresy of the ubiquity of our Lord's Body. Although he had known, and had stated accurately, the doctrine of the "communicatio idiomatum," he now stated it, as if there were an actual communication of the properties of the One Nature to the other. And this he illustrated in an offensive way, such as rather suited a description of the anima mundi of Pantheism, or the particles of the Manichean Godhead[i] confined in vegetation, than even the Divine Omnipresence. He argued that our Lord's Divinity, and so, he said, His Humanity was present every where; then he instanced things of the inanimate creation, "[k]straw, fire, water, a rope, a crab-apple!" Luther himself seems to have laid aside the heresy. He took it up, and laid it down, as his way was. In his answer to the Swiss, 1538, he states in a natural way, his belief in the Article of the Creed, and refers the Presence of our Lord's Body and Blood in the Holy Eucharist to God's Omnipotency.

"[l] As to the third Article of the Sacrament of the Body and Blood of Christ, we have again never yet taught, nor do we now teach, that Christ ascendeth and descendeth from heaven, or from the Right Hand of God, visibly or invisibly. We abide also by the Article of the Creed, 'He ascended into heaven, sitteth on the Right Hand of God, and shall come' &c. and we commit it to His Divine Omnipotency, how His Body and Blood are given to us in the Supper, when we come together at His command, and the consecration takes place. We conceive of no coming or descent, but hold simply to His words, 'This is My Body;' 'This is My Blood.'"

Some of his disciples, after his death, systematised what Luther had but incidentally thrown

---

[i] See S. Aug. Conf. Note. ii. b. p. 324. Oxf. Tr.

[k] See the Real Presence, p. 45, 6.   [l] Briefe, 1784. V. 85. de W.

out; they denied, at least, one article of the Creed; and completed the destruction of the doctrine of the Holy Eucharist, which they defended. It is melancholy to see Brenz, in his later years, plunging himself into heresy, in order to maintain the truth. He taught that our Lord's Manhood is, wherever His Godhead is; that It has all the attributes of God; that our Lord did not locally ascend in His Ascension; that the Right Hand of God, where, the Apostle saith, He hath sat down, is every where; that His Manhood was in heaven as soon as He took our nature in the Virgin's womb [m]; that it is

[m] These statements are continually repeated by Brenz in his controversial works at this time, the de personali unione duarum naturarum in Christo Opp. viii. 831-51. to which he appended a collection of passages on the Holy Eucharist from Luther p. 851-67. de libell. Bullinger, in domo Patris mei p. 868-89. de majestate D. N. J. C. ad dexteram Dei Patris &c. p. 891-970. Recognit. Proph. et Apostol. doctr. de vera Maj. D. N. J. C. &c. p. 976-1101. The following are specimens. "Although the Divine substance is not changed into the human, and each has its own properties, yet these two substances are so united into One Person in Christ, that the one is in fact never divided from the other." p. 834. "*So that wherever the Godhead is, there also is the Humanity of Christ,*" p. 835. "The Right Hand of God is not some bodily or mundane place, to which Christ has, as it were, tied Himself, but is the Omnipotence and Majesty of God. And since this is not shut up in one special place, so as not to fill heaven and earth and all things, it follows that neither is Christ in His Humanity, wherein He is sat down at the Right Hand of God, only placed in this outward heaven. For this saying, 'that the Right Hand of God, at which Christ hath set down, filleth heaven and earth,' signifies not only, that the reign of Christ and His power, extends on all sides, but also that *His Humanity,* which hath set down at the Right Hand of God, *is present with all things,* and that, not only in a heavenly, but also in a human manner, and hath all things in its sight, and, being present, governeth

now in common household bread, as much as in the Holy Eucharist, only that He hath not told us to

them." p. 844. "I have explained that the heaven into which Christ ascended, and in which He dwells, is not a certain place, defined by local spaces, but is the kingdom of God—the heavenly Father, both in heaven *and earth,* wherever God reigns by His Omnipotence and Clemency, nor is it tied to any certain places,"—"diffused everywhere." p. 885. "Since such Majesty could not belong to Christ, if He were not very God and Man, in one individual Person, it follows necessarily, that as soon as the Son of God took, in the womb of Mary, the Man into one Person, immediately He so exalted Him with Himself above all creatures, that *wherever His Godhead is, there also is His Humanity.* For if His Godhead were anywhere, where His Humanity is not, it would be most certain that His Person would be divided; which cannot be." p. 871. "The Father loveth the Son and hath given all things into His Hand, and it follows necessarily, that the Manhood of Christ also, which being taken by the Godhead into unity of Person, is made Almighty, and filleth all things." p. 873. "Wherever is the Substance of the Godhead of Christ, there also is the Substance of His Manhood. Wherefore since it is plain and confessed, that the Divine Substance of Christ filleth all things, all who are possessed of a sound Christian mind, must confess that the Human Substance of Christ also filleth all things." Ib. "Wherever it can be said ' Here is Christ, God, together with His Majesty and Omnipotence,' there it is also said truly, Here of necessity is also Man Christ together with His Body and Soul." p. 874. "The Body of Christ is placed at the Right Hand of God the Father Almighty, so that together with the Son of God, It is above, below, without, within all places." p. 1095. "Although Christ, from the external spectacle of His Ascension into heaven, *is said* to have sat down at the Right Hand of His Almighty Father; yet *the reality* of this *did not then first take place, when Christ ascended visibly into heaven,* and sent the Holy Ghost to His disciples, *but when the Word was made Flesh* and took the Humanity into God. But it was revealed and proved when Christ rose from the dead" &c. p. 1071. "There is a visible Ascent, which took place on Mount Olivet. There is also an invisible Ascent, which took place at the Resurrection." p.

look for it there, and that we have no promise annexed to it there.

"[n] You will say; if the hypostatic union of the two Natures in Christ has such efficacy, that, wherever the Godhead is, there is the Humanity, not indeed—by local diffusion—but in a wonderful and heavenly way, what need is there that I should receive the Body and Blood of Christ in the Supper instituted by Him, when *I have at home bread and wine, in which the Body and Blood of Christ are present,* and I may take them every day, yea every hour ? But hear thou in turn. *Although Christ in His Majesty, together with His Body and Blood, is no wise absent from the household bread and wine,* yet, that thou mayest receive it efficaciously, the word of Christ is to be followed."

Brenz even makes the supposed Presence of our

846. "But what need to speak only of the time of the Resurrection and Ascension, when from the very beginning, at the moment of His Incarnation, He ascended invisibly into heaven, and sat on the Right Hand of the Father? You may marvel perchance what this means; but you will cease to marvel, if you rightly consider the hypostatic union of the two natures in Christ, which took place from the beginning of the Incarnation." p. 847. "To these [such as do not believe in the real communication of the Divine attributes to our Lord's Manhood] the Man Christ will not be very God, but only so entitled; and Christ God will suffer for our sins, not truly but in word only. But in this subject, we understand by 'idiomata' not properties of words only, but of things also; so that when we say of Christ, by the communicatio idiomatum, that 'God suffered and died;' the meaning is not, that God the Word should be said only verbally to suffer and die, yet that the thing itself should not at all belong to God; but that God, although, in His own nature, He neither suffers nor dies, yet so makes the Passion and Death of Christ come to Himself, that, on account of the hypostatic union, He is personally present at that Passion and Death, and is, so to speak, *no otherwise affected* than if He Himself suffered and died." p. 839.

   [n] Opp. p. 849.

Lord's Blessed Body and Blood every where, and
so in all bread, the foundation of the doctrine of the
Holy Eucharist. The words of consecration, according to him, only declare the Body of Christ to
be, where, by virtue of the Omnipresence of Christ's
Human Nature, it was already.

"[o] unless these [our people, who confess a true Presence
of the Body and Blood of Christ in the Supper] believed
that Christ, together with His Body and Blood, was truly
present in the Supper, *before* they recite the words of the
Supper, I do not see how they can escape the magical consecration of the Papists.—We must not think, that the
Body and Blood of Christ, whereas before they were very
far absent, become present in the Supper by the force of
the words; but that, whereas, through the majesty of Christ,
they are truly present with us in the Supper, their presence
is announced to us by the recitation of the Institution of
Christ, and that they are distributed to us for food and
drink, healthful to the worthy, pernicious to the unworthy."

The sayings of other Ubiquitarians, as Marbach,
Schmidlin, Hunius, Andr. Musculus, were equally
monstrous and painful; others as Chemnitz, and J.
Andrea, were more moderate.

Other unallowed forms of speech were also afloat.
The controversy at Bremen was begun by Hardenberg[p], a disciple of Bullinger, but preacher in the
Cathedral Church of the Lutheran Bremen. He[q]
preached against Timann, a pastor of Bremen, who
had, in a book, maintained that "the Body of Christ

[o] Opp. p. 1028.

[p] A native of Hardenberg named Rize (Bretschneider Index
C. R. x. 369), but in those days they liked well-sounding names,
so he took that of his village.   [q] Hosp. ii. 507. sqq.

is every where." The question of ubiquity was dropped, but Hardenberg was asked to accept the statement, "The Body and bread is the essential Body and Blood of Christ." Melanchthon, Bugenhagen, and the other Wittenberg Divines, said that

"They did not know that such a proposition had been used hitherto in the Saxon Churches; but the form, 'the Body is received with the bread' was ever used, and this agrees with that of Paul 'the bread is the communication of the Body.'"

They professed also their adherence to the unaltered Confession.

"We signify to you that in this Church and the whole district subjected to our Magistracy, the Article on the Lord's Supper is unanimously set forth and retained according to the public Confession of the Churches in these regions, *exhibited at Augsburg A. D.* 1530. Nor have we any mind to raise dissensions; but we have determined to abide in the Confession which we have named, and especially we hope that we may ever be one in God, and that the Churches of all Saxony may be and remain temples of God."

They advise adherence to accustomed modes of speech,

"Since it is very necessary, to retain approved and consentient modes of speaking, for the sake of posterity also, we and many others, of highest and lowest orders, have long wished, and still wish, that from all the Churches which have embraced the true doctrine of the Gospel, pious and learned men should meet by public authority, to confer on many necessary things."

The Senate of Bremen upon this, determined that Hardenberg should only be required to adhere to the Confession of Augsburg and the Apology. Hardenberg refused. The Bremen Divines appealed finally to the tenth Article of the Confession of Augsburg, the Apology, the Articles of Smalcald, and the Catechism of Luther. Of the five questions finally put to Hardenberg, three related to these formularies.

"Does he truly think, that these words of the Article of Smalcald, ('the bread and wine in the Supper are the true Body and true Blood of our Lord Jesus Christ, and are given and received, not by the godly only, but by ungodly Christians') are true, and agree with the words of Christ and of Paul?"

"Does he truly think that the Confession of Augsburg, *as it was exhibited A. D.* 1530, is agreeable to the Word of God, and is, in all Chapters, true?

"Does he truly believe and think that these words of the Confession of Augsburg and Catechism of Luther are true; 'under the kinds [speciebus] of bread and wine, the true Body and Blood of Christ are present and are received, are eaten and drunk?'"

This history incidentally shews, in actual life, that the unaltered Confession was still that, to which the Bremen preachers were bound; that the terms of the German Confession "under the form of bread and wine," and of the Catechism "under bread and wine," were accounted the same (for they are quoted together as authorities for the one expression of the German Confession); and that subscription to it was required. It was plainly no hardship that Hardenberg was dismissed, on refusing to subscribe the Lutheran formularies in a Lutheran city.

Melanchthon died in 1560. Peucer and Melanchthon's disciples at Wittenberg hid for a time their

Calvinism under the guise of antagonism to the Ubiquitarian heresy. In 1570, they rejected it openly; in 1571, they drew up the Consensus Dresdensis, and in it united a stronger declaration of belief in the real Presence, and fuller rejection of Ubiquitism. In 1573, the Elector, who accepted the Consensus from them, becoming guardian of the Ducal territories, expelled the Ultra-Lutherans from Jena also. Encouraged by this, the Crypto-Calvinists avowed their belief. They were dispossessed; but Ubiquitism was still condemned in the Articles of Torgau.

Amid the conflict of parties, the "formula Concordiæ" moderated the extremes of Ultra-Lutheranism. It admitted very little of the Ubiquitism of Brenz; but it retained the original Ubiquitism of Luther. Still it was heretical, and committed the Lutheran body to heresy on the Nature of our Lord.

"[r] The foundations, on which in this matter we rest against the Sacramentarians, are these, which also Dr Luther set down in his larger confession on the Lord's Supper.

"The first foundation is an article of our Christian faith, viz. Jesus Christ is true, essential, natural, perfect God and Man in unity of Person, inseparable and undivided.

"The second, that *the Right Hand of God is everywhere*. At this then, Christ, in regard of His Humanity, is truly and indeed placed, and therefore, being present, governs and has in His Hand and under His Feet, all things which are in heaven and earth."

"[s] Now that, as the Apostle attests, He has ascended above all heavens; He both in very deed fills all things and being *present everywhere*, He not only as God, but also *as Man*, rules and governs from sea to sea, and to the ends of the

[r] Libb. Symb. Eccl. Luth. p. 461. ed. Tittm.   [s] Ib. p. 587.

earth." "[t] Wherever thou canst rightly say, 'here is God,' there thou must confess and say; therefore also the Man Christ is present. And if you could shew any place in which God Alone is, and not the Man, forthwith the Person would be divided."

"[u] We believe, that, by the above testimonies of Scripture, the Majesty of the Man Christ is declared, which Christ received, according to His Manhood, at the Right Hand of the Majesty and power of God, so that, according to that Nature also which He had assumed, and with it, He can be present and is present, wheresoever He wills. And especially we believe that He is present as the Mediator, Head, King and High Priest of His Church on earth. For Christ is not halved, nor is one part of Him only present with the Church, but the whole person of Christ. But to this, both Natures, Divine and Human, appertain. Wherefore we have Him present, not only as to His Divine Nature, but as to His Human Nature which He assumed, according to which He is our Brother, and we are flesh of His Flesh, and bone of His Bones. To confirm this, He instituted His Holy Supper, in order to attest, that, according to that nature whereby He hath flesh and blood, He is with us, dwelleth in us, willeth to work effectually in us."

"Resting on this firm foundation, D. Luther of holy memory, set forth the doctrine of the Majesty of Christ according to His Human Nature, faithfully and clearly to the Church."

Almost all which remained Lutheran, accepted the formula of Concord. "It was subscribed " in the first instance, says Walch[v], "by three Electors, twenty-one Princes, twenty-two Counts, four Barons, the Councillors and Magistrates of thirty-five Imperial cities[w], and by 8000 Ministers of God's Word and rectors of schools."

[t] Luth. de cœna Dom. quoted Ib. p. 599.

[u] p. 598.   [v] Libb. Symb. Luth. p. 721.

[w] The names are subscribed at the end of the preface; those of

All these renewed their adherence to the original Confession of Augsburg, both the German and Latin. The Formula Concordiæ, and all the Lutheran symbolical books were signed anew, as at first, in both languages.

With regard to the Article on the Holy Eucharist, not only was the German Confession incorporated anew into the fixed body of Symbolical books, but, in the lengthened argument on the doctrine in the formula itself, even in the Latin copy, the words of the German were incorporated, as those of *the* Confession of Augsburg.

"[x]Contrariwise, [i.e. in opposition to the Sacramentarians] of the Supper of the Lord it is thus taught out of the word of God in the Confession of Augsburg, 'that the true Body and Blood of Christ are truly present, distributed and received, in the sacred Supper of the Lord, under the species of bread and wine, and that those who teach otherwise are disapproved.' In these last words, the error of the Sacramentarians is clearly rejected, who at that very time offered at Augsburg a Confession of their own, which denied the true and substantial presence of the Body and Blood of

the Theologians, at the end of the whole. The title of the German edition is, Concordia. Christliche widerholete, einmütige Bekentnus nachbenanter Churfürsten, Fürsten und Stende Augspurgischer Confession, und derselben zu ende des Buchs underschriebener Theologen Lere und glaubens. Mit angeheffter, in Gottes wort, als der einigen Richtschnur wolgegründter erklerung etlicher Artickel, bey welchen nach D. M. Luthers seligen absterben, disputation, und streit vorgefallen. Aus einhelliger vergleichung und bevehl obgedachter Churf. Fürst. u. Stende, derselben Landen, Kirchen, Schulen und Nachkommen, zum underricht und warnung in Druck vorfertiget. The Latin is Concordia. Pia et unanimi consensu repetita confessio fidei et doctrinæ electorum &c. imperii et theologorum &c. see Bodl. Cat. v. Andreas.   [x] Art. 7. p. 558.

Christ in the Sacrament of the Supper, administered on earth, on the ground that Christ had ascended into heaven."

The Formula Concordiæ then appeals to Luther's lesser Catechism, the Apology, the Concord of Wittenberg, the Articles of Smalcald, Luther's larger Catechism, as declaring one and the same truth of the Real Presence of our Lord's Body and Blood.

The Lutheran system was altogether stereotyped in the Formula Concordiæ. It remained stiff, unchangeable, impressing on the Lutheran mind its form of mingled truth and heresy, until the type wore out, and the whole was broken in pieces. Like the image, whose toes were of mingled iron and clay, it was inherently weak. The heresies which it contained, made the truth joined on with these, powerless. The image was broken for ever. Whatever Germany may become, it can never again be Lutheran.

The form of expression in which the Lutherans combined the belief of the Real Objective Presence with that of the continuance of the outward substances, was brought into England through the negotiations of Henry VIII. with the Confederates of Smalcald. Henry sought only an outward alliance, in order to strengthen himself against the Pope, who threatened him with deposition, and who finally (A. D. 1538) issued the Bull enjoining (in case he should not submit) his subjects to rebel, and foreign princes to make war on him; giving Englishmen (wherever found) who would not join in expelling Henry, to be slaves, their property to be plundered [y].

[y] See the Bull in Burnet. Records i. 3. 9. p. 256. Cherubini Bullarium ii. 704.

The Elector, on the contrary, desired no alliance with Henry, unless they should be united in belief. Henry was anxious also (according to his usual policy) to prevent the German Princes from making terms with any other, and so to keep them dependant upon himself. Accordingly, in 1535, he sent Barnes (whom he put to death in 1540) in great haste to Germany, to break the negotiations between Francis I. and the German Princes. Originally, Barnes was to have been the bearer of instructions from Cranmer also; but Henry expressly directs that he was not to wait for these. The ground of this haste was to stop Melanchthon, whom Henry supposed to be setting out for France, to make terms with Francis, "for the contynuance of the Bishop of Rome's pretended supremacy" and to bring him to England [z];

"laying unto him, how much it should be to his shame and reproach, to vary and go nowe from that true opinion, wherein he hath so long contynued; but allso, on the other side, to persuade him all that he may, to convert his said Jornay hither, *shewing as well the conformitie of his opinion and doctrine here,* and the nobilitie and virtues of the King's Majestie, with the good entertaynement, which undoubtedly he shall have here at his Graces hands."

Barnes was instructed also to persuade the Princes of Germany

"to persist and continue in their former good opinion, concerning the denial of the Bishop of Rome's usurped authoritie, declaring their own honour, reputation and suretie to depend thereupon; and that they now may better mayn-

[z] "Instruction for sending Barnes and others to Germany," from Cotton Library in Burnet, Vol. 3. Records, n. 42.

tain their said just opinion therein, than ever they might, having the King's Majestie (one of the most noble and puissant Princes of the world) of like opinion and judgment with them; who having proceeded therein by great advice, deliberation, consultation, and judgments (of the most part) of the great and famous clerks of Christendom, will in no wise relent, vary, or alter in that behalf."

The further "instruction of the Bishop of Canterbury, his Grace determyned to send after by Mr. Almoner and Hethe." Barnes, however, must have had oral instructions, not only as to the King's second marriage[a], but as to matters of doctrine also. For Melanchthon wrote to Henry VIII.[b];

"Dr Antony with the utmost faith and diligence has discussed with us certain articles; on which I gave him my judgment in writing, whereof I would protest that I do not so love mine own judgment, that if some good and learned men should blame aught, I should not be willing, after the matter had been discussed in common, to prefer their judgments to mine own."

Melanchthon solicited Henry's interference, probably in behalf of the reformed in France[c]. Henry subsequently, July 8, 1535, gave formal credentials to Barnes[d], and through him professed his willingness to join the confederacy, "which" (the Elector writes[e]),

"we have with certain Princes and states of Germany, for the defence of the godly and pure doctrine of the Gospel, if a worthy place be assigned to H. M., and if we first signify certainly to H. M. by embassadors, learned men, *which* Articles we think to defend in the Council, and

---

[a] Mel. Camerar. March 11. C. R. 1263. Seckendorf, iii. 13. § 39. p. 110.   [b] C. R. 1264.   [c] Ib. coll. Ep. 1263.
[d] Ib. 1326. note.   [e] El. Sax. ad Ant. Barnes C. R. 1329.

that we and our confederates will not consent to the Council, without having first communicated with H. M., and with common consent of H. M."

The Elector wrote in answer to Barnes for Henry [f];

"In a few weeks all the confederates will, D. V. meet at Smalcald; we will explain to them the wish of H. M. and deliberate with them on the whole matter; so that H. M. shall understand, that we are wanting neither in zeal nor wish to gratify H. M. and propagate godly and saving doctrine to the glory of God and the well-being of the Church of Christ. For we [g] will never cast away the right and pure doctrine of the Gospel, so needful to the Church, which our most illustrious father and we, together with our allies, confessed at the Diet of Augsburg before the Emperor and the other Princes and states of the Roman Empire."

The Elector, having to go to Vienna to King Ferdinand, arranged for the reception of Henry's embassador, now coming [h];

"And since D. Barnes, among other things, has explained to us that H. M. has commissioned the embassador now coming, to confer calmly on certain Articles with Rev. D. M. Luther, and other Doctors of our school, we, in order to gratify H. M. herein, gladly allow of this conference in our absence, not to waste the time of the embassador. And we will direct the Doctors of our school to meet the embassador, hear his discussion diligently, and confer lovingly with him."

Melanchthon meanwhile was conferring with Barnes [i].

[f] Ib.

[g] The Elector repeats this in his letter to Henry (Ib. 1330), referring for the rest to his instruction to Dr Barnes. Both letters were written by Melanchthon.   [h] 1329. add. 1326.   [i] 1328.

Henry in acknowledging Melanchthon's present of his comment on the Epistle to the Romans, wrote to him[k], " Your friend; " " to our most beloved friend; " and refers him for further information to "letters of our most trusty Privy-Councillor and first secretary, Thomas Crumwell, to which we pray you to give all credence."

At this time the Elector and other German Princes received notice through Verger[l], the Legate, that Paul III. was about to hold the Council at Mantua. Verger promised in the Pope's name, that the Council should be " general, Christian, and free[m]." The Elector agreed with Henry in suspecting the Council, disputing the right of the Pope to convene it, without consulting the kings, suggested to Henry to inform other kings of it. He thanks Henry for his advice to

" [n] establish a solid and sincere harmony in matters of religion, lest dissent in doctrine should give rise to scandal, or occasion to the adversaries to attempt any thing against the doctrine of the Gospel. Yet those comprised in this confederacy know of no dissension of doctrine or opinions among them in matters of faith, and they hope, by the help of God, to abide unanimous and in harmony, in that doctrine which they stedfastly asserted and confessed in the Diet of Augsburg before the Emperor and the whole Empire."

They thank Henry for his wish to agree with them in the cause of religion; mention confidential intercourse of the most reverend Embassador [Fox]

k 1335.   l Verger ad Jo. Frid. C. R. 1351.

m Jo. Frid. ad Leg. Angl. 1356. The term " Christian " must have been the Elector's own, to which the legate assented.   u Ib.

with the Elector and Landgrave, and their Councillors[o].

The preliminary agreement between the English Embassadors and Bruck and Burchard, implies that it was thought that Henry wished to be instructed in matters of religion.

"[p] Having learned that the King of England is from his heart inclined to the Gospel and the word of God, they think good, in order that H. M. may be thoroughly instructed as to religion, that the Elector, Princes and other states of the Christian alliance should send a distinguished embassy, and with it, eminently learned men, to H. M., through whom H. M. may be sufficiently instructed in matters of religion, and whose counsel he might use as to what was to be reformed and ordained in faith and religion in the whole realm."

Dec. 24, the English Embassadors; Edward Fox, Bishop of Hereford, Nicholas Heath, Archdeacon, and Barnes, met the confederates at Smalcald. Fox spoke for the rest[q]. He mentioned the abolition of the authority of the Bishop of Rome in England, and of indulgences. His chief anxiety appears to have been, lest the Protestant Princes should give in to a Council, which should establish the authority of the Roman Pontiff.

The confederacy, on Christmas-day, 1535[r], returned answer in fourteen Articles, of which the two first relate to matters of faith.

[o] T. ii. p. 971, 2. "vetiut" p. 972. 1. 6. must be a misprint for "velint." The letter is written in Burchard's hand and corrected by Melanchthon's.

[p] Ib. 1375. from Burchard's autograph, Dec. 15.   [q] 1382.

[r] C. R. 1383. Translated in Burnet, iii. Records. No 44 (from the State Paper Office),

" That the most serene King should promote the Gospel of Christ, and the sound doctrine of the faith, after such sort as the princes and confederate states confessed it at the Diet of Augsburg, and maintained it in the Apology published, unless perchance it shall seem good, by common consent of the aforesaid most serene King and the princes, that some things thereof should meantime be corrected or changed, out of the word of God."

" That the most serene King should, together with the Princes and confederate states, maintain and defend the aforesaid doctrine of the Gospel, and ceremonies conformable with the Gospel, in a future general Council, if such should be pious, Catholic, free, and truly Christian."

It is remarked that Henry's three Embassadors signed these articles, before the Elector or the Landgrave.

Henry VIII., in his answer, March 12, 1536, acknowledged it as an honour that they offered to him to be " the Protector and defender of your religion," but that first,

" * they must be agreed as to that which is of first moment

---

* C. R. 470. iii. p. 48. Burnet has two sketches of an answer. No. 46 (from the Cotton Library) corresponds with the Latin translation, published by Bretschneider from the Weimar Archives; except that in the copy which they delivered to the Confederates, the Embassadors (as they were allowed) filled out some details as to the proposed subsidies. The other Copy (No. 45, from the State Paper Office) is manifestly the first draft. For the Articles to which the king was ready to accede, are there noted down in the order of the Articles, whereas in No. 46, they are summed up at the beginning; "The 3d, 4th, 5th, 6th, 8th, 9th, 11th, 12th, and 13th Articles do please His Majestie well ynough." The preface is not transcribed in the Weimar copy, but it is probable of course, that No. 46 was sent entire, and that the characteristic preface of No. 45 was never sent. " The said most Noble King

in this treaty, a certain and solid concord in your and our doctrine. And since H. M. earnestly desires that this should be effected, i. e. that the Bishops and learned men, whom H. M. has in his realm, should in all points agree with yours, and since all H. M. counsels look to this, that, in the faith itself and true doctrine, there should be agreement between his divines and those of you all, and since he sees that this cannot be, unless some things in your Confession and Apology be first softened down, through private conferences and some friendly discussions between his and your divines; he would beg your Highnesses to take the trouble to send your Embassadors, and among them some one [t] of excellent learning to H. M., who may confer diligently with H. M. on the Articles of Christian doctrine, and faithfully deliberate, agree, and conclude on ceremonies and other things to be changed, enacted, and ordered in the Church. Which if

answereth, That his Majestie will, and hathe of long tyme mynded to set fourth the Evangelie of Christe, and the trew syncere Doctrine of the same, out of which springeth and floweth our trew Faith, whiche to defende he is most redy both with Life and Goods; but to say, that he being a king reckoned somewhat Lerned (though unworthy), having also so many Excellent well Lerned Men within this Realme, thinketh it mete to accept at any Creature's Hands, the Observing of his and his Realmes Faith thonlye Grounde wherof remayneth in Scripture, surely he doth not; and requiereth his entier Frends herewith not to be greved: But his Highnes is right well contented and much desireth, that for Unyte in Faith and Articles, to be made uppon the same, it wolde please his saide Confedrats and Frends, to sende hither some of their best Lerned Men, to conferre and conclude with him and his Lerned Men, to the Intente to have a parfaite Concorde and Unyon in Faith amongst us. In which his Highnes doubteth not, but at such Tyme as when their Deputs shall come, they shall fynde the most Towardnes in the King, and his Realme."

[t] In the English copy, " the Orators and *some* excellent learned men with them shuld be sent hither to conferre, talke, treate and common upon the same according to the 13th Article," in Burnet, No. 46, p. 146.

your Highnesses do not think it too much to do, H. M. promises that he will so take charge of this business, that all things should succeed, to the glory of God and your wishes."

The Elector of Saxony replied (conditionally on the agreement of the other confederates whom there was no time to consult), that [u]

" If H. M. be willing to propagate in his realm the true doctrine of the Christian religion, conformable to the Confession and Apology which the confederates maintained before H. Imp. M. and the whole Roman Empire, at the Diet of Augsburg, and to receive ceremonies, befitting that same pure doctrine of the Gospel, the Elector would not be wanting to his duty, that, as relates to the confederacy, the king of England should have the highest title and place of defender of the Evangelical alliance, &c. But if the king should be unwilling to admit in his realm, either the pure doctrine of the Gospel, according to the Confession and Apology of the confederates, or the Articles here agreed upon, in a friendly conference between the most Reverend Legates, Dr Martin, Dr Philip and the other Professors of Theology, (which the Elector hopes will not be) or if the king will persevere altogether in the answer and judgment on the Articles of Smalcald, lately, here at Wittenberg, expounded to the Elector by the legates in the name of H. M., the Elector cannot think what good it would be either to H. M. or the confederates, to enter into an alliance, or send legates, as H. M. in his excellent wisdom will readily judge."

The attempts to frame common Articles of belief, meanwhile proceeded. "[v]Luther, Bugenhagen, Jonas, Cruciger, Melanchthon were employed for a quarter of a year in discussion with the Bishop of Hereford, and Heath." Melanchthon was engaged all February and March, 1536. He trusted Heath

<hr>

[u] Ib. 1415. p. 62. about April 22.   [v] Pontan. Elect. 1864.

rather than Fox, and thought Fox indisposed towards them [w]. This probably means no more than
that Fox believed more than Melanchthon. On the
authority of the Church, Heath also had a very different belief from Melanchthon[x]. Seckendorf, on
the authority of Bruck, assigns a prominent place to
Fox[y]. They framed jointly a set of Articles, which
were to be the basis of the further agreement.
Seckendorf's account is[z],

"There [at Wittenberg] they [the Embassadors] ex-
amined all the Articles of the Confession of Augsburg, and
seemed in all respects to agree with the opinion of Luther
and his colleagues. Fox (as Bruck relates, the Elector's
ex-chancellor, who was living at Wittenberg, and whom he
often met at his house) used boldly to assert that the king
would entirely approve of the Wittenberg opinions, and
that he would not himself so freely agree with him, were
he not sure of the king's mind; yet he was very pressing, that

[w] "Nic. Heath, Archdeacon, excels among our guests in urba-
nity and letters; [then in Greek], The rest seem not to have tasted
our philosophy and sweetness; wherefore I avoid them as much
as I can." (Mel. Camer. 1396.) "We have not yet conferred on
the controversies of Evangelic doctrine (Feb. 6). But we shall
come to them. Nicholas the Archdeacon, Embassador, is both a
learned man and equitable towards the purer doctrine. [in Gr.]
But the Bishop has the wont of Arch-priests. He does not seem
well disposed." (ad Vit. 1397.) "We are now (March 9.) disputing
with the English on the doctrine of religion. Nicholas is very
equitable. [in Gr.] The English Bishop does not seem to have
any love for our philosophy." (Vit. 1405.)

[x] Heath wrote to him from England on it, in a letter which M.
answered Apr. 1. 1539. C. R. 1791.

[y] Seckendorf says that Fox, on his return, openly advised the
King to patronize the Protestants and give them a yearly subsidy.
L. iii. lxiii. add. ii. p. 223.   [z] iii. xxxix. add. p. 111.

an embassy should be sent to England, both of Divines, and of others of high rank, of which class Fox desired, above all, George of Anhalt."

Melanchthon had the same impression as to the whole[a];

"The English Embassadors stay on here, longer than any thought. I can in no way leave them, especially since the discussions on doctrine are not finished, for which you know that my help is required earnestly on both sides.— About the divorce we did not agree with them. On the other articles of doctrine there were no slight contentions between us. Still we have agreed on most."

The Embassadors were sent back to king Henry about the end of April, 1536, with the Articles agreed upon, and a friendly letter from the Elector[b], speaking of "their diligence in the matters on which Henry wished them to treat, their distinguished learning, and the zeal with which they were kindled to adorn the Christian religion."

Of the Articles then framed, Seckendorf says;

"There is extant a sort of repetition or explanation of the Confession of Augsburg, elaborated by those of Wittenberg, and accepted and taken home by the English Embassadors. In this, the Article on the Holy Supper is thus conceived;

"[c]We steadfastly believe and teach, that in the Sacra-

[a] Camerar. 1409.

[b] C. R. 1416. from "Melanchthon's autograph, full of corrections."

[c] Constanter credimus et docemus, quod in Sacramento corporis et sanguinis Domini, vere, substantialiter et realiter adsint corpus et sanguis Christi, sub speciebus panis et vini, et quod sub iisdem speciebus vere et corporaliter exhibeantur et distribuantur omnibus illis qui Sacramentum accipiunt.

ment of the Body and Blood of the Lord, the Body and Blood of Christ are truly, substantially, and really present, under the kinds of bread and wine; and that, under those same kinds, they are truly and corporally exhibited and distributed to all those who receive the Sacrament."

No *direct* result (as is well known) came from this conference. Luther and Melanchthon and other Wittenberg Divines had given an answer [d], that the law against marrying the brother's widow was to be retained as a Divine, natural, and moral law; "nor could we in our Churches dispense or allow, especially beforehand, that such marriage should be contracted." But they expressed a doubt about a divorce, and put off any answer about it. Henry was thus disappointed as to a main object of his negotiation; and the death of Q. Catherine (Jan. 20, 1536) set him free from the immediate anxiety about the resentment of Charles V. He had less political interest in the German alliance; and the points of belief unsettled were considerable. The Lutheran embassy was delayed, because the Princes wanted their Divines at home, to consult as to the future Council. At the end of July Ales sent to Æpinus certain Articles for Melanchthon [e];

"From the Articles and my letters to Mr Philip, you will understand what peril we are in. I have not sealed the letters, nor Articles, but have purposely enclosed them open in yours, that you may read them. I pray you, seal the letters, and send them by the next message to Wittenberg to Philip. For it is of moment to the Duke of Saxony and you all, that you should have the Articles.

[d] Seck. l. c. Burnet, i. Rec. 35.
[e] C. R. 1450. July 31.

So I have translated them into Latin.   Beg Philip to answer me as quickly as possible."

It does not seem clear what these Articles were. Melanchthon had them at the end of November.

"[f] We have here the English Articles entire, which I will have transcribed by Cruciger; they are framed most confusedly."

" I am freed[g]," he wrote June 9, " from all anxiety as to the English expedition.   For after those tragic events in England, a great change of counsels followed.   The late Queen [Anne Boleyn], accused rather than convicted of adultery, has been put to death."

The Elector and Landgrave wrote twice[h] to Henry about the Articles " on which the embassadors [of Henry] and the Divines of Wittenberg had agreed." Notice had been given (June 2) of the Council of Trent.   The two Princes consulted Henry (as he had desired) about the answer to be returned.

" Although that deliberation about the Articles of Smalcald is lengthened out, yet, if we knew that your M. was so disposed towards the defence of the pure doctrine of the Christian religion, which we profess, and that you so thought of the Council, as the Bishop of Hereford mentioned, we would adapt our counsels in the intimation of the fixing of the Council, to those Articles composed at Smalcald."

The Princes excuse themselves for not having sent any one to England, both because they had

[f] Vito 1490. Nov. 28. they are in the Acts at Weimar, in Latin, in the handwriting of Burchard and Ales, and also in German. C. R. iii. p. 104, note.

[g] Camerar. 1437.

[h] C. R. 1463. Sept. 1.   They refer in this letter to one sent from Nauburg, June 5.

not received answer from all their confederates, and that " those whom we thought to send, the deliberations about the Synod has detained."

In 1537, Nòv. 14, the same Princes sent another letter [i] to Henry, congratulating themselves, that although there had been no time for consultation, their answer to the invitation of the Council had agreed with that of the King.

Henry sent Christopher Mount to the Elector early in 1538 [k], with the same general professions about pure religion, proposing to unite against the Pope, and to remedy grievances, and asking for the promised embassy. Burchard from Saxony, and Van Boyneburg from Hesse, were sent May 13, with Myconius, " bearing," Melanchthon says [l], " a most weighty commission as to religion."

But Fox, Bishop of Hereford, being now dead, Cranmer's party was on the decline. He complains to Crumwell, that the other Bishops were bent " to break the concord [m]."

" Where that the Oratours of Germany, when thei granted to tarry one Moneth, required that we should go furth in their Booke, and entreate of the abuses, so that the same myght be set furth in wryting as the other Articles arr ; I have syns effectuously moved the Bishops thereto, but they have made me this answer ; That thei knowe, that the King's Grace hath taken upon hymself to answer the said oratours in that Behalf, and thereof a Book is alre-

[i] C. R. 1529. Two sketches of the letter are there given ; one in Melanchthon's hand, which is noted " not sent in this form," another, as Bretschn. conjectures, written by Burchard.

[k] Seck. iii. lxvi. p. 180.　　　　　[l] Jonæ. C. R. 1673.

[m] T. iii. B. iii. Rec. No. 48.

die divised by the Kings Majestie; and therefore they will not meddell with the abuses, leste thei should write therin contraye to that the King shall write. Wherefore thei have required me to entreate now of the Sacraments of Matrimony, Orders, Confirmation, and extreme Unction; wherin they knowe certeynly that the Germanes will not agree with us, excepte it be in Matrymoney onlye. So that I perceyve, that the Bishops seek only an occasion to breke the Concorde; assuring your Lordship, that nothing shall be done, unless the King's Grace speciall Commandmente be unto us therein directed. For they manifestly see, that they cannot defend the abuses, and yet they wold in no wise grant unto them."

On Sept. 7, Myconius, in praying Crumwell to obtain for him a speedy and gracious dismissal, states, "[n] I have now, for many months served the cause of religion together with my Lords, the other Embassadors of the Princes," and

"In the Articles and in the sum of Christian doctrine, we have advanced so as to be now agreed on the chief; and in what remains, 'on abuses,' since we have explained the mind of our Princes, Doctors, Churches, and our own thereon, and the Bishops and Doctors are now in possession of our meaning, they can weigh this, when we are gone."

The joint letter of the three Embassadors, to which Myconius refers, sets forth [o];

"We have, at the requisition of your M., for nearly two months, conferred with some of your M's. most reverend and most learned Bishops, and, by the goodness of God, the

[n] In Strype, T. i. Eccl. Mem. App. No. 95. from the Cotton Library.	[o] In Burnet, T. 1. Records Add. No. 7.

matter has been brought to this point, that we doubt not, that between your Most Serene Royal Majesty, and our Princes, and the confederates of each in the cause of religion, the Bishops, Divines and subjects of each, there will follow sure and lasting concord in the sincere Doctrine of the Gospel."

The sequel of this letter consists of an elaborate argument on the three first subjects, mentioned in the second part of the Confession of Augsburg, under the head of "abuses," viz., on Communion in both kinds; Private Masses; and the Celibacy of the Clergy, with a brief hint about Auricular Confession. To these Henry sent an equally elaborate answer[p], written for him by Bishop Tonstall[q], defending the existing practice on the three points, but omitting all mention of Auricular Confession. For in this, Henry took the side against Tonstall's argument[r], that it was not of Divine institution. With this answer, Henry gave them a courteous dismissal, thanking them for their labour, which he speaks of, as "being now wholly completed." Henry then, considered the negotiation, as being now wholly at an end. A German biographer says, that the conference was held between Myconius, and three English Bishops, with four Divines[s].

It is impossible, without consulting the Articles preserved at Weimar, to fix the relation of the Articles now agreed upon, or in the course of agreement, to those settled by Fox and Heath in Germany in 1535. Those former Articles were undoubtedly

---

[p] Burnet, Ib. No. 8.　　　　[q] Burnet, T. 1. Add., who says that he had "seen a rude draft of a great part of it, written with his hand."　　　　[r] Burnet, Rec. T. 1. Add. No. 10, 11.

[s] Melch. Adam. vit. F. Mycon. p. 179.

made the basis of the present negotiations. For the Embassadors were sent to negotiate an agreement on these; and the article on the Holy Eucharist is exactly the same as that in the copy of the Articles preserved at Weimar. Besides the notice of these discussions for two months, there are extant different drafts of some of the Articles[t], one with corrections in the hand of Henry VIII., another of that on Penitence, in the hand of Cranmer[u]. On the article on the Holy Eucharist, no corrections were suggested.

Personally the king received and dismissed the Embassadors with unusual courtesy. The majority of the English Bishops were not agreed with the Lutherans, nor was the king. This he told the German embassadors plainly. It is said too that he wished not to alienate the French by going further[v]. It would be in accordance with Henry's character, to think that he held out hopes to all, intending to fulfil none. It may have been that he hoped, in the end, to form an Anti-papal alliance, the Landgrave of Hesse being anxious for an alliance on Henry's terms, and the Elector of Saxony alone insisting that the league should be religious, based on oneness of belief[w]. The Elector and Landgrave had taken the opportunity of cultivating Henry's friendship, by sending him information of the secret spread of Anabaptism in England, which they had learned, through a letter found upon an Anabaptist, who had fallen into the hands of the Landgrave[x]. Burchard

---

[t] In Strype, Eccl. Men. App. No. 112, p. 300.

[u] See Jenkyns' Cranmer, iv. 281. [v] Scck. l. c. [w] Id. p. 225.

[x] C. R. 1719. The letter of one "Tasch to Gorge" is given, 1720.

reported, on his return, to Melanchthon, "[y] The king himself spoke much with me, and often said that he desired nothing else than that the Evangelic truth[z]" [should prevail].   Cranmer wrote a letter of encouragement to the Elector.   Henry VIII., in his formal answer, dwelt chiefly upon the points, on which they had come to agreement, and held out hopes for the rest.

"[a] We have arrived at such a shape of counsels and opinions with the said Orators, and, (as your Exc. will know more fully and distinctly from them orally) we have, with God's help, so fitted all things which have hitherto been done and treated on between us, that it rests on most solid foundations and certain reasons, and may, with certain fruit, illustrate the true glory of Christ, and spread most widely.   But when your Exc. shall know more intimately from your Orators, these things which have taken place between us, we doubt not that you will, for your singular prudence and innate desire to promote all good endeavours, exceedingly approve the same; and, in order more happily to complete what has been happily begun, we look, that you will, at a very early time, send to us Dr Philip Melanchthon, on whose excellent learning and sound judgement all good men ground such good hopes; and then we will give all diligence, that your Exc. may see, in those things which in any way regard true piety and belong to the duty of a Christian prince, and which may increase and preserve our mutual good-will, that labor so great on both sides hitherto has not been expended in vain.   The rest your Exc. will learn more largely from the same Orators, who for their good faith and prudence, are most worthy to have the greatest matters committed to them."

[y] C. R. 1744.   [z] The copy breaks off here.   Melanchthon wrote Nov. 1. " Our English Embassaders have returned.   They bring good hopes of amending the Churches." Vito. 1745.

[a] Henry VIII. to the El. of Sax. in Seck. l. c. p. 180.

Early in 1539, [b] Henry sent Mount again to the meeting of the Protestant states at Frankfort, to infuse suspicion of the Emperor's intentions towards them, and to ask them to send a fresh embassy to himself. The Elector and Landgrave declined sending theologians as useless; but sent Burchard, and Binsfort, a privy Councillor, to the Landgrave. These were received courteously, had a conference with the King, Crumwell, the Dukes of Norfolk and Suffolk, the Chancellor and High Admiral and Bishop Tonstall, but were dismissed May 25, as not having sufficient powers.

Brueck indeed thought that it was a mistake, that "[c] against the Elector's instructions, they had entered into the main discussion. For they were not sent to this end, but to prepare the way for the future more solemn embassy, when Philip, Bucer, and others were to have been sent. For such was the answer given to the English Embassadors at Brunswick."

Different embassies were sent about the unhappy marriage with Anne of Cleves, which the Elector dissuaded. Melanchthon wrote to Cranmer [d] to express his grief; to Henry [e], against the six Articles. He "[f] learnt from writings sent to him from England, that the King received his letters ungraciously," and so, although Bucer, whom Brueck designates as "the most political of the theologians [g]," thought that it had been a great mistake not to send Melanchthon sooner [h], Luther, Jonas and Bugenhagen [i]

[b] Seck. iii. lxxiii. p. 22, 6.   [c] Oct. 23. C. R. 1864.
[d] C. R. 1790.   [e] 1792. add 1788.   [f] 1865. p. 800.   [g] 1864.
[h] 1852.   [i] In their joint answer to the Elector C. R. 1865.

agreed with Melanchthon himself, that it was now useless. Brueck said, that, "[j] as to the King himself, it was to thresh an empty ear." Henry thought it of moment enough to " send a messenger to the Elector, to soften to him the six Articles, and request of him that our people," Melanchthon says, " [k] should not write against the six Articles." Melanchthon [l] was employed to write the refusal, and, in so doing to write, against them to Henry himself [m].

In a letter written to Henry by Melanchthon, April 12, 1540, for the Elector and the Landgrave, [n] on occasion of the marriage of Anne of Cleves, they still offered, if Henry would, to send some of their Theologians to hold a conference with English Divines, whom Henry might send to Gueldres, Hamburg, or Bremen. "For," they add, "we greatly desire that a true and pious agreement should be made between the English and German Churches." But Melanchthon's paper [o] which accompanied it, " on the Mass, both kinds, the marriage of priests, monastic vows," being in fact, directed against the six Articles, was conclusive against it. It could not be otherwise. The Elector would accept no other terms than what were equivalent to the Confession of Augsburg. Henry uniformly, and now also, declared that "[p] the Protestants must give way in some points, but that he would always give way to truth." These generalities allured the Lutherans, so that some of them believe that he would give way to conviction [q]. Cranmer and Crumwell in 1539 [r], and

<hr>

[j] 1864.　　　　[k] Mel. Weller. Ib. 1855.　　　　[l] Ib.

[m] Nov. 1. 1539. Ib. 1868.　　　[n] 1950.

[o] Ib. 1951. and Seck. l. c. p. 266.　　　[p] Seck. p. 227.

[q] See 2. q. Bucer. C. R. 1852. iii. p. 779.　　　[r] Seck. l. c.

Cranmer in 1540[s], still encouraged them to persevere. The fall and death of Crumwell, for his part in the King's marriage with Anne of Cleves, and the burning of Barnes, who was a Lutheran, was the close of these negotiations[t]. Barnes wrote that Melanchthon, May 21, 1538, should not come to England, "[u] I would not have him endangered for any hope he has in me. For I too have been deceived. Only ask him to say no word of me. I have a cruel strife with the Bishop of London on justification by faith, and purgatory." On the Holy Eucharist he declared just before his death,

"[v] I ever taught, and still teach, that, by force of the institution and words of Christ, His Body, which His Virgin Mother conceived and bare, is, in a wonderful manner, present in the Sacrament, and by the institution of Christ is given to Communicants."

The formal negotiations came to an end; and the English Church was saved from adopting any Lutheran formulæ. But the statements of faith, which Bishop Fox and Heath brought back, were preserved, and, in a modified form, employed. The Article on the Holy Eucharist, in the collection preserved in England, agrees word for word with that published by Seckendorf from the German Archives[w].

The Articles agreed upon with the German reformers, were 1) "on the Unity of God and the Trinity of Persons," 2) "original sin," 3) "on the two

---

[s] Ib. p. 261.　　　　[t] Ib.　　　　[u] C. R. 1811.

[v] In Luther, Wercke, vii. f. 425. ed. Alt. in Seck. p. 262.

[w] The Articles are given by Jenkyns in Cranmer's Works, T. iv. p. 273. App. compared, as far as they go, with the Confession of Augsburg, and the Articles of Edw. VI.

Natures of Christ," 4) "Justification," 5) "the Church,"
6) "Baptism," 7) "the Eucharist," 8) "Penitence,"
9) "use of the Sacraments," 10) "Ministers of the
Church," 11) "Ecclesiastical rites," 12) "Civil matters," 13) "Resurrection of the body, and the last
Judgment."

Of these Articles, the Lutheran doctrine appears
most distinctly in those on original sin and justification; in the Article on Original Sin, that " concupiscence is *truly sin;*" on Justification, that men are justified when they *believe* that they are justified. "Men
are justified freely for Christ's sake through faith,
when they believe that they are received into grace,
and that their sins are remitted for Christ's sake,
Who by His Death made satisfaction for our sins."
In the Article on the Holy Eucharist, the characteristic word "exhibited" was retained. Melanchthon said generally, that there was much "contention with the English legates," so that their belief
must, in some respects, have been higher than that
of Melanchthon.

In the "[x] Articles devised by the kinges Highnes
Majestie, to stablyshe Christen quietnes and unitie
amonge us, and to avoyde contentious opinons,
which articles be also approved by the consent and
determination of the hole Clergie of this realme,
A. 1536," use was made of the Latin Articles agreed
upon with the Germans, in the articles " on the Sacrament of Baptism, of Penance, of the Altar," and
on Justification. But in the article on Justification,

---

[x] Reprinted from Berthelet's edition, A. 1536, by Bp. Lloyd, in
the " formularies of faith put forth by authority during the reign
of Henry VIII." Oxford 1825.

the Lutheran belief, that " we are justified when we believe ourselves justified," was not expressed ; in that on the Holy Eucharist, Melanchthon's term " exhibited " was retained, not being ambiguous, because joined with the word " distributed[y]".

These Articles of 1536, though set forth by the king and accepted by the greater part of the Convocation, came from the reforming party, and were presented to the Convocation by Crumwell, the King's Vicar General[z].   In this first formulary under Henry VIII., there are Articles on three Sacraments only; perhaps, because Fox and Heath had agreed only upon three Sacraments with the German reformers; perhaps, because such was the mind of Cranmer.   Any how, Articles which treated on three Sacraments only, could not have come from the opposite party, and were probably carried through Convocation (according to their title), through the weight of the king's influences.   The words, then, " under the forms of bread and wine," must plainly be understood in the sense of Cranmer, and those with him, of substances which really remained.   In the Preface Henry states[a]—

" We, being of late, to our great regret, credibly advertised of such diversity in opinions, as have grown and sprung in this our realm, as well concerning certain articles necessary to our salvation, as also touching certain other honest and commendable ceremonies, rites and usages, now of a long time used, &c.—minding to have that unity and agreement established through our said Church—have not only in our own person at many times taken great pains,

[y] See above, p. 59, 60, 108. 136.
[z] See the title, and Wilkins' Concilia, iii. 817.
[a] Formularies, p. xv.   Collier, ii. 122 (iv. 343. ed. 8vo).

study, labours, and travails, but also have caused our Bishops, and other the most discreet and best learned men of our clergy of this our whole realm, to be assembled in our convocation, for the full debatement and quiet determination of the same. Where, after long and mature deliberation, and disputations had of and upon the premises, finally they have concluded and agreed upon the most special points and articles."

The Articles so agreed upon relate to "the rule of faith," "the Sacrament of Baptism," "the Sacrament of Penance," "the Sacrament of the· Altar," and "justification," as being matters of faith; and under the head of "laudable ceremonies used in the Church;" "of images," "honouring of saints," "praying to saints," "rites and ceremonies," "purgatory."

In the following year, 1537, the Articles of 1536 were mostly incorporated in the larger work, "The Institution of a Christian man," commonly called "the Bishops' book[b]". The Bishops enjoined this to be read in Churches[c]. In this, the Article on the Sacrament of the Altar was retained, with a few verbal alterations only. It also had the authority of Convocation[d].

I will set down the Article on "the Holy Sacrament of the Altar," marking in Italics the words taken from the Articles agreed upon with the Germans[e]; and in notes, the slight verbal variations of the Institution of a Christian man and the corrections made by Henry VIII[f], with a view to the third

---

[b] See Bonner's "injunctions" in Wilkins, iii. 864.

[c] See Bishop of Exeter's injunctions, ۱. 1538, in Wilkins, iii. 844; and Bishop Lloyd, Formularies, App. B. p. 380.

[d] Formularies, p. xxv.   [e] Given above, p. 136.

[f] Published by Dr Jenkyns from Cranmer's MS. Works, ii. 40.

of these works, "The necessary Erudition of a Christian man."

The Sacrament of the Altar.

" [g] As touching the sacrament of the Altar, we will [h] that all bishops and preachers shall instruct and teach our [i] people committed by us [k] unto their spiritual charge, that [l] they ought and must *constantly believe, that under the form* [m] and figure *of bread and wine* which we there presently do see and perceive by outward senses, *is verily, and substantially, and really* contained [n] and comprehended *the* very self-same *Body and Blood of* our Saviour Jesus *Christ,* which was born of the Virgin Mary, and suffered upon the Cross for our redemption. *And that under the same form* [m] and figure of bread and wine, the very self-same Body and Blood of Christ is corporally *really* and in the very [o] substance *exhibited, distributed,* and received [p] of all *them which receive the said sacrament.* And that therefore [q] the said sacrament is to be used with all due reverence and honour; and that every man ought first to prove and examine himself, and religiously [r] to try and search his own conscience, before he shall receive the same, according to the saying of St. Paul [s], Quisquis ederit panem hunc aut biberit de poculo Domini indigne, reus erit corporis et sanguinis Domini; probet igitur

Cranmer makes no remark on these suggestions of Henry VIII.

[g] Articles, p. xxv. and p. 2. Institution, p. 100.

[h] *Think it convenient* Inst.   [i] *The* Inst.   [k] *By us* om. Inst.

[l] *In the Sacrament of the Body and Blood of the Lord.* Germ. Art.

[m] *Kinds speciebus* G. A.   [n] *Present* G. A.   [o] *Same* add Inst.

[p] *Unti and* add Inst.   [q] Farther.   [r] Straitly.

[s] The Institution substitutes a translation of St. Paul. "Whosoever eateth this Body of Christ unworthily, or drinketh of this

seipsum homo, et sic de pane illo edat, et de poculo
illo bibat; nam qui edit aut bibit indigne, judicium
sibi ipsi manducat et bibit, non dijudicans corpus
Domini."

A. D. 1539, June 2, Crumwell laid before the lower
House of Convocation, questions on the subjects
which were finally embodied in the six Articles.
The question on Transubstantiation was[t]:

" Whether there be, in the Sacrament of the Altar, transubstantiation of the substance of the bread and wine into
the substance of flesh and blood, or not?"   "[u]Whether,
in the most blessed Sacrament of the Altar, remaineth,
after the consecration, the substance of bread and wine,
or not?"

The answer of the lower House was[v];

" That, in the [w]blessed Sacrament of the Altar, by the
strength and efficacy of Christ's mighty word, it being spoken
by a priest, is present really the natural Body and Blood of
our Saviour Jesus Christ, conceived of the Virgin Mary,
under the form of bread and wine.   And that after consecration there remaineth no other substance but the substance of his foresaid natural Body."

Blood of Christ unworthily, shall be guilty of the very Body and
Blood of Christ; wherefore let every man first prove himself, and
so let him eat of this bread, and drink of this drink [that he may do
it worthily and to his salvation. add Henry VIII.].   For whosoever
eateth it or drinketh it unworthily, he eateth it and drinketh it to
his own damnation : [because he putteth no difference between the
very Body of Christ, and other kinds of meat. om. Henry VIII].

[t] Wilkins, Conc. iii. 845.   [u] " In the next page." Wilkins, Ib.
  [v] Ib.   [w] In the king's draft, Ib. p. 849. it runs,
" In the *most* blessed Sacrament of the Altar, by the strength
and efficacy of Christ's Almighty word, *that* being spoken "—
omitting " by a priest."   But Henry may have omitted the words,
from his wish to depress the Clergy.

This answer of the lower House, the king embodied (with one variation) in his draft of the six Articles.

The question was, in the same year, proposed to the Lords, in a different form.

"[x] Is the Eucharist the true Body of Christ without transubstantiation?"

So that (as has been remarked[y]) they who raised the question would have been content with the affirmation of the doctrine of the Real Presence, leaving the mode of the Presence undefined. Cranmer, Goodrich, Holgate, and Dr Petre (afterwards Secretary of state) were appointed by the Lords to draw up one bill on the six Articles; Lee, Abp. of York, Tonstall, Gardiner, and Dr Tregonnel, another[z]. Lee and his Committee embodied in their bill the answer which had before been given by the lower House of Convocation and had been adopted by Henry VIII. in his draft. They strengthened, however, the Article on Transubstantiation, in that they stated distinctly, that "no substance of bread and wine remaineth;" else, in form, the Article was the same as that of the lower House of Convocation, adding to the affirmation of the doctrine of the real Presence "under the form of bread and wine," another distinct and separate affirmation, that "[a] after the consecration, there remaineth no *substance of bread and wine*, or any other substance, but the substance of *Christ, God and Man.*"

[x] Lords' Journals, i. 109. May 16. "An Eucharistia verum sit corpus Dominicum absque transubstantiatione?"

[y] Burnet and Collier, A. 1539.   [z] Lords' Journals, i. 113.

[a] Statutes at large, T. i. p. 652. I have marked the altered words in Italics. The words "substance of Christ, both God and Man" are substituted for "the substance of His foresaid natural

The king accepted the form, which he had already privately approved of; and it became law, until it was repealed in the first year of Edward VI.

In 1543, the " Necessary Doctrine and Erudition of a Christian man" was put out, in which the article of the Holy Eucharist was entirely re-written, and all traces of the Article, as Cranmer had first framed it, were effaced. In this book, the words "under the form" &c. are no longer used in the positive declaration of the doctrine of the Holy Eucharist, but only, negatively, in denying the necessity of receiving the Holy Eucharist in both kinds. As far as it is used, it is taking in the other sense of "kind, species[b]." In stating the doctrine positively, it is affirmed, that "the creatures used do *not* remain still in their own substance," and that " the form of bread and wine" *appear* only. It even sets therein chiefly the "incomparable dignity" of the Holy Eucharist, that in it alone the natural substances do not remain.

It " [c] among all the Sacraments, is of incomparable dig-

Body." In the Article on private masses, the Act substitutes the words " this *the king's* Church and congregation," for " our Church " used by Convocation and the king; and in the article on Auricular Confession, it affirms that it is " expedient and necessary," the lower House of Convocation having declared it " expedient," the king " necessary." Wilkins, l. c.

[b] " Although our Saviour Christ Jesus—did minister it to His disciples there present, under both the kinds of bread and wine; " " the fashion or manner of receiving it, under one or both kinds; " " He that receiveth this Sacrament worthily under the one kind or under the form of bread only; " " cause them to think that the whole Body and Blood of Christ were not comprehended in that only form of bread, as well as in both the kinds." Formularies, p. 265, 6.

Formularies, p. 262, 3.

nity and virtue, forasmuch as in the other Sacraments the outward kind of thing which is used in them remaineth still in their own nature and substance unchanged. But in this most high Sacrament of the Altar, the creatures which be taken to the use thereof, as bread and wine, do not remain still in their own substance, but, by the virtue of Christ's word in the consecration, be changed and turned to the very substance of the Body and Blood of our Saviour Jesus Christ. So that, although there appear the form of bread and wine after the consecration, as did before, and to the outward senses nothing seemeth to be changed, yet must we, forsaking and renouncing the persuasion of our senses in this behalf, give our assent only to faith, and to the plain word of Christ, which affirmeth that substance there offered, exhibited and received, to be the very, precious, Body and Blood of our Lord, as it is plainly written by the evangelists, and also by S. Paul: where they, entreating of the institution of this Sacrament, show how our Saviour Christ, sitting at His last Supper with His Apostles, took bread, and blessed it, and brake it, and gave it to His Disciples, and said, Take ye and eat, this is My Body. And also when He gave the Cup, He said, This is My Blood of the New Testament, which shall be shed for many for the remission of sins.

" By these words it is plain and evident to all them which with meek, humble, and sincere heart, will believe Christ's words, and be obedient unto the faith, that in the Sacraments, the things that be therein, be the very Body and Blood of Christ in very substance."

This was the last formulary put out under Henry VIII. The anti-reforming Bishops had thus twice shewn their conviction, that the words 'under the form of bread and wine' were inadequate to express the belief in Transubstantiation. In the six Articles, they subjoined to that statement a distinct paragraph, denying that "the substance of bread

and wine remained." In the " Necessary Doctrine "
they changed the whole statement of doctrine.

In the first year of Edward VI., Cranmer and
the Bishops who acted with him, put out the first
volume of Homilies, against the protest of Gardiner,
who wrote against it. At the close of this book,
Cranmer in giving notice of the second book, re-
verted to that form of expression, which had been
put forth in the Confession of Augsburg, accepted
by Bishop Fox and Heath, as Henry's legates, in
the Articles agreed on, thence transferred into the
" Articles " and the " Institution," under Cranmer's
influence. The form which he adopted at the close
of the first book of Homilies, to express the doctrine
of the Holy Eucharist, " of the due receiving of His
Blessed Body and Blood under the form of bread
and wine," was at that time, a recognised Theological
phrase, maintaining, at once, the objective Presence,
and the continuance of the natural substances,
which God employs to convey His unseen Gift.

To sum up this history, as far as it bears upon the
language of the notice in our Homilies;

1) The German Confession of Augsburg which
contains the words, " the true Body and Blood of
Christ are truly present *under the form of bread and
wine*," was of equal, if not of greater, authority than
the Latin; having been the copy read in the Diet,
laid up in the Imperial Archives, and alleged by
Melanchthon himself, in his Apology, as an authentic explanation of the Latin, where the two differed.

2) The German copy of the Confession of Augsburg, equally with the Latin, expressed the deliberate
meaning of the chief Lutheran Divines; was dis-

cussed and formally accepted by the Lutheran Princes and States ; was authenticated by their subscriptions, as their own belief, and the teaching of their preachers ; it was continually subscribed by those teachers ; and was, next to the Creeds, equally with the Latin copy, their fundamental symbolical book.

3) Those alterations, in both the Latin and German Confessions, which are mentioned with praise, are chiefly expansions of the Confessions according to their original meaning.

4) The German Confession was even more popular than the Latin.

5) The German copy of the Confession was, all along, published, both publicly and privately, for Visitations and for religious instruction ; it was formally re-signed at subsequent periods ; was incorporated into the Lutheran "bodies of doctrine," and finally being (with the original Latin) inserted into the Formula Concordiæ, was a rule of teaching and faith to the Lutherans, as long as they acknowledged any.

6) The Article on the Holy Eucharist in that Confession was never varied, never questioned, never explained away; but its language "under the form of bread and wine" was even embodied in the Latin Formula of Concord, as that of *the* Confession of Augsburg.

7) The change in the Latin did not involve any change of belief in the Lutheran body, which continued to acknowledge the unaltered Latin and the German Confession, and understood the altered Latin in the sense of the original Confession.

8) After the Article in the Latin had, in 1540,

been published in an altered form, the German, remaining unaltered in the Article on the Holy Eucharist, became the basis of the negotiation with Roman Catholics at Regensburg.

9) The German words "under the form of bread and wine" meant, and were understood by all Lutherans (i. e. by those who framed the Articles and those for whom it was framed) to mean, a sacramental invisible presence of the Body and Blood of Christ, under the Bread and Wine, whose substances remained.

10) "Under the form of" was altogether equivalent to "under" or "in."

11) Roman Catholic Divines, in shaping the Article of Augsburg so that it should express their belief, added to it the distinct mention of Transubstantiation, shewing thereby their sense that that doctrine did not lie in the Article itself.

12) This statement "under the form of" as used of a form whose substance remained, was not specially Lutheran, but occurred in the older writers. What was peculiar to Lutheranism, was the inadequate end, assigned to the Presence of Christ, the *mere* assurance of faith; and the ground whereby it was supported, the heresy of Ubiquitism.

13) Ubiquitism having been embodied in "the formula of Concord," the Lutheran belief in the Holy Eucharist was thenceforth bound up with heresy; not on the ground of the form in which it was originally proposed, but of false doctrine by which it was supported.

14) The formula "under the form of bread and wine" was introduced into England, apart

from all which injured that belief in the Lutheran system.

15) The language was introduced by Cranmer, when he had ceased to believe in Transubstantiation; and the Article in which it was embodied, was twice accepted by both Houses of Convocation, viz. in the Articles of 1536, and the Institution of a Christian man, 1537.

16) In the six Articles, when Henry VIII. wished to establish Transubstantiation, he added to this statement, words distinctly expressing that the substances ceased to be.

17) In the " Necessary Erudition of a Christian man," A. D. 1543, in which Transubstantiation was laid down at much greater length, this phrase " under the form of bread and wine " was laid aside, except in speaking of " receiving under both kinds," and the like.

18) When, under Edward VI., Cranmer and those who held with him, had the greater influence, they recurred to the old form; and, in the book of Homilies of 1547, Cranmer and other Bishops re-introduced the language, " of the due receiving of the Body and Blood of Christ under the form of bread and wine."

19) This form was not admitted in Mary's reign; but in two sets of Articles, then put out [d], Gardiner required subscribers, not only to assert the Real Presence, but to deny that the substance of bread and wine remained.

[d] Four Articles signed by the Vice-Chancellor of Cambridge, and fifteen subscribed by all, " regents and not regents:" Lamb's Collection of Documents, p. 172, 3.

20) In Elizabeth's reign, the writers of the second book of Homilies recognised the notice in the first book, which embodied the dogmatic statement on the Holy Eucharist; the first book has been twice revised, but this statement of doctrine has remained undisturbed until now.

The fact that the words occur in a distinct statement in a notice at the end of the Homilies, rather adds, I think, to their weight. For a writer expresses himself, for the most part, even more carefully when he is formally stating the subject on which he purposes to treat, than he may perchance do, in the flow of a homily or a sermon.

If any one is disposed to dismiss the words lightly, on the ground that they occur, not in a homily, but in a formal notice of the subject of a future homily, let him make the case his own. Let him put it to himself what he would have thought of the title, if instead of the words "of the due receiving of His Blessed Body and Blood under the form of bread and wine," the statement had been that of a different School. Supposing, for instance, it had run thus, " [e] of the use of the Holy supper of our Lord Jesus Christ as a sign of the love that Christians ought to have among themselves, one to another;" or, again, had it been [f], " of the admonishing and exciting our faith, by means of the visible symbols, in like way as by the preaching of the word, that it should lift itself up, and mount up above all heavens, and thus, being present in heaven, feed on the

[e] The statement rejected in Article xxviii.

[f] I have taken the words of the statement from the Status controversiæ quæ est inter nos et Sacramentarios in the Formula Concordiæ, p. 556.

Body and Blood of Christ, yea on Christ Himself
and all His benefits; the Body and Blood of Christ
being as far removed from the signs, as the earth
from the highest heavens," would this have been
thought no sanction of Zwinglianism? If any one,
entangled in the Zwinglian heresy, had been brought
before a Court, can any one doubt that the statement would have been cited in his behalf? I certainly cannot doubt it. Such a formula would express the meaning of the Zwinglian School, into
which Crammer, afterwards, unhappily fell, but
which God did not allow him to impress upon any
formulary of the Church of England. As the statement stands, it is—not at all an essential, but still
it is—one form of declaring the ancient faith, as it
is in God's word, and as it is attested by Councils
and the ancient Fathers, and as we ourselves believe
it. We do not wish to force upon any one the
adoption of that particular formula; but we claim
it as expressing our own belief.

With regard to that mode of accounting for the
continuance of those words until now, that " [g] they
were repeated by succeeding *printers* in *their* editions
of the book," I would gladly have passed it over,
were it not *said* to have been employed to prevent
English justice [h].—Of course, the bounden duty of
" printers " is to print faithfully, what is set be-

[g] Mr Goode, p. 41.

[h] In the abstract of Dr Bayford's argument for the Prosecution
of Archdeacon Denison, this occurs as the second argument, and
even in an exaggerated form; " that the title of a Homily, given in
the notice at the end of the first Book of Homilies, ' Of the due
receiving of His Blessed Body and Blood under the form of bread

fore them.   Neither printers, nor publishers, have, plainly, any authority to alter what has once been sanctioned.   But the very excuse offered for the continuance of the phrase, is an admission that some one has been responsible for it.   And who?   The Bishops who put forth the second book of Homilies, recognised and sanctioned those titles at the close of the first.   The Homilies themselves have been more than once revised.   Yet these words "of the due receiving of His Body and Blood under the form of bread and wine," have remained.   They have been sanctioned deliberately.   No authority less than a Synod of Bishops or Convocation can remove them.   And while they remain, they give the sanction of those who wrote them, authorised them, retained them, to speak that belief in the sacred Presence of our Blessed Lord Jesus Christ, which those words express.

and wine,' which was admitted by Dr Bayford to support the doctrine excepted to, was part of a printer's note, and had been introduced without authority." (Defence of the Archdeacon of Taunton, p. 278.)   It is hardly conceivable that Dr Bayford should have made *this* statement.   But it is plain that Mr Goode's assertion was in some way employed.

CHAPTER II.

The Doctrine of the Real Presence, as contained in the Catechism, Liturgy, and Articles of the Church of England.

Whenever it has been my duty to instruct any one for their first Communion, I have always, next to Holy Scripture, and in explanation of it, employed the formularies of the Church. I have always found them adequate, and suited to the very simplest minds, whether the unlettered, or the very young. First, in order, comes to them, what they have long since learned, the answer of the Catechism.

Question. What is the inward part, or thing signified?

Answer. The Body and Blood of Christ, which are verily and indeed taken and received by the faithful in the Lord's Supper.

The answer in the Catechism tells them, that "the inward part" of "the Sacrament of the Lord's Supper," is not merely "grace," but the Body and Blood of Him who is the Author of grace, "the Body and Blood of Christ;" and that these "are verily and indeed taken and received by the faithful in the Lord's Supper." The Catechism does not

enter *directly* upon the question of the Objective
Presence.   But whereas, in the answer on the Sacrament of Baptism, it speaks first of " the outward
and visible form," and then of " the inward and spiritual grace," in the Sacrament of the Lord's Supper it
employs a different division.   And this is the more
remarkable, because it interrupts, although it does
not disturb, the careful order which reigns throughout the Catechism.   In this latter part of the Catechism, first stands the question as to the number of
the " Sacraments generally necessary to salvation,"
the meaning of the word, and the parts in each Sacrament.   Then follow, as to each, the questions,
what is the outward part; what the inward; and
what the preparation required for the reception of
each.   This order is preserved accurately in the
Sacrament of Baptism.   It is not interrupted; only
a question is added at the close, to meet an objection as to Infant Baptism.   As to the Sacrament
of the Lord's Supper, there are two deviations from
this, both of which bear upon doctrine.   First, there
is a question as to the object of the Sacrament of the
Lord's Supper as a whole, as distinct both from
the inward part, and from the benefits of which we
are individually partakers through the Communion.
Before any enquiry as to either the outward or inward part, or the benefits of which we are partakers
thereby, is placed the answer as to the meaning of
the whole, " the continual" ever-renewed " remembrance " or memorial " of the Sacrifice of the Death
of Christ," whereby we ever give thanks before God
and plead to God the Death of His Son, as the
sacrifices, under the Old Testament, foreshadowed,

and pleaded that Sacrifice, yet to be offered. "Ye do shew forth the Lord's Death, till He come."

The other deviation from the order is, that, instead of the one question, "What is the inward and spiritual grace," we have two; "What is the inward part, or thing signified?" "What are the benefits whereof we are partakers thereby?" Now, of these two, the last plainly corresponds with the question, as to Baptism, "what is the grace of the Sacrament?" The first question enquires not into the "*grace*," but into "the *thing* signified." It is no longer "What is the inward and spiritual *grace?*" but first "What is the inward *part* or *thing* signified?" And after this, then follows the question as to the *Grace*, "the strengthening and refreshing of our souls by the Body and Blood of Christ." The "inward part" then, or "thing signified" is, in the Lord's Supper, something distinct from the "benefits" or "grace." The framers of the Catechism maintained the correspondence of the two Sacraments, as far as the case admitted. They deviated, just as the Ancient Church and St. Augustine, with whom they were so familiar, deviated. It has been noticed that the division as to the two Sacraments in St. Augustine does not exactly agree. There is an outward part and an inward; but the inward part of Baptism is the grace of Baptism; the inward part of the Lord's Supper, is not merely a grace; it is more; it is the Body and Blood of Christ. In the Holy Eucharist, the *grace* of the Sacrament comes through the right reception of the *res Sacramenti*, or "the inward part or thing signified." To the faithful recipient, the "thing signified," and the "grace" of the Sacrament, come in one. In receiving the outward part we receive the inward, the Body and Blood; in receiving the inward part, we, if faithful, receive "the grace;" only that grace may be indefinitely fuller and larger and deeper, according to the faithfulness or preparation of the communicant. In its largest sense, a Sacrament is a "sign of a sacred thing." There is the visible sign, and there is that which is invisible. It is plainly right and instructive to point out the correspondence between the Sacraments as far as it exists; but where the correspondence of the things ceases, there the correspondence of the language must cease. The Sacrament of the Lord's Supper has something more than the Sacrament of Baptism. Notwithstanding the division which lies in the very nature of a Sacrament, that there is that which is seen and that which is not seen, St. Augustine was obliged, in regard to the Lord's Supper, to make a further sub-division. There is 1) "the Sacrament, the bread and wine;" 2) the *res* or substance of the Sacrament, "the Body and Blood of Christ;" 3) the grace of the Sacrament, "the strengthening and refreshing of our souls by the Body and Blood of Christ." It is idle to object, that "this is not a logical division." The mysteries of God's gifts exceed our logic, as they do our capacities. But the objection means, in fact, nothing more than this, that it is not right to point out the resemblance which exists between two things, or to call them by a common name, unless that resemblance is complete. Why not? The two Sacraments which flowed from our Lord's pierced Side, have these

things in common ; 1) that He instituted them, "ordained by Christ Himself; " 2) that they have that
which is outward and visible, and 3) that which is
inward and invisible; 4) that the outward part is
the means of conveying the inward to the soul, "a
means whereby we receive the same; " 5) that the
reception of the outward part is a pledge on God's
part, that we, if we are fitted, shall receive the inward to our soul's health; "a pledge to assure us
thereof." Plainly there is no reason, why these
points of resemblance between the two Sacraments
should not be taught (as is done in our Catechism)
because there is yet a great point, in which the Sacrament of the Lord's Supper has something more
than the Sacrament of Baptism, the Real Presence
of the Body and Blood of Christ, the Author of grace.
The Catechism, however, does teach us wherein they
agree, and what the Lord's Supper has in itself beyond Baptism ; and it does this in the very words of
S. Augustine. The *res* Sacramenti, according to St.
Augustine, is "the Body and Blood of Christ." Our
Catechism translates his word, and says that "the
inward part or *thing* signified" is "the Body and
Blood of Christ, which are verily and indeed taken
and received by the faithful in the Lord's Supper."

But as the inward part or grace of Baptism is a
thing bestowed upon those who worthily receive the
Sacrament *through* the Sacrament; so is the inward
part of the Sacrament of the Lord's Supper. The
outward and visible part or sign is (our Catechism
teaches us) "a means whereby we receive the inward." As, through the Baptism of water in the
Name of the Trinity we receive the inward part of

Baptism, "the death unto sin and the new birth unto righteousness," so, through the outward elements of the Lord's Supper, "the bread and wine," received as Christ has commanded, we receive the "inward part," "the Body and Blood of Christ." But in order that we may receive them, they must be there, for us to receive them.

This, as it is the first teaching of our childish years, training us to look on, and to long for, what we are to receive thereafter, comes naturally, as the first, immediate instruction, preparatory to the first Communion. We had repeated from our early childhood, that "the Body and Blood of Christ are verily and indeed taken and received by the faithful in the Lord's Supper." And now, at the first Communion, comes the great reality itself. "Verily and indeed;" in deed and in truth; really and truly, are "the Body and Blood of Christ taken and received in the Lord's Supper by the faithful," and so by each one of us, if we are faithful. "If this be not the Real Presence," I heard in my youth from an old clergyman, "I know not how it could be expressed."

The gift, then, in the Sacrament of the Lord's Supper, according to our Catechism, is not *only* grace, nor even any spiritual union with our Lord wrought by God the Holy Ghost; it is no *mere* lifting up our souls to Him at the Right Hand of God; but it is His Body and Blood, in deed and in truth, received by us, if faithful. And, at present, we are concerned with what it is to the faithful, not what it becomes to the unfaithful.

From the Catechism we should, in preparing for a first Communion, naturally turn to the service itself.

Communion Service.

1) In the first exhortation, we meet with the emphatic words, that "in that Holy Sacrament" "Christ is our Food." This is the first exhortation of the Church addressed to us, when giving notice of "the most comfortable Sacrament of the Body and Blood of Christ."

" It is our duty to render most humble and hearty thanks to Almighty God our heavenly Father, for that He hath given His Son our Saviour Jesus Christ, not only to die for us, but also to be our spiritual food and sustenance in that Holy Sacrament."

This is addressed to all those who are not hitherto communicants, as well as to communicants.

Very great stress has been laid upon the fact that in the prayer "We do not presume, &c.," the words "*in* these holy mysteries," have been omitted after the words "so to eat the Flesh of Thy dear Son Jesus Christ and to drink His Blood." It has been said,

" [a] these words might convey the idea, that we ate Christ's Flesh and drank His Blood in eating and drinking the bread and wine, and accordingly in the subsequent revision the words ' in these holy mysteries ' were omitted."

But then, according to the argument of that writer, the words "*in* that holy Sacrament," convey to us that same belief that "God has given His Son our Saviour Jesus Christ to be our spiritual food and sustenance *in* that Holy Sacrament." It is not, again, grace, nor effluences, nor gracious influences,

[a] Mr Goode, p. 619.

derived in whatever way they might be, from our Divine Lord; but it is Himself, who is declared to have been given to us to be "our Food" "*in* that Holy Sacrament." And how "our Food?" In no other way, than we learnt before in our Catechism, because "*in* that Sacrament, we verily and indeed receive the Body and Blood of Christ."

2) And so again, in the Exhortation, just before communicating, the Church tells those who "mind to come to the Holy Communion of the Body and Blood of our Saviour Christ," that, if we "receive that holy Sacrament with a true penitent heart and lively faith," "*then* we spiritually eat the Flesh of Christ and drink His Blood; then we dwell in Christ and Christ in us; we are one with Christ and Christ with us." The words are of the more moment, not only for their own fulness of teaching, but because our Church, in them, sends us to our Lord's own teaching in that great chapter of St. John, whence the words are taken. That sixth chapter is our Church's authority for saying, that *then*, in the Holy Sacrament, we "eat the Flesh of Christ and drink His Blood." And so our Church, with the ancient Fathers, teaches us to take to ourselves all our Lord's other blessed words in that chapter, of His gifts in the Holy Communion. Let who will, dispute or doubt whether our Lord in that discourse is telling us of the fruit of that Sacrament of His Body and Blood, which was then as present in His mind as when He instituted it. Our Church certainly teaches us, not to doubt, but to believe. The words in our Exhortation are almost the repetition of those of our Lord; " He that eateth My Flesh and drinketh My Blood

dwelleth in Me, and I in Him." And these words are, so to speak, that very centre of His whole discourse. Other verses tell us of the fruit of that union with our Lord. "Whoso eateth My Flesh and drinketh My Blood hath eternal life, and I will raise him up at the last day." "He that eateth Me, shall live by Me." "I am the living Bread which came down from heaven. If any man eat of this Bread, he shall live for ever; and the bread that I will give is My Flesh, which I will give for the life of the world."

In these words our Lord tells us, that, through eating His Flesh and drinking His Blood, we shall live for ever; that we shall live by Him, even as He lives by the Eternal Father. In the words selected by our Church, He declares how that eternal life becomes ours; that it is not a mere immortality of being, but a life by Him, in that we, receiving Him within ourselves, "dwell in Him and He in us."

It is a part, then, of this teaching of our Lord, (which our Church has embodied in her Communion Service) that there especially, we "eat the Flesh and drink the Blood of our Lord and Saviour Jesus Christ;" and by so eating, "we dwell in Him and He in us;" and this indwelling is so great and so near and so close, that "we are one with Him and He with us." We bring with us, only "a true penitent heart and lively faith." All besides, we *receive* there. "We spiritually eat His Flesh and drink His Blood;" and not only by the operation of God the Holy Ghost, but through that eating of His Flesh and drinking of His Blood, we have that union and oneness with Himself, and He, our Redeemer, dwelleth in us.

3) This teaching, the prayer, "We do not presume," makes our own, and directs us to ask of our Lord for ourselves, what we had before been taught that He would give. In the exhortation we were taught, that if we come to the Holy Eucharist with certain dispositions, true penitence and faith, Christ would dwell in us, and we should dwell in Him. In this prayer we are taught to ask for cleansing and His indwelling through the participation of His Body and Blood.

"Grant us therefore, gracious Lord, so to eat the Flesh of Thy Dear Son Jesus Christ, and to drink His Blood, that our sinful bodies may be made clean by His Body, and our souls washed through His most precious Blood, and that we may evermore dwell in Him and He in us."

We are not, then, according to this prayer, only in a general way cleansed by the Precious Blood of Christ, through faith in Him. Our cleansing comes to us through our actual contact with that Sacred Body and Blood. It is "Christ within us," His Body and Blood within us, Who cleanses us. We pray God the Father, "Grant us, *so* to eat the Flesh of Thy dear Son Jesus Christ and to drink His Blood, that our sinful bodies may be made clean by His Body," plainly by His Body which we have eaten, "and our souls may be washed by His most Precious Blood," plainly His Blood which we have drunken. This is precisely the teaching of the Ancient Church, so often repeated in the Liturgies and the Fathers. "Let us drink our Ransom," says S. Ambrose [c], "that by drinking, we may be

---

[c] Doctrine of the Real Presence, p. 462.

redeemed." "[d] He receiveth, who proveth himself, but whoso receiveth, shall not die the second death; for the bread is the Remission of sins." Or S. Augustine[e], "I drink my Ransom." Or S. Ephrem[f];

"Because Thou hast given me Thy Body to eat, and Thy living Blood to drink, by Thy Body may I be pardoned, and by Thy Blood have my sins forgiven, and rise to praise Thee among the assemblies of Thy Saints."

"That sea of fire disturbeth me and terrifieth mè, and I am in fear by reason of the iniquity I have done. May Thy Cross, O Son of the Living God, be to me a bridge, and from Thy Body and Thy Blood may Hell go away ashamed, and I by Thy mercies be redeemed!"

Or the Mozarabic Missal;

"[g] O Lord my God, grant me *so* to receive the Body and Blood of Thy Son our Lord Jesus Christ, that through It I may be accounted worthy to obtain forgiveness of all my sins, and to be fulfilled with Thy Holy Spirit, O our God, who livest and reignest for ever and ever. Amen."

4) In the prayer of Consecration we again ask the same, that

"we, receiving these Thy creatures of bread and wine, according to Thy Son our Saviour Jesus Christ's holy institution, in remembrance of His Death and Passion, may be partakers of His most Blessed Body and Blood."

His mere "creatures of bread and wine" they are, when we use those words of prayer; for they are not yet consecrated. His "creatures of bread and wine" the outward elements "remain, in their na-

---

[d] Ib. p. 457.   [e] Ib. p. 501.   [f] Ib. p. 419.

[g] Bibl. Patr. Tom. 27. p. 669. Miss. Mos. p. 7. ed. Lesl.

tural substances." But now we, "receiving them, according to our Saviour Jesus Christ's holy institution," i. e. consecrated with the words with which He consecrated them, and yet invisibly consecrateth them, "become partakers of His most blessed Body and Blood."

5) The words with which the consecrated elements are given, carry on the prayer, "We do not presume." There, we had prayed that we might "so eat the Flesh of Christ and drink His Blood, that our sinful bodies may be made clean by His Body and our souls washed by His most Precious Blood." Here, the Priest, delivering the Bread and the Cup, is to say the ancient words of the Church; "The Body of our Lord Jesus Christ which was given for thee—The Blood of our Lord Jesus Christ which was shed for thee—preserve thy body and soul unto everlasting life." Plainly not, in this place, "The Body of our Lord Jesus Christ" as it is in Heaven, at the Right Hand of God; from which we have no direct influence; which does not, in any way that has been revealed to us, "preserve" us. In that Sacred Body, indeed, our Lord intercedes for us, and continually exhibits, in the Presence of the Father, those glorious Scars, the tokens of His Cross and saving Passion. In it He is present there, our High Priest for ever, "who ever liveth to make intercession for us." "In His Blood we have redemption." Yet no where in Holy Scripture is any benefit spoken of, as derived directly from His Body, except as received by us in the Holy Eucharist. "The bread which we break," says S. Paul, "is it not the communion of the Body of Christ?" i. e. is it not

that, whereby we are partakers of the Body of Christ; which, coming between, unites us with that Body and with Him? Our Saviour too speaks so often in that sixth chapter of S. John, of our eating His Flesh and drinking His Blood. But, apart from His Gift of Himself, His Body and Blood, in the Sacrament of His Body and Blood, no benefit is spoken of in Holy Scripture, as issuing to us directly from the Body of Christ. It is also an actual prayer for the present, and the future. It is not, "mayest thou be saved, for His merit's sake who bore thy sins in His own Body on the Tree." It is, "The Body of our Lord Jesus Christ preserve (now, henceforth and for ever) thy body unto everlasting life." That bread is being given to us, over which our Lord's words have just been uttered, "This is My Body." That Cup is being given to us, over which His word of power has just been pronounced, "This is My Blood." The prayer, "The Body of our Lord Jesus Christ preserve thy body and soul," can mean no other than that Body which had just been spoken of in the prayer of consecration, "the Body of our Lord Jesus Christ" present (as the ancient Church believed, whose words they are) by virtue of His word, "This is My Body." It can mean no other Body than that which we had just prayed to eat aright.

It is, again, a prayer formed from our Lord's words in the sixth chapter of St. John. He said, "Whoso eateth My Flesh and drinketh My Blood, hath eternal life, and I will raise Him up at the last day." "He that eateth this bread shall live for ever." The Church of old formed their words of benediction from our Saviour's promise. As He said, that by "eating His Flesh and drinking His Blood" "we shall live for ever," the Church prayed that the Body which we eat and the Blood which we drink should preserve our bodies and souls for ever. What the Church originally meant, when she framed those words of benediction, that, of course, must be their meaning now. To take them in any other meaning would be to strain them from their own.

As early as the time when S. Augustine sent S. Gregory to preach the Gospel here, the older form [h], "The Body of Christ, Amen," "The Blood

[h] The Eastern Liturgies still for the most part retain the form of asserting the Real Presence. That of S. Mark is ; "When he communicated the Clergy ["any one" Neale, ii. 680] he says 'The Holy Body,' and at the Chalice, he says, 'The Precious Blood of our Lord and God and Saviour.'" (Assem. vii. 41.) S. Chrysostom and S. Basil; "I communicate to thee the Precious, Holy and immaculate Body of our Lord and God and Saviour Jesus Christ, for the remission of sins, for life everlasting." "Thou, deacon, servant of God [by name] receivest the Precious and Holy Body and Blood of our Lord and Saviour Jesus Christ, to the remission of thy sins, and to life everlasting." [S. Chrys. lit. Ven. 1644. pp. 72, 5.] See further S. Basil below note k. The Syriac Liturgies generally, especially S. James; "And when he communicates priests, deacons and people, he says, 'The Body and Blood of our Lord Jesus Christ is given to thee for remission of debts and forgiveness of sins in both worlds, Amen'" (Assem. v. 209. Renaudot. ii. 42); and while the Communion is being administered with a spoon [to the people] "the deacon chants with the rest of the Choir: 'My Brethren, receive the Body of the Son, crieth the Church: drink His Blood with faith, and sing His Glory: This is the Chalice which our Lord mingled upon the wood of the Cross: approach, ye mortals, drink thereof, unto remission of sins, Alleluia, and praise to Him, of Whom His flock drinketh, and attaineth purity.'"

of Christ, Amen," had been enlarged into the benediction.   In St. Gregory's time (A. D. 600) it was

Renaudot gives as "the common order of the Syrians," both
Orthodox and Jacobite; " He [the priest] ascends the foot-pace,
and, taking a portion out of the Chalice with a spoon, saith, ' I
hold Thee, Who holdest the ends of the earth: I have Thee in
my hands, Who rulest the depths: Thee, O God, I place in my
mouth; by Thee may I be freed from the undying fire, and be
made worthy to obtain remission of sins and of offences, even as
the woman that was a sinner, and the robber, O Lord our God
for evermore.'   And when he communicates, he says: 'A propitiatory portion of the Body and Blood of Christ our God, is given
to His weak and sinful servant, for pardon of offences and remission of sins in both worlds, for ever, Amen.'   And when he
drinks out of the Chalice, he says 'A propitiatory portion of the
Body and Blood of Christ our God, is given to the venerable priest,
steward of God's House, who poureth out prayers that are heard
and offereth acceptable sacrifices, and is kept by Christ the Chief
Shepherd.   His prayers be with us, Amen " (ii. 24).

The Nestorian " Liturgy of the blessed Apostles," and that of
Theodore the Interpreter [ii. 596. and 621], have ; " And he signs
the people with the cross.   Meanwhile the responses are said,
' Brethren, receive the Body of the Son, crieth the Church, and
drink His Chalice with faith in the house of the Kingdom.' "   The
Mozarabic (which is thought to be a connecting link between the
Eastern and Western), has the precatory form;

" Then he takes the paten and places it on the Chalice, and
cleanses his thumb with his finger, and saith this prayer,

" ' Hail for ever, heavenly drink, sweet to me beyond and before
all things.

" ' The Body and Blood of our Lord Jesus Christ preserve my
body and soul unto eternal life, Amen."   (Neale's Introduction, ii.
675, and Missale Mozar, p. 7. ed. Leslie 1755).   So also the
Armenian; " Full of reverent fear, he eats of the Body and drinks
of the Chalice, saying, ' Thy Incorruptible Body be to me
life, and Thy Holy Blood be the propitiation, and remission of
sins.' " Liturgia Armenia trasportata in Ital. p. 115, ed. 2. Venez.
1832.

at least enlarged into[i], " The Body of the Lord
Jesus Christ preserve thy soul."   No unprejudiced
person can doubt, that when, in giving the consecrated elements, they said, " The Body of Christ,"
" The Blood of Christ," and the people who received
them said, " Amen," they meant and believed that
what was given was the Body and Blood of Christ.
"[k] So then thou dost not idly say Amen, already

[i] So much was said by St. Gregory to the woman who first
mocked, and then was converted (Joann. Diac. Vit. S. Greg. ii. 41) ;
but the words may have been broken off by her smiling.

[k] Author of de Sacramentis, Doctrine of Real Presence, p. 285 ;
see Tertullian, Ib. p. 331, S. Cyril, p. 390, S. Aug. p. 534.   The
Liturgy of S. Basil draws out this.   " The priest says the Confession, ' The Holy Body and the true precious Blood of Jesus Christ,
Son of God, Amen.'   The people say, Amen.   ' The Body and
Blood of Emmanuel our God, This is in truth.'   *People*, 'Amen.'   ' I
believe, I believe, I believe and confess to my last breath, that this
is the life-giving Flesh of Thine only begotten Son our Lord and
God and Saviour Jesus Christ.' "   Assem. Cod. Lit. vii. 78.   This
is followed in all the Egyptian Liturgies, and the Ethiopic, derived
from them.   (Renaud. i. 271.)   The Ethiopic is somewhat
fuller.   (Ib. 520.)   " The Holy, Precious, Living, and True
Body of our Lord and Saviour Jesus Christ, which is given for
the remission of sins, and eternal life to all who receive It with
faith.   Amen.   The Holy, Precious, Life-giving and True Blood
of our Lord and Saviour Jesus Christ, which is given for remission of sins and eternal life to those who receive It with faith.
Amen.   This is the Body and Blood of Immanuel, in actual
verity, Amen.   I believe, I believe, I believe from henceforth
for ever.   Amen.   This is the Body and Blood of our Lord
and Saviour Jesus Christ, which He took of our Holy Lady, the
holy and pure Virgin Mary, &c.   I believe, I believe, I believe
that His Divinity was not separated from His Humanity; not for
an hour, or the twinkling of an eye.   He delivered Himself for
salvation, remission of sins, and eternal life to those who receive
Him with faith.   Amen.   I believe, I believe, I believe from hence-

thereby confessing in spirit, that thou receivest the Body of Christ. The priest saith to thee, The Body of Christ, and thou sayest Amen, i. e. true. What thy tongue confesseth, let thy affections retain." As little then, when this same form of words was enlarged into the blessing, " The Body of our Lord Jesus Christ preserve thy body and soul unto everlasting life," can it be doubted that it was said of the same Body and Blood, sacramentally given under the bread and wine, as before.

The words, by which the reception of the Body and Blood of Christ, whether by the celebrating priest or by other communicants, was accompanied, varied in different Rituals; the substance remained the same.

They were such as these; "[l] The Body of our Lord Jesus Christ be to me a sinner, the way and the life." " [m] The Body of our Lord Jesus Christ be to me an everlasting remedy to life eternal " "[n] be a remedy to my soul to life everlasting." "[o] The Body and Blood of our Lord Jesus Christ avail to me a sinner to an everlasting remedy to life eternal." "[p] The Blood of our Lord Jesus Christ preserves me to life

forth for evermore. Amen. And when the priest has communicated the Body of Christ, he shall distribute the Communion to the people, saying: 'This is the bread of Life, Who hath come down from heaven, of a truth the Precious Body of Immanuel our God. Amen.' And the recipient shall say, Amen. The Deacon shall give the Chalice, saying, 'This is the Cup of Life which came down from Heaven, which is the Precious Blood of Christ.' And the recipient shall say, Amen, Amen."

[l] Sarum and Bangor in Maskell's Ancient Liturgy of the Church of England, p. 122.   [m] Ebor. Ib.   [n] Hereford, p. 123.

[o] Sarum and Bangor, Ib. p. 124.   [p] Ebor. Ib.

eternal." " ᵠ The Body and Blood of our Lord Jesus Christ guard my body and my soul to life eternal." " The Blood of our Lord Jesus Christ preserve my soul to life eternal." Other manifold forms of communicating, used in the Latin Church, are preserved ʳ; but, however the actual word may vary, in which the benediction is conveyed, there is no Western liturgy, in which the Body and Blood of Christ are not given with words of benediction, " The Body of Christ," " the Blood of Christ," "preserve," " guard," &c.

The celebration of the Mass was daily ; Communions, at the time of the Reformation, are said to have been infrequent. The form then with which the Priest communicated himself, was a part of the daily service and was incorporated in it. The words for communicating the people were not preserved there, but are preserved in the Sarum Manual in the service for the sick ˢ. " The Body of our Lord Jesus Christ guard [custodiat] thy body and soul unto life eternal."

In the service of the Mass itself, the words to be used in communicating the people were handed down by tradition ; as now in the Roman Missal, they are given, not in the " Canon of the Mass," but in the " Order for celebrating the Mass."

But with such words of blessing, the consecrated elements were delivered to every communicant in every Church in our land. What those words meant during nine centuries, what they meant in the reign

ᵠ Heref. p. 125.   ʳ See Martene de Eccl. rit. i. 4. 9. p. 152.   Georgius Lit. Rom. pontif. T. 3. L. iv. c. 19.
 ˢ Manual. Sarisb. Rouen, 1543. London, 1554. f. 79.

of Henry VIII. *that* they must still have meant, when, at the very beginning of Edward VI.'s reign[t], the old words of benediction sounded to us again in our own tongue, "[u] The Body of our Lord Jesus Christ, which was given for thee, preserve thy body unto everlasting life." "The Blood of our Lord Jesus Christ, which was shed for thee, preserve thy soul unto everlasting life." All around was the same. The Mass was still said according to the old form ("[v] until other orders shall be provided,") with some few additional exhortations and prayers. The Bishops and Priests who celebrated, were still the same. Cranmer too still believed in the Real Presence of "our Lord's Body and Blood under the form of bread and wine." All else being unchanged, the same words must mean the same as before. The same they must have meant in Edward VI.'s first book, when they were yet again filled out to the fulness of the present benediction. "The Body of our Lord Jesus Christ preserve thy body and soul unto everlasting life." "The Blood of our Lord Jesus Christ preserve thy body and soul unto everlasting life." The same must those same words mean still.

Nor does the subsequent mention of our duty change the prayer which had preceded it. Each is a whole in itself. The prayer declares God's gift and purpose; the exhortation, "take and eat this," tells us of the gratitude with which we should receive it.

[t] The Order of the Communion in K. Edw. VI.'s time, 1547, in Bp. Sparrow's collection of Articles &c. p. 18-24.   [u] p. 24.

[v] p. 20. Mr Goode overlooks this notice of an intended change, p. 47.

When in the evil days towards the close of the reign of Edward VI. they wished to lower the doctrine of the Church of England, they omitted the Benediction, "The Body of our Lord" &c. and substituted an Exhortation, "Take and eat this in remembrance" &c. They made the change effectually for their purpose. As far as the words went (for they did not remove the Consecration) they substituted a "remembrance" for a Communion. The omission of the words in those times is an evidence of their meaning. Those of that day preferred Alasco and his Zwinglians to the Ancient Church, and substituted Alasco's form for that of the old Liturgies. They held that there was only "a commemoration," and so they removed the ancient words which expressed the belief in a real objective Presence. The holy Eucharist is *also* a remembrance; so the reformers in Queen Elizabeth's reign retained the words which express this. But they restored the words which had been struck out, because they expressed the Presence of our Lord's Body and Blood in the consecrated elements. By so doing they gave back to the Church of England another expression of that doctrine.

6. The second Thanksgiving after the Communion contains two points of teaching; 1) the thanksgiving

"We most heartily thank Thee for that Thou dost vouchsafe to feed us, who have duly received these holy Mysteries, with the spiritual food of the most precious Body and Blood of Thy Son our Saviour Jesus Christ."

2) the fruit of the Communion,

"And dost assure us thereby of Thy favour and goodness

towards us, and that we are very members incorporate in the Mystical Body of Thy Son."

All harmonises; all speaks of the actual gift of the precious Body and Blood of our Saviour. It speaks not of our feeding on Him, by faith, but of our being fed by Him. We are, so far, passive in this, not active. Faith may ascend in mind to the Right Hand of God; it may behold its Saviour; it may plead with Him, speak to Him, adore Him, entreat His favour, His gracious look, it may appeal to His love and compassion for us sinners; it will cling to *Him*, as its Intercessor and Redeemer, Who shall be our Judge. All this is unspeakable mercy and forbearance and compassion of Him, to allow such access to His throne of grace, to us poor sinners. But to contemplate Him, believe in Him, hope in Him, love Him, are acts of ours, although fruits of His grace. They obtain grace from Him who said, 'Ask and ye shall receive.' But to obtain grace is to obtain one gift of God; to be fed with the food of His most precious Body and Blood is quite another gift of God, wholly distinct. To have what we ask for, is a gift of God: to obtain grace, is another gift of God; to receive the Holy Ghost to dwell within us, is yet a third gift ; to be fed with the food of Christ's most precious Body and Blood, is yet a distinct gift. Faith receives it, but faith cannot gain it, except by receiving it in the way which Christ has appointed, in the Holy Eucharist. To "feed on Christ," as it is said, is not "to be fed by Christ;" to be fed by Christ is not, in itself, so much as to be "fed with His most precious Body and Blood."

Our Prayer Book teaches us of no act of ours, except to receive. We pray God, that we, "receiving His creatures of bread and wine according to our Saviour Jesus Christ's holy institution, may be partakers of His most blessed Body and Blood." The bread which has been consecrated by the word of Christ, is given to us with the prayer, "The Body of our Lord Jesus Christ, which was given for thee, preserve thy body and soul." We receive it, and thank God that He "has fed us with the most precious Body and Blood of His Dear Son."

2) By the reception of His Body and Blood we are "very members incorporate in the mystical Body" of Christ.

It is again the very language of the Ancient Church. "[w]By one Body, His Own, blessing through the mystical Communion [the Eucharist] those who believe in Him, He makes incorporate with Himself and with one another." "[x]He commingleth Himself with us, and not by faith only, but in very deed maketh us His Body." "We are called Christ's Body and members, as receiving, through the Eucharist, the Son Himself within us." "He Himself is in us through His Flesh, and we are in Him." We are first incorporated into Christ by Baptism. But, being so made members of Him, we are, through receiving His Holy Body and Blood, brought into closer union with Him. The special doctrine of these places is, that not only through His Spirit, but through the reception of His Body in ourselves, we are made yet more, members of Himself.

[w] S. Cyril, see Real Presence, p. 642. add p. 639. p. 635.
[x] S. Chrysostome, Ib. p. 571.

Again, what is spoken of, throughout, is not any influence or grace from His Divine Person, but His very Body and Blood. "Spiritually" indeed, for it is a spiritual Body, and is given to us in a Divine and spiritual way. But this we are taught, that "the inward part of the Sacrament is His Body and Blood, which the faithful do verily and indeed take and receive;" that "we spiritually eat His Flesh and drink His Blood;" that God has given "Christ to be our Food in those Holy Mysteries;" that if faithful, "we *so* eat His Flesh and drink His Blood," as to be cleansed by them; that they "preserve our bodies and souls unto everlasting life;" that God the Father Himself feeds us with that most precious Body and Blood.

No words of the Ancient Church could state more clearly what is that wherewith we are fed, viz. the Body and Blood of Christ. The words of the Catechism, those with which we receive the Communion, and the declarations that we receive the Body and Blood "*in* those Holy Mysteries," teach moreover, that that Presence is not in our souls only, but that the heavenly part is conveyed to us, through the earthly symbol consecrated by His word of power.

It is through these formularies that we have all come practically to the knowledge of the Articles. The Articles were not framed directly for the laity. Although full of valuable dogmatic statements, we come to them, at all events, whether we be Clerks or laity, through the Catechism and the Liturgy. The Catechism is the instruction of our childish minds. Its clear statements of truth grow and expand with us, as we grow. We all, by requirement of the Church, learn our Catechism, and must know it, before we are confirmed. We all must be confirmed, before we are Communicants. What we learn earliest, sinks the deepest. "Quo semel est imbuta recens, servabit odorem Testa diu." This we drank in, when our minds were freshest. May they retain it to the end, deepening, as the grace which we receive! We learnt and repeated our Catechism, we studied and dwelt on the Communion service, while looking on to solemn seasons. The first Communion should be, above all, a turning point in our lives. It is the means of the highest union with our Saviour, the pledge of His love; it is, if we be faithful and persevere to the end, the earnest of everlasting union with Him. We ought not to conceive that our Church contradicts herself; or that she would teach us, in any indirect way, what should unsay the simple teaching, by which she moulded our thoughts in our earliest years. She *does* not, if we will but draw *her* meaning out of her own Articles, not bring our own preconceived theories into them. As many of us as have been taught, as the Church would teach us, have been brought by the Providence of God to the Articles, through and out of the teaching of the Catechism, and through the teaching and prayers of the Communion service, which incorporates that teaching into our belief through our devotion. Prayer is ever the deepest teacher. Prayer speaks, face to face, with God; prayer pleads to God, asks of God, looks to God with full assurance of faith for what it asks. Legally, some argue that the Articles are the interpreters of the Prayer Book. I know not on what ground. For our recognition of the Prayer Book is full, distinct, and independent. As the condition of our ministering in any office, we are bound solemnly to "[y] declare our unfeigned assent and consent to all and every thing contained and prescribed in and by the Book of Common Prayer and administration of the Sacraments." But whatever be the rule of law, it is the order of nature and of grace, that our prayers are the interpreters of the Articles. Through her Prayer Book does the Church teach the people, and, among them, ourselves. Through it she continually teaches. "[z] The law of our Prayer constitutes the law of our faith." We sign Articles, and we sign them conscientiously. We speak our prayers straight to Almighty God Himself. We must, as we are Christians, believe in our inmost souls, what we speak to Him. We need no comment to explain it. Words were but ill suited for prayers, which needed a commentary. We do not need fine-turned sentences with which to approach Almighty God; but simple, yet it may be, deep words (for the simplest are always the deepest) in which to ask of Him what He is more ready to give than we to ask.

But for myself, I have never doubted that the

[y] "Every person who shall hereafter be put into any ecclesiastical benefice, within this realm of England, &c., shall openly and publicly, before the congregation there assembled, declare his unfeigned assent and consent to the use of all things therein contained and prescribed, according to the form before appointed." "I, A. B., do hereby declare my unfeigned assent and consent, &c."—*Act of Uniformity*.

[z] S. Cœlestin. Auctoritt. de grat. Dei. c. 8. Conc. iii. 475.

Articles, understood in their natural sense, with no foreign meanings introduced into them, contain no other doctrine than the Catechism and the Liturgy.

The Articles.

The Records, which remain of the Convocation of 1562, which re-cast the forty-two Articles of Edward VI., contain no details which might express the minds of the individuals who framed them. The Records of the lower House perished by fire. The upper House debated in private. Yet we know that there were then, as now, two parties in the Church, of the one of which Archbishop Parker himself, Bishop Geste, and Bishop Chesney were representatives, who were termed by their opponents " Lutherans, or semi-papists." The other was the extreme reforming party, who had been exiles at Geneva. Some of these were so discontented with the state of things, of which they formed a part, that they retained their sees, only to exclude those whom they accounted " Lutherans or Semi-papists [a]." Even Grindal, who became Archbishop, and Bishop Horn so speak. They professed to Bullinger, that they retained their Episcopates, to hinder " a papistical, or Lutherano-papistical ministry," i. e. of those of whom Archbishop Parker was the representative.

" [b] If we were to acquiesce in the inconsiderate advice

---

[a] Grindal to Bullinger, in Zurich Letters, i. 169. P. S.

[b] Ib. i. 177, quoted by Hardwicke on Eng. Ref. p. 251. n. 6. " We well knew that either avowed papists, or Lutherans would succeed into their places, and introduce greater follies and corruption of doctrine at the same time." Gualter to Beza. Z. L. ii. 143. quoted Ib. The expression of Turner

of our brethren, and all unite our strength illegally to attack
the habits by law established, to destroy and abolish them
altogether, or else all lay down our offices at once; verily
we should have a papistical, or at least a Lutherano-papistical ministry, or none at all."

Of those two parties, Archbishop Parker, who
wrote with his own hand the most important changes
in the Articles of the Sacrament, belonged to that
which, from its belief as to the Sacraments, was
called Lutheran. Five weeks only before his de-
cease, Parker mentions, in a letter written to Lord
Burleigh, that he himself, Lord Burleigh and others
were "[c]named great papists." In his will, dated
April 5, about a week earlier, he says[d],

"I profess that I do certainly believe and hold whatsoever the Holy Catholic Church believeth and receiveth, in
any articles whatsoever pertaining to Faith, Hope, and
Charity, in the whole sacred Scriptures. And where, in
these, I have offended my Lord God in any ways, either by
imprudence, will, or weakness, I repent from my heart of
my fault and error, and ask forgiveness with a contrite
heart."

Under him, as the President, the Convocation of
1562 was assembled, which brought our Articles
into what is, in all material points, their present
form.

We know the stages, through which the altera-

(Ib. ii. 125. quoted Ib.) "our principal ministers have exposed
the flock of Christ unarmed to wolves, papists, *Lutherans,*
Sadducees and Herodians," shews what question really lay under
the controversy about externals.

[c] Strype's life of Parker, App. iv. n. 99. p. 185.

[d] Ib. B. iv. c. 45. App. iv. 100.

tions from the Articles of 1552 took place, but not,
by whom any of the alterations were made.

An authentic notice is preserved of the instructions to form such articles in the session of 1562 [e];
but not to whom the office was to be committed.

Concerning the form of doctrine. "Certain Articles,
containing the principal grounds of Christian religion, are
to be set forth (in the which also is to be determined the
truth of those things which in this age are called into controversy). Much like to such Articles as were set forth a
little before the death of King Edward. Of which Articles, the most part may be used with addition and correction, as shall be thought convenient."

A note in the Margin said, "These Articles are
to be drawn with speed."

We find the Articles, accordingly, in the hands
of a committee to the lower House. The Records
of that House having been burned in the fire of S.
Paul's, we have only one brief notice of their proceedings in this respect, in the Records of the upper.
The Convocation was opened on the 12th of January.
A week afterwards, on the 19th [f], the Prolocutor

"in a communication to the most reverend father [the
Archbishop] and other bishops, his suffragans," set forth,
"that the Articles published, (as he asserted) in the Synod
of London, in the time of the late King Edward VI., were
delivered to certain other [g] persons of the assembly of the
lower House, who had also been chosen to this end, that
they should diligently look through, examine, and consider

[e] Strype's Annals, i. c. 27. from MS. G. Petyt Arm.

[f] Act. in Convoc. A. 1562. in confic. Art. Rel. in the App. to
Gibson's Synodus Anglic. p. 192.

[g] i. e. other than those to whom the matters of discipline had been
referred, of whom he had just spoken.

them, and, as they should see good, correct and reform them, and exhibit them at the next sitting."

The time having been so short, it is probable that some preparations had been made beforehand. It is, in itself, improbable, that alterations so extensive could have been made in the week which had elapsed since the assembling of Convocation. For of the xlii Articles of 1552, fifteen only came up from the lower House, wholly unaltered, viz. Art. i. iv. xii. xiii. xiv. xv. xviii. xx. xxi. xxii. xxiv. xxvii. xxxii. xxxvii. xxxviii. The alterations in others, are sometimes slight in extent; many are intended only to bring out, what already lay in the Articles of 1552. Such was the addition of *et credenda* in the Article "on the three Creeds," which did, in fact, lie in its words *omnino recipienda sunt.* But this very minuteness of alteration shews that each Article was separately considered. Besides this, four of the Articles of 1552 were omitted, viz. Art. x. "of grace;" xvi. "Blasphemy against the Holy Ghost;" xix. "all men are bound to keep the moral commandments of God" (partly incorporated in Article vii.); xli. Millennarians. Four were added, viz. Art. v. "of the Holy Ghost;" xii. "of good works;" xxix. "The wicked eat not the Body of Christ in the use of the Lord's Supper;" xxx. "of both kinds." These changes, moreover, they had not made simply of themselves, as they considered each Article; but they had employed, in part, another document, selecting from it what they thought good. This would take more time. Then also Bishop Geste says[h], that he himself had written a new part in

---

[h] See his letter below.

Article xxviii. "Corpus tamen Christi datur, accipitur et manducatur in cœna, tantum cœlesti et spirituali ratione." But, according to the numbering of the lines at the end, these words were in the copy, as it came to the upper House. The Committee of the lower House must then have had aid, external to their own body.

In this stage the Articles did not receive any sanction from the lower House. The revision was simply the work of a Committee. On Jan. 19, the Articles were in the hands of the persons, chosen by the lower House, "to be exhibited to the next Sitting," viz. of the upper House, to whom the Prolocutor was reporting, and in those hands they were, the next day. For the Journals of the upper House record that, on Jan. 20 [i], the Archbishops and the Reverend Fathers, treated together for about three hours, on certain Articles, concerning the all-holy religion (of which mention was made in the Acts of yesterday). On Jan. 22, 25, 27, the Bishops held private conferences of three, two, three, hours respectively; and on Jan. 29, "[k] after some discussion, the Bishops whose names are subscribed to them, agreed unanimously, as to certain Articles of Orthodox faith, entitled 'Articles on which, in the Synod of London A. D. 1562, the Bishops agreed for the removal of dissent of opinions, and for the establishing of consent in religion.'"

Amid this ignorance, who were the individuals to whom the office of "adding to or correcting the Articles" of 1552 was entrusted, the way in which

----

[i] Acts, p. 194.   [k] Ib. p. 196.

the office was executed, shews that two different parties had been engaged in it.

On the one hand, the fifth Article, " on the Holy Ghost;" part of the tenth, " on Freewill;" of the eleventh, " on Justification ;" and a characteristic phrase in the twelfth, " on good works ;" part of the sixth, "on Holy Scripture;" and the twentieth, "on the authority of the Church " (whenever this was introduced); together with the statement of the Eternal Generation and Consubstantiality of the Son with the Father in the second, are taken from a Lutheran document, " the Confession of Wittenberg,[1]" although with no admixture of Lutheranism. On the other hand the twenty-eighth Article " on the Lord's Supper " was re-cast; that part of it which condemned the doctrine of "the real and corporal Presence," was re-written, yet the condemnation was retained. The Article was now tacitly pointed against the Lutheran Ubiquitism. A statement about our Lord's Nature, so directed[m], and supported out of S. Augustine, was substituted for the general declaration in the former Article, as to the properties of human bodies. Divines of the Calvinist party, who alone could have condemned the doctrine of the Real Presence, would not have had recourse to a Lutheran formula, by aid of which to amend the Articles of 1552.

The debates in the upper House were (it is noticed in its Journals) kept secret. The omission of the text in S. Peter, of " the preaching to the

---

[1] See Archbishop Lawrence's Bampt. Lect. ii. note 15. p. 233-5.

[m] The words "non in multa, vel omnia simul loca *diffundi* oportet " embody a characteristic phrase of Ubiquitism.

spirits in prison," in proof of our Lord's descent into Hell, was doubtless owing to some disputes in the diocese of Exeter, reported by Alley[n], its Bishop. The doctrine of the descent into Hell (which some denied, " alleging especially the authority of Calvin and Bullinger") was retained, as being an Article of the Creed; but the text was omitted.

The alterations made in the upper House were chiefly omissions[o].   Three Articles at the end which had been directed against the Anabaptists were omitted, probably because that sect was no longer of the same account.   The Articles were. thus reduced to their present number.   But all the alterations were made by Parker's own hand.   Single words, whether added or substituted, are in his handwriting; the erasures are made by " [p] a red lead pen which the Archbishop commonly used for noting, as he read any book."

The part of the re-cast xxviii. Article, which condemned the doctrine of the Real Presence, was not only crossed out, transversely, but was underlined throughout, with Parker's "red-lead pen."   The underlining was, in this copy, no mark of omission. Passages were erased without being underlined, and underlined without being erased.   In Article xxv, the clause " quomodo nec pœnitentia," was underlined, but retained.   For it appears in the English edition of 1563[q], " In which sort, neither

[n] Strype, Annals, i. c. 31. He gives the Bishop's paper from the MS. endorsed by himself.

[o] The Articles, with the marks of the original MS., are printed by Dr Lamb, in his Historical account of the Thirty-nine Articles.

[p] Strype. Ann. i. c. 28.   [q] Both are reprinted by Dr. Lamb. Ib.

is penaunce." The underlining, as well as the erasures, being made as Parker made them, it is probable, that he first underlined the words, as objecting to them, and afterwards, with the concurrence of the Synod, finally erased them.

In order to prevent mistakes, the number of the lines in each page of the draught had been noted at the end of the copy, as submitted to the Bishops. [r] Parker, with his own hand, adapted the number to the alterations made in the upper House. When thus completed, the " two Archbishops" and eighteen "Bishops, of bothe Provinces lawfully gathered in a sacred Provincial Synod [s]," (as they say) " received and approved them." Chesney, Bishop of Gloucester, and Geste, Bishop of Rochester, signed them subsequently [t]. It was in this amended form, that the lower House, as a whole, first received them from the upper, accepted and subscribed them [u].

The condemnation, not of the " Real Presence " only, but of the " corporal Presence " also, was thus formally proposed to the Synod of 1562; and

---

[r] See Artic. in Synod. Lond. A. D. 1562, p. 19, 20. in Dr. Lamb. Burnet, although he had seen this MS., with his usual carelessness, attributes these omissions to " the Queen and her Council " after the Articles had been subscribed in Convocation. (T. ii. B. iii. p. 728, 9). In his corrections of his History (T. iii. L. iii. p. 518) he altered his mind as to the object of the changes, which he thinks to have been out of regard to the Lutheran Churches; but he still supposes the changes to have been made after the Articles had been approved by Convocation; though, he says, it no way appears to him whether it was done by consent of Convocation, or order of the Queen.

[s] Ib. p. 20.

[t] Strype, i. c. 21, from Convoc. Regist. in possession of Atterbury, then Dean of Carlisle.   [u] Strype, Ib.

that condemnation of both was distinctly rejected by it.   I subjoin a translation of the Article, as it was submitted to, and rejected by, the Synod of 1562, marking in Italics the words which, in the original, are retained verbatim from the Article of 1552.

" Christ, ascending into heaven, gave immortality to His own Body; the Nature He did not remove; for (according to Scripture) He retaineth for ever the verity of human nature, which *must needs be in one defined place*, and not be diffused into *many* or all *places at once. Since* then *Christ*, being *taken up into heaven, will abide there to the end of the world*, and will come thence, not from elsewhere (as Augustine speaketh) to judge the quick and dead, *no one of the faithful ought either to believe or profess a real or (as they speak) corporal Presence of His Body and Blood in the* Eucharist."

The whole statement in the Article of 1552 was;

" Forasmoche as the trueth of mannes nature requireth, that the bodie of one and the selfsame manne cannot be at one time in diverse places, but must nedes be in some one certaine place; Therefore the Bodie of Christ cannot bee presente at one time in many and diverse places.   And because (as holie Scripture doeth teach) Christe was taken up into Heaven and there shall continue unto the ende of the worlde, a faithful manne ought not, either to beleve or openlie to confesse the reall and bodilie presence, (as thei terme it) of Christes Fleshe and Bloude in the Sacramente of the Lordes Supper."

Our present Articles on the Sacraments (xxv. xxvii. xxviii.) have this in common; that they begin by rejecting the Zwinglian heresy, whether as to the theory of Sacraments generally, or as to the two great Sacraments specially. Then they make positive statements of belief in the benefits conveyed through the Sacraments. Then the twenty-fifth and the twenty-sixth Articles make statements as to practices or belief, in the Roman Church.

In the *twenty-fifth* Article, "of the Sacraments," the rejection of the Zwinglians, and the positive statement of doctrine, are retained almost verbatim from the Articles agreed upon by Bishop Fox and Heath with the Lutheran Divines. The statement itself is an enlargement and correction of the Article in the Confession of Augsburg, both strengthening its language as to the efficacy of the Sacraments, and correcting it, where it laid down a wrong and inadequate object of them. To shew this more vividly, I will mark in Italics those words of our Article, which the Confession of Augsburg also has.

" *Sacraments, ordained* of Christ, *be not only badges* and tokens of *Christian men's profession, but rather* they be certain sure witnesses and effectual *signs of* grace and *God's* good *will* towards us, by the which He doth work invisibly in us, and doth not only *quicken,* but also strengthen and *confirm our faith* in Him."

Our Article inserts the words, "ordained of Christ," because it mentions others, which "have not," it says, "the like nature of sacraments" with Baptism and the Lord's Supper. But while it strengthens each statement, its important additions are the word "efficacious," and that, "through which He doth work invisibly in us." Both confessedly belong to the ancient doctrine; both were strongly objected to by all the Reformed bodies; according to whom the Sacraments were sealed to attest past grace, symbols to awaken faith; not "efficacious signs *through* which God worketh in us."

The Confession of Augsburg was erroneous, in that it made the quickening of faith *the* object of Sacraments. This was the special error of the Lutheran system. They made a man's own faith, it's increase or confirmation, not union with Christ or increase of that union, the end of Sacraments. The Confession of Augsburg laid down this as *the* object of the Sacraments, that they should be "signs and testimonies of the will of God towards us, *in order to* excite and confirm faith, in those who use them." Our Article states, as the chief object of the Sacraments, that "God by them worketh invisibly in us," and subjoins the mention of the confirmation of our faith, as a subordinate object, in a distinct statement; "*and* doth not only quicken, but also strengthens and confirms our faith in Him."

The *twenty-sixth* Article condemns the Donatist heresy, which had been revived by the Anabaptists, that the efficacy of the Sacraments depended on the character of the minister.

In this Article also, the Articles agreed upon by Bishop Fox and Heath, remarkably corrected that of the Confession of Augsburg. I will again set down the words of our Article, as taken from that of Bishop Fox and Heath, marking in Italics the words which occur in that of Augsburg.

"*Although* in the visible *Church, the evil be ever mingled with the good,* and sometimes the evil have chief authority in the ministration of the word and Sacraments, yet forasmuch as they do not [v] the same, in their own name but in

---

[v] **Ministrent, non suo &c.**

Christ's—*we may use* their ministry, both in hearing the word of God, and in receiving of *the Sacraments.* Neither is the effect of Christ's ordinance taken away by their wickedness, nor the grace of God's gifts diminished from such as by faith and rightly do receive the Sacraments ministered unto them; which *be effectual because of Christ's* institution and promise, *although they be* ministered *by evil men."*

The words, as they stood in the Confession of Augsburg, countenanced the belief, universal among the Zwinglians and Calvinists, that the Word of God and the Sacraments operate in the same way on the soul. The Augsburg Article was, "that the Sacraments *and Word* be effectual because of Christ's ordinance and command." Our Article reverses the Lutheran statement, inserting the mention of the "word" where the Lutheran omits it, and omitting it, where the Lutheran inserts it. Where the Lutheran Article says, "we may use the Sacraments which are ministered by the bad," our's says, "we may use their ministry [i. e. of the bad], both in *hearing the Word* of God, and in receiving of the Sacraments." Both are lawful, and the lawfulness of both is asserted in our Articles, because the lawfulness of both was denied. But "the efficacy of the Sacraments" alone depends upon "the *institution* and promise of Christ." And so, although twice before, in our Articles, mention had been made of the "Word" as well as "the Sacrament," the mention of "the Word" is here omitted, in order to bring out the doctrine, that the *Sacraments* especially owe their efficacy to "the institution of Christ;" whereas, contrariwise, the Zwinglians and Calvinists believed that the Word and Sacraments had their effect in one

and the same way, by kindling faith; the "Word,"
by hearing; the Sacraments, by sight.   The English
Article again carefully corrects the Lutheran.

The beginning of the *twenth-eighth* Article is retained from the twenty-ninth of those of Edward VI.
First, Zwinglian statement is rejected; secondly,
the benefit of the reception is stated in words of
Holy Scripture, the same which Melanchthon chiefly
used in his later years.

"The Supper of the Lord is not only a sign of the love
that Christians ought to have among themselves, one to
another; but rather is a Sacrament of our Redemption by
Christ's death : insomuch that to such as rightly, worthily;
and with faith, receive the same, the Bread which we break
is a partaking of the Body of Christ; and likewise the
Cup of blessing is a partaking of the Blood of Christ."

These words of Holy Scripture in the Article must
of course mean all which they do in Holy Scripture.
S. Chrysostom, in his loving way, dwells forcibly on
the word " Communion," as S. Paul uses it."

" [w] The bread which we break, is it not the Communion
of the Body of Christ?   Wherefore said he not, ' the participation? '   Because he intended to express something
more, and to point out how close was the union : in that we
communicate, not only by participating, but also by being
united.   For as that Body is united to Christ, so also we
are united to Him by this bread."

S. Chrysostom knew the force and meaning of
the word, κοινωνία, in his own tongue, in which he
spoke so eloquently.   "The communion [x]," or *fel-*

[w] Ad loc. see Doctrine of the Real Presence, p. 580.
[x] 2 Cor. xiii. 14. Phil. ii. 1.

lowship " of the Holy Ghost," is the participation of the Holy Ghost, who dwells in the souls of the faithful. "To be called by God to the *fellowship* [y] of His Son Jesus Christ," means, to be brought into communion with Christ Himself, to become members of Him, to partake of Him, that He should dwell in us, and we in Him. So also, when S. John uses the same word, " [z] our *fellowship* is with the Father and with His Son Jesus Christ," he speaks of actual participation of men with God, God giving, man receiving; and especially " [a] God sending forth the Spirit of His Son into our hearts, crying, Abba Father;" by which Spirit we became "partakers of the Divine Nature," in that the Father and the Son dwell in us through the Spirit. So, in its way, " communion" or communicating, is, in the New Testament, used of man's actual imparting of gifts to man. In this sense it it used by S. Paul [b]. "It hath pleased them of Macedonia and Achaia to make a certain contribution [lit. *communion*, participation, communication, i. e. of their goods] to the poor Saints;" "Your liberal *distribution;*" " praying us with much intreaty that we would receive the gift and the *fellowship* of the ministering to the Saints;" "to do good and to *communicate*, forget not." As the word " communion" signifies an actual communication everywhere else, as also here. " [c] It is called and is truly a 'communion,' because through it we communicate with Christ, and partake of His Flesh and

---

[y] 1 Cor. i. 9.   [z] 1 John i. 3.   [a] Gal. iv. 6.

[b] Rom. xv. 26. Cor. ix. 13, viii. 4. Heb. xiii. 16. Although we must use different words in English, the one word κοινωνία stands in all these places.   [c] Damasc. iv. 14. quoted by Suicer, sub v.

Godhead; then too, because we communicate with, and are united with, one another; for since we all are partakers of the one bread, we become the one Body and Blood of Christ, and are members of one another, in that we are incorporate with Christ."

The words of the English Article are indeed so plain, that they can hardly receive either illustration or proof. Our Article explains "communion" by "partaking of;" and says, with the Apostle, that "the bread which we break is a partaking of the Body of Christ; the Cup of blessing is a partaking of the Blood of Christ." The Apostle does not only affirm that the bread "is a partaking of *Christ*," which would of course be also true, but he expresses the way in which we become "partakers of Christ." He says "the bread," i. e. that bread over which Christ saith the words, "This is My Body," "is a communion or partaking of *the Body of* Christ." "The Cup of blessing," i. e. the Cup which Christ blessed, saying, "This is My Blood of the New Testament," "is the communion, partaking of, *the Blood of* Christ." We become partakers of Christ, because we are partakers of His Body and Blood. "According both to the declaration of our Lord," says S. Hilary[d], "and our faith, it is truly Flesh and truly Blood. And these, received and drunk into us, cause that both we are in Christ, and Christ is in us." Hence the participation of the Holy Eucharist is, probably, in Holy Scripture[e] too, called "the Communion," "because," says S. Isidore[f], "it gives us a oneness with Christ and admits us to the com-

---

[d] See Doctrine of the Real Presence, p. 392.

[e] Acts ii. 42.   [f] Real Presence, p. 666.

munity of His Kingdom."   But "the bread" would not be "the communion of the Body of Christ," unless, through it, that Body was conveyed to us.

This statement is made yet more definite by the subsequent part of the Article.

The Article first rejects the Doctrine of Transubstantiation, and, in stating why it rejects it, explains what doctrine, and what doctrine only, it rejects.

" Transubstantiation (or the change of the substance of bread and wine) in the Supper of the Lord cannot be proved by Holy Writ; but is repugnant to the plain words of Scripture, overthroweth the nature of a Sacrament, and hath given occasion to many superstitions."

The " repugnance to the plain words of Scripture " must be, as I said [g], to " those words in which our Lord and S. Paul speak of the natural substance, as remaining."   The " overthrowing of the nature of a Sacrament," must consist therein, " that the outward and visible part is supposed to have no real substance."

The Article then proceeds to state how the Body of Christ is given, taken, and eaten;

"The Body of Christ is given, taken, and eaten, in the Supper only after an heavenly and spiritual manner."

Now, as has been already pointed out, the words " given " and " taken " are correlatives, and mean more than " received."   No one who meant to speak of " reception " only, would have used the words " given and taken."   Nor does any Zwinglian or Cal-

[g] Sermon, The Presence of Christ, p. 14.

vinist Confession so use them. A thoughtful lay-
man has stated clearly the force of the terms.

"[h] The Body of Christ is not said, in a general way, to
be 'received,' but to be 'given, taken, and eaten;' as if
there were a solicitude, in correcting the abuses of the Sacrament, explicitly to maintain the union between the
heavenly and spiritual blessings, and the outward and visible
sign. *This* is 'given' by the minister and 'taken' by the
communicant. To use these precise expressions therefore
respecting the Body of Christ is, by clearest implication,
to combine that 'heavenly and spiritual' blessing, with the
given and taken symbol."

The words "given and taken" occur repeatedly
in the Concord of Wittenberg, [i] and appear there,
from the context itself, to be used of man "giving
•and receiving."

The explanation, that " the Body of Christ is
given *only* in a spiritual and heavenly manner," was
added, probably, in order to remove the imputation
of the opposite party, that something carnal, or
circumscribed, or some earthly conception, was intended. For Archbishop Parker had removed the
statement in the forty-two Articles, which rejected
the Real Presence.

Bucer had been obliged to make the same explanation in accepting the Concord of Wittenberg,
and in part, in the same words.

"[j] The first part was so expressed, that it might be
evident that we do not acknowledge mere signs, the earthly
matter, bread and wine in the Supper, as many have suspected of us. Nor do D. Luther and his people teach,

[h] Essays by A. Knox, Esq. ii. 173.　　　　[i] See above, p. 90-93.
[j] C. R. 1492. iii. 79.

that Christ is naturally united with the elements of bread and wine, or that these things are exhibited after any fashion of this world. It is a heavenly thing; it is exhibited *after an heavenly manner.* Hence there is no place for imaginings as to change or local inclusion, or as to any weakness consequent on the transitory nature, either of ourselves who receive these Mysteries, or of the symbols by which we receive them. The Lord acts with us who live in the body, in a way adapted to our weakness."

We know, from the framer of the Article himself, that he intended by these words, "after a spiritual and heavenly manner," "[k] only to exclude the

[k] In a letter to Lord Burleigh, Dec. 22. 1566, preserved in the State-Paper Office, Domestic Correspondence, T. xli. No. 51. An account of it is given in the "Calendar of State Papers." The letter was printed in the "Guardian." I have had it collated with the original and have myself verified it.

Edmund Gheast, Bishop of Rochester, to Cecil.

" Greeting in ye Lord

" Right Honourable—I am verye sorye yt you are so sick: God make yow whole, as it is my desyer and prayer. I wold have seen yow er this, accordinge to my duetye and good will, but when I sent to knowe whether I might see yow, it was often answeered yt yow were not to be spoken with.

" I suppose yow have hard how ye Bisshop of Glocestre [i. e. Cheney] found him selue greeved with ye placynge of this adverbe *onely* in this article, 'The bodye of Christ is gyven, taken and eaten in ye Supper after an heavenly and spirituall manner onely,' by cause it did take awaye ye presence of Christis bodye in ye Sacrament; and prively noted me to take his part therein, and yeasterdaye in myn absence more playnely touched me for the same. Whereas betwene him and me I told him plainely, that this word *onelye* in ye foresaid article did not exclude ye presence of Christis Body fro the Sacrament, but onely ye grossenes and sensiblenes in ye receavinge thereof. Ffor I saied unto him, though he tooke Christis bodye in his hand, receaved it with his mouthe, and that corporally, naturally, reallye, substantially, and carnally, as ye doctors doo

grossness and sensibleness in the receiving of Christ's Body." He says that he did not mean to exclude, " the taking Christ's Bodye in the hand, nor receiving it with the mouth, and that corporally, naturally, really, substantially, and carnally.—"

Mr Goode has ridiculed the belief[1] that in the Holy Eucharist, the Body and Blood of Christ are present, yet not after the manner of a body, but as I have often repeated, "[m] spiritually, sacramentally, Divinely, mystically, ineffably, through the operation of the Word of Christ, and of God the Holy Ghost."

write, yet did he not, for all that, see it, feale it, smelle it, nor taste it. And therfore I told him I wold speake against him herein, and ye rather by cause ye article was of myn owne pennynge. And yet I wold not, for all that, denye therebye any thing that I had spoken for ye presence. And this was the some of our talke.

"And this that I saied is so true by all sorts of men, that even D. Hardinge writeth the same, as it appeareth most evidently by his wordes reported in ye Bisshoppe of Salisburie's [Jewel's] booke pagina 228, wich be thees: then we may saye, yt in ye sacrament his verye bodye is present, yea, really, that is to saye, in deede, substantially, that is, in substance, and corporally, carnally and naturally, by which wordes is ment that his verye bodye, his verye fleshe, and his verye humaine nature, is there, not after corporall carnall or naturall wise, but invisibly, unspeakeably, supernaturally, spiritually, divinely, and by waye unto him only known.

"This I thought good to write to yowr honour for myn owne purgation. The Almightye God in Christ restore yow to your old health, and longe keepe yow in the same, with encrease of vertue and honour.   Yours whole to his poor powre,

Edm. Roffens."

Endorsed " 22 December, 1566, B. of Rochester to myself."

Superscribed, "To the Right Honourable and his singler good freind Sir Willm. Cecill knight, principall Thresaure to ye Quenes Ma*tie*."   [1] p. 49, 50, 53, &c.

[m] Sermon, The Presence of Christ, p. 46.

The same doctrine is repeatedly stated by Bertram, to whom Ridley and Cranmer frequently referred, and whose disciples they wished to be.

Bertram had two questions put to him by Charles the Bald; 1) whether "the mystery of the Body and Blood of Christ, celebrated daily in the Church, took place, under no figure or veil, but with a naked manifestation of the mystery [n];" in other words, whether what we *see*, is the Body of Christ; 2) whether what we receive, is "that very Body, which was born of Mary, suffered, died, and was buried, which, rising and ascending to heaven, sitteth at the Right Hand of God."

Bertram, in his answer, asserts most distinctly the Real Presence of the Body and Blood of Christ, but *that*, with the very distinction, which I have taught, of a spiritual Body, but not received after the manner of a body.

"[o] Since they confess that it is the Body and Blood of God, and that this could not be, unless a change for the better took place, and that change not corporally but spiritually, it must needs be said figuratively, since under the veil of corporeal bread and corporeal wine, there is a spiritual Body and spiritual Blood. Not that there are two existences of two diverse things body and spirit; but one and the same thing is, in one respect, the kind of bread and wine, in another is the Body and Blood of Christ. For as either [element] is corporeally touched, it is the kind of a corporeal creature; but according to the power that they are spiritually made, they are the mysteries of the Body and Blood of Christ."

Bertram sums up his answer to the first question;

"[p] All which has hitherto been said, shews that the Body

[n] § 2. p. 58. ed. Par. 1686.　　[o] c. 16. p. 49.　　[p] c. 49. p. 124.

and Blood of Christ which are received in the Church by the mouth of the faithful, are figures, according to their visible form, but, according to the invisible substance, i. e. the power of the Divine Word, they are truly the Body and Blood of Christ. Whence, according to the visible creature, they feed the body; according to the virtue of the mightier substance, they feed and sanctify the minds of the faithful."

Yet Bertram, who repeatedly insists on the Real Presence, and that what we receive in the Holy Eucharist is the Body and Blood of Christ, insists also that the Body is a " spiritual Body," and is present " not corporally,"—or after the manner of a body. He is commenting on a passage of S. Ambrose[q].

"[r] He saith in what follows; 'what we eat, what we drink, the Holy Ghost hath, in another place, told thee by the Prophet, saying, Taste and see that the Lord is good; blessed is the man that trusteth in Him.' Is it by being corporally tasted, that the bread, is it by being corporally drunk, that the wine shews that the Lord is good? For whatsoever savoureth and delighteth the palate, is corporal. Is then to 'taste the Lord,' to have any corporal perception? He inviteth therefore to make trial of the savour of a spiritual taste, and in that, whether drink or bread, to think of nothing after a corporal sort, but to be affected wholly after a spiritual sort; seeing that the Lord is a Spirit, and blessed is the man that trusteth in Him.

"He proceeds: 'In that Sacrament Christ is: because it is the Body of Christ: it is not therefore bodily Food, but spiritual.' What plainer? what more manifest? what more Divine? For he says, 'In that Sacrament Christ is.' For he does not say: 'That bread and that wine is Christ.'

[q] De myster. quoted in Doctrine of Real Presence, p. 464.
[r] § 58-63.

Had he so said, he would have preached a Christ corruptible, (which God forbid) and subject to death: for in that food whatever is discerned or tasted corporally, is confessedly subject to corruption.

"He goes on: 'Because it is the Body of Christ.' On this, you are up, and say: 'Lo clearly he confesses that that bread and that drink are the Body of Christ.' But mark how he subjoins: 'therefore it is not bodily Food, but spiritual.' Do not therefore apply the carnal sense; for by this nothing is here discerned. It *is* indeed the Body of Christ; yet not corporal, but spiritual: It *is* the Blood of Christ; yet not corporal but spiritual. Nothing therefore is here to be thought of corporally, but spiritually. *It is the Body of Christ, but not corporally : and it is the Blood of Christ, but not corporally.*

"He proceeds: 'whence too the Apostle saith of its type, our fathers did eat spiritual meat, and did drink spiritual drink. For the Body of God is a spiritual Body: the Body of Christ is the Body of the Divine spirit: since Christ is Spirit, as we read; The Spirit before our face is Christ the Lord[s].'

"Most clearly has he taught, how we ought to understand the Mystery of the Body and Blood of Christ. For when he had said that our fathers did eat spiritual food, and drink spiritual drink; while yet no one doubts that that Manna which they eat, and that water which they drank, were corporal: he adds, as to the Mystery which is now wrought in the Church, defining in what respect it is the Body of Christ, 'for the Body of God is a spiritual Body.' Christ is, in truth, God, and the Body which He took of the Virgin Mary, which suffered was buried, rose again, was indeed a true Body, that is, remained visible and palpable. But the Body, which is called the Mystery of God, is not corporal, but spiritual; and if spiritual, neither visible nor palpable. Hence blessed Ambrose continues; 'The Body of Christ is the Body of the Divine Spirit.' But the Divine

[s] Lam. 4. 20.

Spirit is nought that is corporal, nought corruptible, nought palpable. But this Body, which is celebrated in the Church, is, according to its visible kind, both corruptible and palpable.

"How then is it said to be 'the Body of the Divine Spirit?' In respect truly of that which is spiritual, i. e. of that which has its existence invisible and impalpable, and so incorruptible."

Paschasius Radbertus (with whom Bertram has been so often popularly contrasted, and against whom he has ever been supposed to have written) uses the same language[t];

"I have, as I hear, aroused many to the right understanding of this mystery, because it was said, that the flesh profiteth nothing; so that they learnt and understood to think worthily of Christ, Whose Body is not corrupted, because It is spiritual, and the whole which is celebrated in this Sacrament is spiritual, because 'it is the Spirit which quickeneth,' and worketh, in it, life to those who believe and receive worthily; but to those who believe not, and eat it unworthily, truly [worketh] the judgment of condemnation."

S. Bernard[u] not only employs the word "spiritually," but denies the word "carnally."

"Jesus Christ the same yesterday, to-day, and for ever. 'Yesterday,' from the beginning of the world to the Lord's Ascension; 'to-day,' thence to the end of the world; 'for ever,' after the common resurrection of all. To none of these is Christ wanting; to none, is Jesus wanting; to none is anointing; to none, salvation. To Patriarchs and Prophets He was exhibited in vision; to the Apostles in His Humanity; to Martin in faith; to Angels now in Person. Which

---

[t] Ep. ad Frudegard. Bibl. P. xiv. 755.

[u] Serm. de fest. S. Martini § 10. 11. Opp. i. 1058.

Person He has promised that He will shew to all the elect not 'to-day,' but 'for ever.' 'Yesterday' had passed away, and our 'to-day' had dawned, when the Apostle spake, 'Although we have known Christ after the Flesh, we now know Him no more.' Yet in the dawn, something of the Flesh of the Lamb seemeth to be retained; but 'the residue' is already given to the fire; because even unto 'to-day, is the Flesh exhibited to us; but *spiritually, not carnally.* Nor ought we to complain, that either that manifestation, made to the Fathers of the Old Testament, is denied to us, or that Presence of His Flesh which was exhibited to the Apostles. For the true Substance of His Flesh is present with us now also; beyond question, it is in the Sacrament."

When the Calvinists used the word "spiritually," they meant at most "wrought by the Holy Spirit;" their theory being, that life is derived to us from the Flesh of Christ in heaven through the agency of God the Holy Ghost. This is Calvin's own statement.

" ᵛ It is said that the Body of Christ is given to us spiritually in the Holy Supper, because the hidden virtue of the Holy Ghost effects the union of things which are severed by space : and so, that life from the Flesh of Christ should penetrate from heaven to us, which power and property of quickening may, without inconvenience, be said to be something abstracted from the Substance, if only this be soundly and rightly understood, that the Body of Christ remains in heaven, and yet that, to us who sojourn upon the earth, life emanates and reaches from His Substance."

The Calvinist belief was, that Christ was no otherwise present in the Holy Eucharist, than He was to the Patriarchs or holy men, before He came in the Flesh ; that He was no otherwise present in the

---

ᵛ Diluc. expl. doctr. de vera partic. carnis et sang. Xti. cont. Hesshus. fin. Opp. viii. 744. et ap. Hosp. ii. 479.

Sacrament, than out of the Sacrament; that Sacramental and non-Sacramental Communion were one and the same act; and that Sacraments had no other office than to kindle faith. They knew, in some sort, of what is truly a " spiritual Communion " that Christ, by His Spirit, dwells in the souls which long for Him, and call Him into themselves by their longing and prayer. But " spiritual Communion " is quite different from Sacramental Communion : it may be made at every moment, with every breath, if we had devotion enough to be ever longing for Him.

It was in this sense, and in this sense only, that the Lutherans rejected the word " spiritually " as inadequate. The author of the Formula Concordiæ states the case fairly [w].

" In order to the solid explanation of this controversy, it must first be said that there are two kinds of Sacramentarians. Some are gross Sacramentarians. These profess openly in clear, plain words, what they in their hearts believe : namely that in the Lord's Supper nought else, save bread and wine, is present, or distributed, or received orally. But other Sacramentarians are ingenious and subtle, and indeed the most pernicious. These, speaking on the subject of the Lord's Supper, in part use our words, and make a shew as though they too believed the true Presence of the true, substantial and living Body and Blood of Christ in the holy Supper, yet this Presence and eating, they say is spiritual, and takes place through faith. And these last-mentioned Sacramentarians conceal and retain under these specious words, the same gross opinion as the former, i. e. that beyond bread and wine nothing is present, or orally received in the Lord's Supper. For the word ' spiritually ' to them signifies nothing else, but the Spirit of Christ, or the virtue of the absent Body of Christ, and Its merits,

[w] c. 7. de cœna Dom. p. 460. ed. Tittm.

which, they, say is present; but the Body Itself of Christ they think is in no wise present, but is only contained in the highest heaven above; and they affirm that we ought, by thoughts of faith, to rise above, and ascend into heaven, and that there, (but in no way with the Bread and Wine of the Holy Supper) that Body and Blood of Christ are to be sought."

The Council of Trent itself does not reject the word "spiritually" simply, but only when opposed to "sacramentally and really."

"x If any man say, that Christ, exhibited in the Eucharist, is eaten spiritually only, and not sacramentally and really also, let him be anathema."

Indeed, it has no other terms for worthy Communicants, than that they receive our Lord's Body both "sacramentally and spiritually," whilst the unworthy receive It only sacramentally.

But the Church of England teaches, that we receive Christ, not spiritually only, but "really," since she teaches that "the faithful do in the Lord's Supper verily and indeed take and receive the Body and Blood of Christ."   She teaches that we receive Him also "sacramentally," since she teaches, that "the Father has given His Son our Saviour Jesus Christ not only to die for us, but also to be our spiritual Food and sustenance *in* that holy Sacrament."

Bucer appeals to the Bishop of Avranches, that he himself allowed that the Body of Christ was present in a spiritual manner.

"y Thou thyself confessest, O Bishop, that the Body of Christ is not present in the Sacrament in a bodily manner,

x Sess. xiii. de Euch. c. 8.

y Def. doctr. Xt. c. Robert. Ep. Abrinc. 1534. fol. H. 6 verso.

but hath a spiritual mode of being; such as either that according to which the soul is in the body, or that by which an angel is in space."

Beza, on the other hand, would have "spiritual" to mean only supernatural, in a way incognizable to our senses, and apprehended by faith only. This he does in the Gallican Confession, in which he states the reformed belief, in a way which is said by a reformed writer[z], to have satisfied neither the French Catholics, nor the Lutherans, nor the reformed.

"[a] We affirm that the holy Supper of the Lord, to wit, the other Sacrament, is a testimony to us [not, "a means"] of our union with our Lord Jesus Christ, seeing that He not only once for all died and rose from the dead for us, but also truly feeds us and nourishes us with His Own Flesh and Blood, that we being made one with Him, may have a common life with Him. For although He is now in heaven, there to remain, until He come to judge the world; yet we believe, that by the hidden and incomprehensible virtue of His Spirit He nourishes us with the substance of His Body and Blood, apprehended by faith. But we say that this is done *spiritually,* not that we substitute imagination or meditation for efficacy and truth: but rather, because this Mystery of our union with Christ is so sublime, as to overpass all our senses, yea, and the whole order of nature; further, because, since it is divine and heavenly, it cannot be laid hold of, save by faith."

In our own Liturgy and Article, the word "spiritual" is not contrasted with any particular word. It occurs four times in all. 1) In the Exhortation, we are told that "it is our duty to render most humble and hearty thanks to God the Father—that

[z] Augusti Diss. de libb. symbol. ref. p. 630.
[a] Conf. Gall. c. 36.

He hath given His Son our Saviour Jesus Christ—
to be our spiritual Food and sustenance in that Holy
Sacrament." Plainly, the word "spiritual" here
means food for our spirits, food whereby our souls
are nourished; as our Catechism says, that they are
" strengthened and refreshed by the Body and Blood
of Christ."

2) In the same sense, plainly, we thank God for
having "vouchsafed to feed us with the spiritual Food
of the most precious Body and Blood of" His " Son
Jesus Christ our Lord." For His Body and Blood
are the Food, not of our bodies, but of our spirits.

S. Athanasius has left proof of his belief in the
Real objective Presence. He says,

" [b] so long as the supplications and prayers have not yet
taken place, bare is the Bread and the Cup; but when the
great and wonderful prayers have been completed over it,
then the bread becometh the Body, the Cup the Blood of
our Lord Jesus Christ."

Yet he repeatedly speaks of it as "spiritual Food."

" [c] Our Saviour also, since He was changing the typical
for the spiritual, promised them, that they should no longer
eat the flesh of a lamb, but His own, saying, 'Take, eat and
drink, this is My Body and Blood.'"

" [d] Partaking of the Flesh of the Lord, as Himself said;
'The Bread which I will give for the life of the world.'
For the Lord's Flesh is life-giving Spirit."

S. Ambrose speaks (as is well known) very
strongly on the Real objective Presence; yet he uses
the same word " spiritual." He infers that it is
spiritual Food, *because* it is Christ's Body.

[b] **Real Presence, pp. 237, 8.**   [c] Ib. p. 374   [d] Ib. 376.

"ᵉ In that Sacrament Christ is : because it is the Body of Christ.   It is not *therefore* bodily food, but spiritual."

3) In the Exhortation, "at the time of the celebration of the Communion," occur the words that, " if with a true penitent heart and lively faith we receive that holy Sacrament," " then we spiritually eat the Flesh of Christ, and drink His Blood."   This is the very expression, with which the compilers of the Prayer Book were so familiar, as S. Augustine's. "ᶠ Who dwelleth not in Christ, and in whom Christ dwelleth not, without doubt doth neither spiritually eat His Flesh, nor drink His Blood."   The word occurred in S. Augustine, as they read him, in the very same connexion in which they used it, of those who so ate the Body of Christ and drank His Blood, that they dwelt in Christ and Christ in them.

Again S. Augustine says,

"ᵍ Then shall the Body and Blood of Christ be each man's life, if what is taken in the Sacrament visibly is, in the truth itself, eaten spiritually, drunken spiritually." " Look to it, then ; eat ye spiritually the heavenly Bread, bring innocence to the Altar."

Take S. Athanasius again ʰ;

" He [Christ] saith, ' The words which I have spoken unto you, are spirit and life,' as though He said, That which is visible and is given for the salvation of the world, is the Flesh which I bear, and Its Blood shall be given by Me spiritually as Food, so that it may be distributed spiritually in each, and may become to all a protection, to the resurrection of life eternal."

What the word " spiritually " meant as used by

ᶜ Ib. p. 464.   ᶠ Ib. p. 512.   ᵍ Ib. p. 527, 510.   ʰ Ib. p. 377.

S. Augustine, S. Athanasius, 'or S. Macarius, who says, "[i] They who partake of the visible bread, spiritually eat the Flesh of the Lord;" *that* must that self-same word mean in our Articles. . As the words "spiritual," "spiritually," do not, in S. Ambrose, S. Athanasius, S. Augustine, S. Macarius, exclude the Real objective Presence, which those Fathers taught, so neither can it, by the mere force of the word, in our own Exhortation. But there is nothing besides, to limit it.

4) Lastly, the words in our Articles, "after an *heavenly and* spiritual manner," in themselves, give the idea which their writer said that he intended they should convey, i. e. of a Presence, not after any way of this earth, or cognizable by our bodily senses; not in a gross or carnal way, but in a way befitting Him, Whose Body and Blood are given to us. Those who wished to exclude the belief in any real reception of Christ's Body and Blood, did not content themselves with the word "spiritually," but, in contrast with the word "spiritually," which they affirmed, they expressly denied[k] the word "corporally." "It is received by the faithful, *not corporally*, but spiritually," says the Helvetic

[i] Ib. p. 104.

[k] Mr. Jenkins (Strictures on Mr. Grueber's letter, p. 11) contrasts with our Article, the statement of the Bremen Clergy; "which Flesh and Blood is not merely received spiritually in faith or with thanksgiving, but is truly and actually present in the Supper." "Truly and actually" are the "verily and indeed" of our Catechism. Hardenberg, against whom this statement was framed, believed that there was no Presence in the Sacrament; but that our Lord's Body being (as it is locally) in heaven, an influence came down from It, like a ray from the sun. See further on his history ab. p. 119 sqq.

Confession.   In our Articles, moreover, not only is there no denial of what is " corporal," but the very addition of the word "heavenly" ("after an heavenly and spiritual manner,") marks the contrast to be,—that which Bishop Geste says that he intended it to be,—to "exclude only the grossness and sensibleness in the receiving thereof."   The Body of our Lord, being spiritual and heavenly, is received " in a manner heavenly and spiritual."

It is also much to be observed that in the statement of Bp. Geste's in the Article, the word "spiritual" does not occur in any technical way, or so that it can be thought to express any opinion of a school of Divines.   No emphasis is laid upon it.   It does not stand per se, or in the chief place in the sentence. It stands subordinate, as a synonyme of the word " heavenly," and as carrying on the meaning of that word.   This in itself shews that the word "spiritual" must be taken in its general, not in any specific, sense. The word " spiritual," as used of Communion, has either a very definite dogmatic meaning, viz. that which is effected through communication of the Spirit, i. e. of God the Holy Ghost; or it must be used in its popular untechnical meaning.   But the fact that the word " spiritual" is, in the Article, subordinated to the word " heavenly," shews to any simple and unprejudiced mind, that it is used in the same general sense as that word "heavenly."   It is the language of Bucer in his comment on the Lutheran Concord of Wittenberg to which he had assented.   " [1] It is a heavenly thing; it is exhibited

---

[1] See above, p. 203.

after a heavenly manner." It is *not* the language which Calvinists use to express *their* belief.

This, however, may be said rather in justification of Bishop Geste, that he did not use self-chosen or ambiguous words. He used words of the Fathers, in the sense of the Fathers. But for ourselves, although those who subscribe to the Articles cannot be bound to any meaning of the writer, beyond what he has expressed in his words, no honest man can again contend, that we are bound to a meaning, which the writer himself expressly disclaimed, as *not* being his meaning in those words.

There remains one more sentence in the twenty-eighth Article, to be considered here;

" And the mean whereby the Body of Christ is received and eaten in the Supper is faith."

The Homily " concerning the Sacrament " gives a good commentary upon it, setting forth why faith is essential to the reception of the inward grace of the Sacrament. The Article calls faith "the mean;" the Homilies, " a necessary instrument."

" ᵐ That faith is a necessary instrument in all these holy ceremonies, we may thus assure ourselves, ' for that,' as S. Paul saith, ' without faith it is impossible to please God.' When a great number of the Israelites were overthrown in the wilderness, Moses, Aaron, and Phinees, did eat manna and pleased God, for that they understood, saith S. Augustine, the visible meat spiritually. Spiritually they hungered it, spiritually they tasted it, that they might be spiritually satisfied. And truly, as the bodily meat cannot feed the outward man, unless it be let into a stomach to be digested, which is healthy and sound : no more can the in-

ᵐ P. i. fin.

ward man be fed, except his meat be received into his soul and heart, sound and whole in faith. Therefore, saith Cyprian, when we do these things we need not to whet our teeth, but with sincere faith we break and divide that whole bread. It is well known that the meat we seek for in this Supper is *spiritual* food, the nourishment of our soul, a *heavenly* refection, and not earthly; an *invisible* meat, and not bodily: a ghostly *substance*, and not carnal, *so* that to think that *without faith* we may enjoy the eating and drinking thereof, or that *that* is the fruition of it, is but to dream a gross carnal feeding, basely objecting and bending ourselves to the elements and creatures."

The writer of the Homily must have had the Article in his mind; for he uses its words; and explains the connexion of its statements. Bishop Geste had said, in the Article, that the "Body of Christ is given, taken, and eaten, *in the Supper*, only after a *heavenly* and *spiritual* manner." The writer of the Homily says, "the meat we seek for *in this Supper*, is *spiritual* food, a *heavenly* refection." To the statement, that "the Body of Christ was given, taken, and eaten, only after a *heavenly* and *spiritual* manner," the Article adds, "and the mean whereby the Body of Christ is received and eaten in the Supper is faith." The writer, of the Homily *infers*, that *since* it is a *spiritual* and *heavenly* food therefore it would be to "dream a gross carnal feeding" to think that we may "*enjoy* the eating of it," or that *such* "eating is the fruition of it" ("that *that* is the fruition of it"). These things then plainly appear from the author of this Homily, writing, as he did, contemporaneously [n] with the publication of the Ar-

---

[n] The second Book of Homilies was published in 1564, but printed in 1563, and finished in 1562. Strype's Annals, i. c. 39.

ticles; 1.) that he took the words, "spiritual, heavenly, ghostly, invisible," as equivalent to one another, which is the very way in which Bishop Geste explained his own words in the Article. 2.) He calls faith "a necessary instrument," as the writer of the Article calls it "the mean." 3.) He lays down that faith is essential, not to *any* reception of our Lord's Body and Blood, but to "the *fruition*" of it, or the benefits resulting from it. 4.) In that he denies, that "eating without faith" is "*the* fruition of it" ("that *that* is the *fruition* of it") he even implies, that it may be a *reception* of it, although not the *fruition* of it. He lays the emphasis upon the words "enjoy," "fruition." 5.) He lays down, that the ground why faith is a necessary instrument to its enjoyment, is that it is a spiritual and heavenly food. He does not lay down, that "through faith, we ourselves feed on Christ, in the Sacrament, as out of the Sacrament," which the Calvinist assigns as the office of faith; but he says only, "the inward man cannot be fed, except his meat be received into his soul and heart, sound and whole in faith." He lays down that a condition of soul, spiritually sound and healthy, is essential to profiting by the reception of "spiritual food;" and that "faith" is (as, of course, it is) essential to that sound condition of soul. Faith is "the mean," according to him, by which a man healthily receives the "spiritual food" of the Body and Blood of Christ. 6.) So far from countenancing those who venture to ridicule a real, Divine, spiritual, actual Presence of our Lord's Body, he himself affirms that the Food we seek for in this Supper, is "a ghostly *substance*."

But there can be no other " ghostly *substance* " there, except what we believe, the *substance* of the Body and Blood of Christ, present after a spiritual, ineffable, supernatural, Divine manner.

It is almost to weaken the clearness of this authentic and authoritative evidence as to the meaning of the Article, to illustrate it from any other sources. Yet it is remarkable that Roman Catholic writers have themselves accepted this same statement of the reception by faith. Bucer preserves the words of Robert Bishop of Avranches, who, in accepting the phrase, uses the same illustration as the writer of the Homily.

" º As to what I here allege, that the Body of Christ was given to His Disciples, to be received mentally through faith, he thus writes : ' This opinion we accept ex animo, yet so as further to add, that the very, true, Body of Christ is present, and that Its Presence, spiritual indeed and invisible, but real and true, is of the same avail to the mind, yea more, than food can be to the body. And this, of a surety, the more blessedly and nobly, in that that Food is not converted into the recipient, but converts into itself him who is nourished by It. Nor do we moreover deny that Christ made use of bodily signs.' "

Bossuet has been quoted as expressing the same, even while criticising Burnet's statement as to our English Articles.

" ᵖ The first part of the Article is very true, if we take ' spiritual manner ' to be a manner above sense and nature, as the Catholics and Lutherans take it; and the second is

º Def. doctr. Xt. c. Rob. Ep. Abrinc. fol. I. 6. verso.
ᵖ Variat. x. 6.

no less certain, if we take the reception to mean a profitable reception, and such as S. John speaks of, when he says of Jesus Christ, that 'His own received Him not,' although He was in the world, in Person, in the midst of them; that is, that they received neither His doctrine nor His Grace."

Indeed, the Roman missal remarkably asserts the office of faith in this Sacrament, in that, in the very midst of the words by which the Cup is consecrated, it declares that this is " the mystery of faith."

"[q] Likewise, after Supper, taking also this excellent Cup into His holy and venerable Hands, and giving Thee thanks, He blessed and gave it to His disciples, saying, 'Take and drink ye all of this; For this is the Cup of My Blood, of the new and eternal Testament *(the mystery of faith)*, which shall be shed for you and for many, for the remission of sins.' "

None insist more on the office of faith, than they who believe what faith alone can learn or know, that what we receive is the Body and Blood of Christ. Take the fervid words of S. Isaac the great, a writer contemporary with S. Augustine.

"[r] I beheld, that her cup was mingled, and, instead of wine, it was full of Blood; and instead of bread, a Body was placed for her, in the midst of her table. I saw the Blood, and trembled; and the Body, and fear seized me; and she [Faith] made a sign to me, ' Eat, and be silent; drink, child, and scrutinize not.' She shewed me a Body slain, and placed thereof between my lips; and cried to me sweetly, ' See what it is, thou art eating.' She gave me the pen of the Spirit, and bade me subscribe; and I took, I wrote, and I confessed, ' This is the Body of God.' So,

[q] Canon of the Mass.   [r] Real Presence. p. 493, 4.

again, I took the Cup, and I drank in her feast, and from the Cup the scent of that Body, of which I had eaten, struck me; and what she said of the Body, that 'This is the Body of God,' that again I said of the Cup, that 'This is the Blood of our Redeemer.'"

And again;

" Faith spake to me, and called to me, and said to me, that the Sacraments of the Church came forth from the opened Side of Christ."

Rubrics.

The Declaration at the end of the Communion Service belongs chiefly to another part of the subject, the adoration of Christ present in the Sacrament. I will consider now, however, so much of it as belongs to the mode of Christ's Presence in the Holy Eucharist.

The Declaration itself, in its original form, never had any authority from the Church. It was "[s] added to the Communion Service by King Edward on his own authority after the publication of his second liturgy;" " the order in Council, requiring the insertion of the rubric, bears date on Oct. 27, only four days before the book was to be generally used throughout the kingdom." It is found accordingly to have been inserted by cancelling the leaf or some similar contrivance. " The Rubric does not appear in either of the copies published by Whitchurch in 1552, but it does appear in each of two editions by Grafton printed in Aug. 1552."

The Declaration was, accordingly, struck out by

[s] Cardwell Hist. of Conferences p. 34, 5.

the Divines who revised the Prayer Book of Elizabeth's accession in 1559. On the restoration of Charles II., kneeling at the Holy Communion was one of the eight gravamina of the Non-Conformist party [t]; the requirement of it, as a condition of communicating, was afterwards alleged as *the* point of "sinfulness" in the Liturgy, and was the subject of a day's disputation [u]. The Non-Conformists especially desired, that "the Rubric in the Common Prayer-book, in 5 and 6 Edw. VI., established by law," they say [v], "as much as any other part of the Common Prayer-book, may be restored for the vindicating of our Church in the· matter of kneeling at the Sacrament (although the gesture be left indifferent)."

The Bishops, at first, declined [w]. Afterwards, in the review of the Prayer Book, the substance and words of the Declaration were retained. One only alteration was made, which was more than verbal. Whereas the declaration of Cranmer and Edw. VI.'s Council had the words "any *real any essential presence, there being*, of Christes natural flesh and bloude," the present words were substituted, "any *Corporal* Presence of Christ's natural Flesh and Blood." Thus, just after the Bishops and Priests of the English Church had been expelled, and when they were scarce restored, it was again proposed to them to deny " the *Real and essential* Presence of Christ's natural Flesh and Blood, there being," and was again refused.

[t] Baxter's Life p. 341. Cardwell p. 245, 6.
[u] Collier, ii. 889. Cardw. p. 364.
[v] Cardw. p. 322. [w] Ib. p. 354.

We have not then to consider the word, " corporal," merely in itself; we have it, as a substitute for the words, " Real and essential." The Bishops rejected the demand, which involved the condemnation of the words, " Real and essential," and they substituted the word " corporal." Plainly, the word " corporal," which they admitted, could not, in their minds, mean the same as " Real and essential," which they rejected. What they refused to deny was, " the true and essential Presence of Christ's Body and Blood being there." They would *not* deny that our Lord's Blessed Body and Blood were *there*, " really and essentially." When then they denied " a corporal presence of Christ's natural Body and Blood," they must have meant to deny that our Lord's natural Body and Blood were there " corporally," i. e. after the manner of a body. This they denied, and this only. They did not deny " the Presence of Christ's natural Body and Blood." This would have been all one with denying " the Real and essential Presence." They were, some of them, learned men, and well versed in controversy and scholastic language. When then they struck out the words " Real and essential," and inserted the word " corporal," it is a mere paradox to say, that they meant the same, as if they had left in what they struck out, and left out what they put in. An historian of these Conferences, whose aim seems to have been to hold a middle course on this great truth, says [x];

" Its [this rubric's] removal [in 1559 clearly shews that

[x] Cardwell Hist. of Conf. p. 35.

the Church could not then be brought to express an opinion adverse to the Real Presence. It was restored in 1661, and its reappearance may likewise be employed to shew, that the Church at that time also was unwilling to make any declaration on that important tenet. To prevent misapprehension on this point, the words, ' or unto any real and essential presence, there being, of Christ's natural flesh and blood,' were altered to the *very different expression,* ' or unto any corporal Presence of Christ's natural Flesh and Blood.' "

2.) Another Rubric is alleged (although with much misgiving), to shew that the English Church holds Sacramental and non-sacramental Communion to be one and the same.

" ʸ If a man, either by reason of extremity of sickness, or for want of warning in due time to the Curate, or for lack of company, to receive with him, or by any other just impediment, do not receive the Sacrament of Christ's Body and Blood, the Curate shall instruct him, that if he do truly repent him of his sins, and steadfastly believe that Jesus Christ hath suffered death upon the Cross for him, and shed His Blood for his redemption, earnestly remembering the benefits he hath thereby, and giving him hearty thanks therefore, he doth eat and drink the Body and Blood of our Saviour Christ profitably to his soul's health, although he do not receive the Sacrament with his mouth."

Mr. Goode who alleges this, does not lay much stress upon it, because 1, it is manifestly an exceptional case ; 2, precisely the same doctrine was taught in the Sarum Manual, and from this, which they had habitually used, the framers of our Service had, of course, learned it.

ʸ The Communion for the Sick.

Q

" ᵃ Then let the sick man be communicated, if he have not been communicated before, and there be no probable fear of vomiting or any other irreverence; in which case, let the priest say to the sick man, 'Brother, in this case, true faith and good will sufficeth thee; only believe, and thou hast eaten.'"

Mr. Goode says;

" ᵃ This rubric in the Salisbury Manual was probably inserted there, before the Doctrine of the Romish Church was fixed according to its present form, and would not probably be received, much less inserted, by the present Church of Rome."

Whatever change there has been in the statement of Roman doctrine, has related, not at all to the doctrine of the Real Presence, but to that of a change in the elements. But the Salisbury Manual, which contains that rubric, continued to be published during the reigns of Edward VI., Mary, and James I., 1543, 1554, and 1610 ᵇ. So far, moreover, from that ritual bearing the stamp of an older date, it has, brief as it is, a mark of later times. For the older rituals prescribe that the sick should be communicated in both kinds ᶜ (which was the older practice in England also ᵈ), the Salisbury Manual gives directions as to one only.

So far, indeed, from this rubric not being "received

ᵃ f. 97. quoted by Palmer, Orig. Lit. ii. 230.　　　ᵃ p. 621.

ᵇ See Martene de ant. Eccl. rit. 1. 7. 4. ordo 2-5. 7. 10. 12-16. 23-27. The one kind is prescribed only in the Ordo 29. in the 15th cent. and the Ambrosian ritual of 1645. Ib. 32.

ᶜ Mr. Palmer quotes from the Bodleian copies, Rouen, 1543, Lond. 1554. The Douay edition, 1610, repeats the same rubric.

ᵈ Martene i. v. 2. § 4. sub qua specie.

by the present Church of Rome, " it contains the doctrine laid down by the Council of Trent, in distinguishing the three kinds of Communicants; those who communicate only spiritually, as those who wish to receive but receive it not; or only sacramentally; or both sacramentally and spiritually.

"[e] As to the use [of the Sacrament] our fathers rightly and wisely distinguished three ways of receiving this holy Sacrament. For they taught that some received it only sacramentally, as sinners; others only spiritually, those namely, who, *through the wish (voto) eating that heavenly bread* set before [us] *feel its fruit and benefit* [fructum ejus et utilitatem sentiunt]; the third, both sacramentally and spiritually; and these are they, who beforehand so prove and prepare themselves, that they come to this Divine table clad with the wedding garment."

The rubric is, indeed, simply an application of the principle, that Almighty God accepts us, "according to that a man hath, not according to that he hath not." He who imputes not to us, what does not spring from a perverse will in us, but who accepts the wish which He inspires, counts the will for the deed, the wish for the Sacrament, the same as the Sacrament itself. In like way S. Augustine, and others following him, laid down that "[f] faith and conversion of heart could supply what was lacking of Baptism, if, in the straitness of the time, any one could not be holpen by the celebration of the mystery of Baptism." From him, Hugo de S. Victore lays it down as a maxim as to Sacraments, necessary to salvation; "[g] Where there is faith

[e] Sess. xiii. c. 8.　　　　[f] De Bapt. c. Don. iv. 22.
[g] De Sacram. L. 1. P. 9. fin. add on Baptism L. ii. P. 6. c. 7.

with love, as the good deserts are not lessened, even
if the work, which is religiously and devoutly purposed, be not outwardly completed; so the saving
effect is not hindered, even if the Sacrament, which
is longed for in truth of will, is shut out by the
point of death.   S. Bernard argues the question at
length[h].   To give one passage only.   "[i] Paul saith,
'No man can say, Lord Jesus, except by the Holy
Ghost.'   Shall we say then, that he who, at the point
of death, not only calleth on the Lord Jesus, but with
the whole longing [of his heart] desireth His Sacrament, either doth not speak by the Holy Spirit (in
which case the Apostle would have spoken falsely),
or that, with the Holy Spirit, he is damned?   He
hath the Saviour, dwelling in his heart by faith, and
in his mouth by confession; and shall he, with the
Saviour, be damned?   Certainly since, on no other
ground than the good desert of faith, hath martyrdom that prerogative, that it especially may be
received fearlessly, in place of Baptism; I do not see
why faith may not, even without martyrdom, be of
the same avail with God, to Whom, without question, it is known without the proof of martyrdom.—
We read, 'Whosoever hateth his brother, is a mur-
derer.'   What is plainer, than that the will is taken
for the deed, when the deed is excluded by necessity?   Unless we are to think that with God Who
is Love, the will hath more avail in evil than in
good, and that the merciful and gracious Lord is
more ready to avenge, than to reward!"

Hence the threefold division of Baptism, formally

---

[h] **De Bapt. ad Hug. de S. Vict. Opp. i. 631.**
[i] **c. 2. p. 635.**

recognised by the Schoolmen, "the Baptism of water, of blood, of the Spirit[j]," Who gives the faith and love required, and suggests the desire of the Sacrament.

On the same principle, the Council of Trent[k] admits that through "contrition, perfected by love, man is reconciled to God, before the Sacrament of penitence is received *in fact*," yet so, "that that reconciliation is not to be ascribed to contrition itself, without *the wish* for the sacrament [sine voto sacramenti] which," it says, "is included in it."

3.) Another rubric is alleged by a writer, who calls for a revision of the Liturgy, on the ground that it teaches the doctrines of Baptismal regeneration, Absolution, and the Real Presence.

"And if any of the bread and wine remain unconsecrated, the Curate shall have it to his own use; but if any remain of that which was consecrated, it shall not be carried out of the Church, but the Priest and such others of the Communicants as he shall then call unto him, shall, immediately after the Blessing, reverently eat and drink the same."

On this the writer remarks[l],

"This change, it will be observed, is in perfect keeping with those already noticed. Some indeed may be disposed (and not altogether without reason) to consider it as one of the most important alterations which the Communion Service has undergone; involving, as it does, so palpable a recognition of that mysterious virtue, which is supposed, according to the theory of Rome, to be infused into

[j] Baptismus sanguinis, fluminis, Flaminis. see Aq. 3. p. q. 66. art. 11. Bonav. 4. dist. iv. p. 2. art. 1. q. 1. Durand, q. 8. &c.

[k] Sess. 14. c. 4.

[l] Liturgical purity our rightful inheritance, by J. C. Fisher, Esq. P. ii. c. 5. p. 400.

the elements by the priestly act of consecration. It is indeed, in this respect, all that the most zealous adherent of the Tridentine doctrine could desire. Such is the mystical sanctity of the newly 'consecrated' bread and wine, that they are not, we are told, to be used even by the priest himself, anywhere except within the hallowed precincts of the altar."

To one who believes in the Real Presence, this is strange and sorrowful language. But it is a remarkable admission on the part of one opposed to that truth, how even a rubric may bear testimony to it. Plainly, unless there were an abiding Presence in the elements, there would have been no ground, why Communicants should (as they did in the second century[m]) carry home what remained, that they might communicate when they could not come to Church; or for reserving it for the sick (as may still be done in the Scotch Church), or for making any distinction (such as is here made) *between that which was consecrated, and that which remains unconsecrated.*" A prayer is used in the Baptismal Service, that God would "sanctify this water to the mystical washing away of sin." But any water, used in the Name of Trinity, by any person, is valid for the Sacrament of Baptism. When used, no directions are given, what should be done with it. It is allowed to sink into the earth. In the Kirk of Scotland, where the bread, although used as a sacred symbol, is still, and is believed to be, common bread, it is taken away after the supper, and eaten, as being, what it is, ordinary bread. The Church

[m] Tert. de Orat. 19. p. 313. Oxf. Tr. and note b. ad Uxor. ii. 5. p. 439. O. T. and note z. Bingham, 15. 4. 13.

of England directs, that if any remain of "that which was consecrated," the Priest and certain of the communicants should "eat the same;" and that, "*reverently*," at the same Altar where they had just communicated. The word "reverently" doubtless means, "kneeling, &c." For they who so receive, communicate twice. Yet they may also, like Elisha, pray for a double portion of His Spirit. For although the gift in the Holy Eucharist, our Lord's Blessed Body and Blood, is one, the grace is manifold.

Such acts are a witness to belief. No such direction would be found in bodies (such as the Lutheran also) where there is no belief in any Presence after the Communion. They too among ourselves who believe that Presence to be withdrawn after Communion, while they must obey the direction of the Church, do not, often, "eat and drink the same," in any sense, "reverently."

The mode of receiving, after the Communion, may often be an index, whether the priest believes that that Presence still abides there or no. But then, the very care, that what remains should not be exposed to irreverence, nor be received by non-Communicants (to whom it would be a Communion), but that it should be received *reverently*, shews that the Church of England believes an abiding objective Presence of the Body and Blood of Christ in the elements, apart from the act of reception. Here, again, she has guarded her doctrine, in a way which Melanchthon and the later Lutherans emphatically repudiated.

4) The little simple direction as to the covering of the consecrated elements, contains the same

doctrine of the Real Presence of our Lord's Body and Blood.

"When all have communicated, the Minister shall return to the Lord's Table, and reverently place upon it, what remains of the consecrated elements, covering the same with a fine linen cloth."

Except on the belief in the Real Presence, there would be no ground whatever for such provision. Prayer had been used for the consecration of the font. The water had been used for the Sacrament. There is no direction for reverent care as to what had not been employed. But, further, the direction as to the "fine linen cloth" is a symbolical instruction, descending from the earliest ages of the Church. As Joseph of Arimathea "wrapt our Saviour's Body in a clean" and fine "linen cloth[n]," so the Church directed that the Sacramental Body of Christ should, when replaced on the Altar, be enveloped in the pure fine white linen. This was called "the Corporal," as enfolding the Lord's Body. It is mentioned in the Liturgy of S. Chrysostome[o] in the East, and by his disciple, S. Isidore. The use of the linens on the Altar is mentioned by S. Optatus[p], and a prayer for their consecration is found in the Sacramentary of S. Gregory[q]. I have already given the passage of S. Isidore, in which he explains "the fine linen spread out underneath the ministry of the Divine gifts," by reference to the act of Joseph of Arimathea[r].

[n] σίνδονι.

[o] Under the name εἰλητόν Opp. xii. 786. see Suicer sub v.

[p] L. vi. p. 92. quoted in not. 562. on S. Greg.　　[q] Opp. iii. 150. ed. Ben.　　[r] Ep. i. 123. in Real Presence, p. 665.

"For as he, having wrapped the Body of the Lord in fine linen, committed to the tomb that Body, through which our whole race has gained the fruit of the resurrection, so we, consecrating the shewbread upon fine linen, find undoubtedly the Body of Christ, gushing forth for us with that incorruptibility, which He whom Joseph attended to the tomb, the Saviour Jesus, rising from the dead, bestowed."

In like way Germanus explains the term used in S. Chrysostome's Liturgy. "[s] It signifies the fine linen in which the Body of Christ was enveloped, which was taken down from the Cross and was placed in the tomb."

In Bede's time, this explanation of the ritual was an ancient tradition of the West. He says in his comment on the history of our Lord's Burial [t];

"According to the spiritual meaning, we may think that the Body of the Lord is not to be enveloped in gold, or gems, or silk, but in pure linen; although it signifies this too, that *he* enwraps Jesus in a pure fine linen, who receives Him in a pure heart. Hence it has been the custom of the Church, that the Sacrifice of the Altar should not be celebrated on silk or on dyed cloth, but in linen from the earth, as the Body of the Lord was buried in a pure linen cloth, as we read in the Pontifical acts to have been enacted by the blessed Pope Sylvester [u]."

The same explanation was given by Alcuin [v]; and

[s] Theoria, p. 153, quoted by Suicer.

[t] In Marc. xv. [u] Spurious.

[v] "The corporal, on which the Body of the Lord is placed, should be no other than linen, because we read that Joseph brought clean linen, wherein he wrapped the Body of the Lord." De Div. Off. T. ii. P. 2. p. 500.

subsequently, by Rabanus Maurus[w], and yet later by Rupertus[x], Hugo de S. Victore[y], Innocent III.[z], and Aquinas[a], and from him by the Schoolmen generally. The complaint made by Walerann to S. Anselm[b] on variations of practice in this respect, shews how much value was attached to it. It was not only part of the acknowledged and popular meaning; but, at that time when the people were so much taught by the eye, it pictured to them the mysteries of the Redemption.

There now remains only, to sum up the teaching of the Church of England on the Real Presence in the Holy Eucharist. She teaches then, that "[c] Sa-

---

[w] "It signifies the linen, wherein the Body of the Saviour was enveloped." De Inst. Cler. i. 33.

[x] "For if there were no spiritual meaning in this too, why are costly palls, and dorsals all of silk, hung upon the walls, and the all-holy Body of the Lord, laid on a linen corporal, is covered thereby? For if we regarded Its dignity, we should do well to wrap around It whatsoever we have that is most precious. Some mysteries then, worthy of being sought out and understood, are noted by this distinction. For the linen corporal, whereon we celebrate the memorial of the Lord's Passion, signifies His Tribulations, and the wondrous Purity of His Flesh therein." "The more diligent investigators observe, that the corporal is twofold, signifying the linen folds round the Lord's Head, in which Joseph enfolded the Body which he had embalmed with spices." De Div. Off. ii. 23. [y] De Off. Eccl. ii. 38.

[z] "The Deacon, meantime, disposes the Corporal palls, which signify the linens, wherewith the Body of Jesus was wrapped. But the part which is placed, folded, above the Chalice, signifies the napkin, which had been over His head, wrapped together in a place by itself." (Then as in Bede.) De Myst. Miss. ii. 56.

[a] 3 p. qu. 51. art. 2. from Bede.

[b] Ad Walerann. querelas Resp. c. 3.

[c] Art. xxv. Catechism.

craments, ordained by Christ Himself," are means "whereby God doth work invisibly in us;" "means whereby we receive" "the inward part or thing, signified" by "the outward and visible sign;" and that they are "pledges to assure us thereof;" that "[d] the inward part or *thing* signified in the Sacrament of the Lord's Supper, is the Body and Blood of Christ, which are verily and indeed taken and received by the faithful *in* the Lord's Supper;" that "[e] Almighty God, our Heavenly Father, hath given His Son our Saviour Jesus Christ to be our spiritual *Food* and sustenance *in* that holy Sacrament;" that this is "a Divine thing to those who receive it worthily;" that, then, "[f] we spiritually eat the Flesh of Christ and drink His Blood; then we dwell in Christ and Christ with us, we are one with Christ and Christ with us;" that we "[g] come" there "to the Body and Blood of Christ;" "[h] receive His Blessed Body and Blood under the Form of bread and wine;" that, "at His table, we," if we be faithful, "[i] receive not only the outward Sacrament, but the spiritual *thing* also; not the figure only, but the truth; not the shadow only, but the Body;" "spiritual Food, nourishment of our soul, a heavenly refection, an invisible meat, a ghostly *substance*;" that "Christ" is our "refection and meat;" that that Body and Blood are present there; for "in the Supper of the Lord, there is no vain ce-

---

[d] Catechism.   [e] Liturgy, 1st Exhort.

[f] Lit. Exhort. at "time of the celebration."

[g] Hom. on the Sacram. P. ii. init. from S. Basil.

[h] Notice at the end of the 1st B. of Homilies.

[i] Hom. on the Sacr. P. i. fin.

remony, no bare sign, *no* untrue *figure* of *a thing ab-sent* [j];" that "the bread" which "is blessed" or "conse-crated [k]" with our Lord's words, "This is my Body," "[l] is the Communion or partaking of the Body of Christ;" that the Cup, or wine, which is blessed or consecrated with His Word, "This is My Blood of the New Testament," "is to such as rightly, wor-thily and with faith, receive the same," "the Commu-nion or partaking of the Blood of Christ;" that, if we receive rightly, "[m] we *so* eat the Flesh of Jesus Christ, the Son of God, and drink His Blood, that our sinful bodies are made clean by His Body, and our souls washed through His most Precious Blood;" we are made "[n] partakers of His most Precious Body and Blood;" and so, "[o] partakers of Christ" Himself, God and Man; that " God [p] Himself vouch-safes to feed those, who duly receive these holy Mysteries, with the spiritual Food of the most Pre-

[j] Mr. Goode says (p 82), " He [I] says, It is an unauthorised inference from our ' Lord's words ' that they mean only, ' This re-presents, is a figure of, My absent Body.' But who authorised him to insert the words 'absent' ? " and again, p. 35 ; " Dr. P. writes as if he were defending ' the presence of Christ in the Eucharist' against those who denied it. " I should be thankful to know that none denied it. The contrast which I had in my mind was pre-cisely that of the Homily.

[k] " If the *consecrated* Bread or Wine be all spent, before all have communicated, the Priest is to consecrate more, according to the form before prescribed, beginning at [Our Saviour Christ in the same night, &c.] for the *blessing* of the Bread ; and at [Likewise after Supper, &c.] for the *blessing* of the Cup."

[l] Art. xxviii.   [m] Liturgy Prayer, " We do not presume."

[n] Prayer of Consecration.   [o] Art. xxix. Plainly, in denying this of the wicked, the Article means to assert it of the faithful.   [p] Second Thanksgiving after Communion.

cious Body and Blood of His Son our Saviour Jesus Christ;" that "[q] the Body and Blood of Christ which were given and shed for us," thus "given to us," "[r]taken, eaten," and drunken by us (plainly, if we persevere), "preserve our bodies and souls unto everlasting life," and (as is implied by the very prayer) are a means towards that perseverance; "a[s] salve of immortality and sovereign preservative against death;" "a deifical Communion;" "the pledge of eternal health, the defence of faith, the hope of the Resurrection;" "the Food of immortality, the healthful grace, the conservatory to life everlasting."

These statements of our faith chiefly relate to that Holy Gift which we *receive*, the Body and Blood of Christ. For the object of the framers of the Liturgy was, as they themselves imply, to restore the *Communion.* The whole service was framed with a view to Communicants. Yet while, alike in the Liturgy, Catechism, Articles, and Homilies, these are attestations to the Real objective Presence, there is not one word to contradict it. On the contrary, we know that those who re-cast the Articles, and revised the Liturgy, did, at different times, formally reject [t] phrases, directed against " the Real, essential Presence of our Saviour Jesus Christ's natural Flesh and Blood." They stated, indeed, that "[u] the Body of Christ is given, taken, and eaten, in the Supper, only after an heavenly and spiritual manner." But we know, that they intended by

---

[q] Form of communicating.

[s] Hom. on the Sacr. P. l.

[u] Art. xxviii.

[r] Art. xxviii.

[t] See ab. p. 192 sqq.

these words, only to "exclude 'the grossness and sensibleness of the receiving thereof." They themselves " explain the words "heavenly and spiritual," by "invisible," and, in so doing, speak of a "ghostly *substance*." They say, that "the mean whereby the Body of Christ is received and eaten, is faith." But this too they explain to relate to its benefits to the faithful, of which Art. xxviii. is speaking. They state as the ground, why faith is a necessary instrument" "that, as S. Paul saith, 'without faith it is impossible to please God ;'" that "the inward man cannot be fed, except his meat be received into his soul and heart, whole and sound in faith; that, since it is spiritual food, the nourishment of our soul,—heavenly refection, an invisible meat, a ghostly substance," "to think that *without faith* we may *enjoy* the eating and drinking thereof, or that *that* is the fruition of it, is but to dream a gross carnal feeding."

In every way, then,—in Catechetical instruction of the young; doctrinal teaching as well of those who are not Communicants, as of those who are; popular homilies; Articles for avoiding difference of opinion; and the Liturgy, wherein the teaching is interwoven with our thoughts and prayers, and becomes our own voice in speaking to Almighty God—the Church of England teaches us, that we, in deed and in truth, receive *in* the Sacrament, the Body and Blood of Christ. She also teaches the Real objective Presence of the Body and Blood of Christ in that Sacrament. The objections raised against that truth have been solely inferential, con-

<hr>

' Ab. p. 203, 4.   " Hom. on the Sacr. P. l. fin.

fronted by the fact that that rejection was twice formally rejected, and contradicted by the positive statement of the writer of the Article.

We might appeal to those who cast out our names as evil, whether they would themselves have framed formularies, such as our Liturgy and Cate- chism; whether any body who does not believe what we maintain that the Church of England believes, has done as the Church of England has done.

CHAPTER III.

On the Sacramental reception of the Body and Blood of Christ by the wicked; and on the Adoration of our Lord Jesus Christ present there.

The awful question of the reception of the Holy Eucharist by the wicked, is only partially touched upon in our Articles. They lay down carefully the practical, rather than the theoretic side of the doctrine. They state that the wicked lose all good, and purchase to themselves endless evil. And for this, the framers of the Articles had adequate ground. Men are unwilling to part either with their sins or with God. And so they take up with any outward act, which God enjoins, in order to soothe their consciences, and persuade themselves, that they are not under God's displeasure. The Jews, in the time of the Prophets, offered sacrifices for sins. With " hands full of blood,[a] " they offered sacrifice to God. Strange, to think that sacrifice, whereby a man looked on to the great Sacrifice for sin, whereby he owned that his own life was justly forfeited by his past sins, could propitiate God,

[a] Is. i. 11-15.

while he who offered it was heaping sin upon sin, and incurring that heaviest sentence of God's displeasure, "Whoso sheddeth man's blood, by man shall his blood be shed."

We need not then to look for any special ground, why, after our Articles had stated that "to such as rightly, worthily, and with faith, receive the same, the bread which we break, is a partaking of the Body of Christ, and likewise the Cup of blessing is a partaking of the Blood of Christ," another Article should be added, declaring, that "the wicked and such as be void of a lively faith," although they receive "the Sacrament of the Body and Blood of Christ, are in no wise partakers of Christ."

The fear that people, who would not part with their sins, would thrust themselves into holy things to their own hurt, was very vivid at the time that our Articles were framed. The mistake, into which so many fell, both here and on the Continent, about the "opus operatum," is an evidence of this. Those who condemned that phrase, meant to condemn a doctrine, that "Infidelity [b] or unbelief, is no hindrance to the *grace* of the Sacraments;" that "neither grace, nor faith [c], hope or charity [d], are re-

[b] Luther. Calvin, Antidot. Conc. Trid. in 7. Sess. in vi. Inst. 4. 14, 14.

[c] Luther, "not faith." Conf. Augsb. Calv. Barlow, Def. of the Art. of the Protest. Rel. p. 147, quoted by Mr Goode on Baptism, p. 293.

[d] "If wee obtaine the effects of the Sacrament by receiving Christ in faith, hope and charity, togither with the entrance of his body into ours, as he sayd before, then the Sacrament giveth not that grace *by the very worke wrought*, as he sayth heere. If it give grace *by the very worke wrought*, as he saith heere, then it is not

quired;" "that [e] men, coming without faith, void of knowledge, without repentance or any good motion, may receive the effect of the Sacrament;" that men are "justified by a ceremony without any good motion of the heart [f];" men, "in whom not only there is no grace, but not so much as any inward disposition or motion of grace beforehand [g];" and

to be ascribed to faith, hope and charity, as he sayth there." Bp. R. Abbot's Mirror of Popish Subtleties, p. 183.

"It is plaine that *Baptisme hath his* force not of *the verie worke done* but of true and unfayned faith working in the heart good conscience towards God." Ib.

"[e] A miserable doctrine it is whereby men are borne in hand that comming without faith, voyd of knowledge, without repentance or any good motion, yet they may receive the effect of the Sacrament: whereas the Scripture so plainly affirmeth that whatsoever is not of faith, is sinne, and that 'without faith it is unpossible to please God.'" Ib. p. 184.

[f] Apol. Conf. Aug. de num. et usu Sacram.

[g] *Bp. Downame* ("on certainty of perseverance" quoted by Mr. Goode on Baptism, p. 308). "Here therefore is cohfuted that most pernicious doctrine of the papists, that the Sacraments of the Gospel, which they call the new law, do confer grace, and that *ex opere operato*, to them in whom not only there is no grace (for then it were *opere operantis*), but not so much as any inward disposition or motion of grace beforehand. By which doctrine, they have turned Christian religion to a mere outward formality, consisting in outward rites and observations, without any truth or religion in them, according to that prophecy of them" (2 Tim. iii. 5). *Bp. Cooper* (Sermons, p. 31. ap. Mr. Goode on Bap., p. 280). "First, they teach that Baptism doth confer grace and wash away our sins, *ex opere operato*, that is, even by the very washing only of the water, though there be no good motion of faith or belief in the heart of him that is baptized." *Bp. Carleton,* "The Pontificians teach that grace is so tied to the Sacraments and other institutions, that there is no need of faith or any good motion, inasmuch as they may obtain grace, as they speak, from

this, " without the power of the Spirit [h] ; " not " the work of God Alone [i]," but " by a power which remaineth in the outward signs,—not of the free grace of God [k]." As the doctrine was *then*, and is, even now frequently, imagined, the " work wrought " in the Sacrament was opposed to, or independent of, Him Who worketh it, and irrespective of any quality in him who receiveth it.

the very opus operatum. This is Pontifical grace." (Cons. Eccl. Cath. de Grat. c. 4, p. 412.) " This, then, is the common tenet of the Schoolmen, that Sacraments confer grace from the opus operatum, so that no good meritorious motion of the mind is required.'" (Ib. 415, 6.) Of course, this is true, in that it excludes " merits ; " but Bp. Carleton supposes it to exclude " faith " also. " They who exclude all inward meritorious motion, certainly exclude faith; for faith is a meritorious motion, *if any is.*" Ib. " It is certain that the tenet of the Pontificians on the opus operatum is, that Sacraments confer or cause grace, as they speak, after the manner of an instrument [see Art. xxvii.] from the opus operatum, without faith." p. 420.

[h] *Bp. Barlow*, l. c. " Briefly, we so highly extol the dignity, necessity, and efficacy of Baptism, that Duræus pleaseth himself triumphantly, in hope that some of our writers are proved, in this opinion, Romanists, saving he misliketh our detestation of that magical conceit of *opus operatum*, videlicet, that the very act of Baptism, without either the parties' faith, or the Spirit's power, should confer grace of itself."

[i] *Bucer ;* " yet, in order not to glide into the opinion of the 'opus operatum,' we are wont so to set forth these things, as to own that all this is the work of God alone, and that the ministration alone belongs to the minister." De Concord. Euch. (Opp. Angl. p. 655.) *Abp. Ussher* (Sum and substance, &c. p. 419, ap. Dr. Bayf. p. 175), " especially that Baptism doth confer grace by the work done (for they *commonly look no higher*)."

[k] *Becon* (The Catechism. Works, f. 438. ed. 1564. p. 218. P. S. quoted by Dr. Bayford, p. 152), " If our Sacraments,—which, of themselves, are nothing else than (as St. Paul termeth them), the

The " opus operatum " had been condemned, as meaning this, not only by Melanchthon, in the Apology for the Confession of Augsburg, by Luther and Calvin, but (although less definitely) in the 26th Article of 1552; "and yet not that, of the woorke wrought, as some men speake, which worde, as it is straunge and unknowen to holie Scripture, so it engendereth no godlie, but a verie superstitious sense."

The clause was struck out in the Articles of 1562, yet the prejudice remained; and the "opus operatum" continued to be condemned, as containing an error, or a series of errors, the very opposite of what was really designated by that name.

The term "ex opere operato" did, indeed, mean the very opposite of all this. It was not used 1) to ascribe any efficacy to the Sacraments, in themselves; nor 2) to exclude the necessity of faith or repentance in the receiver, whensoever, by reason of age, he was capable of either; nor 3) to express any inherent created virtue in the Sacrament; nor, 4) that the Sacraments are any physical means of grace. The real doctrine expressed by the words " ex opere operato," in contrast with the " ex opere operantis," is that, whereas every prayer, and every

' seals of righteousness,' or of our righteous-making—by faith, and witnesses of God's favour towards us, were of such virtue that they could give grace, that is, the favour of God, remission of sins, justification, the Holy Ghost, everlasting life, etc, by the work wrought, as they say, or by any power that remaineth in the outward signs; so should it follow, that our justification depend not only of the free grace of God, but of works; which is most false."

act of religious service, having God for its end, and proceeding from faith and love, wrought through God the Holy Ghost, obtains a blessing from God in proportion to that faith and love, God, in His Sacraments, bestows upon those who with faith receive them, gifts beyond all proportion, not grace generally, but the grace special to the Sacrament, not a mere reward of their faith, but that gift also, which our Saviour Christ has, by His Institution and promise, annexed to the right reception of the Sacrament which He ordained.

Gerson says concisely [1],

"I find not how any better or more efficacious food of love and grace can be given to the flock of Christ, than through the due bestowal of the Sacrament. For there grace is bestowed on the receiver, by virtue of 'the work wrought,' i. e. beyond or above the merit of the receiver, in virtue of the Merit of Christ who instituted the Sacrament, and endowed it with spiritual privilege."

This was its ordinary meaning. But it stood contrasted with all agency or goodness of man, whether of the recipient of the Sacrament, or, more rarely, of the priest who celebrated. In this last sense it was employed by Innocent III. in his well known words, as to the Eucharistic Sacrifice [m].

[1] Serm. de off. Past. in Conc. Rem. A. 1408. 3. part. Opp. ii. 554. ed. Antw. 1706.

[m] De myst. missæ iii. 5. Scotus [quodlib. q. 20. init. referred to by Mr. Jenkins] uses it in this same contrast, as does Biel, Expos. Missæ Lect. 26.; but in the other, in iv. dist. 1. q. 3. as does Gerson, and Aq. iv. d. i. q. i. art. 5. d. ii. q. i. art. 4. fin. d. iv. q. i. art. 4. (In his Summa, referred to by Mr. J., he does not use it at all, nor do Albertus M. or S. Bonaventura in the

"The Sacrament is made, not through the merit of the priest, but through the word of the Creator. Although then the 'work which worketh' [opus operans] is sometimes unclean, 'the work which is worked' is always clean."

Still it was a common error at that time, that the Schoolmen had deliberately held, and that "the Pontificians" still held, that the Sacraments could be of avail, "without grace or faith or any good motion of the heart" on the part of the receiver, even although, by reason of age, he was capable of them. This has indeed continued to be a vulgar error to this day [n]. Bishops R. Abbot, Cooper, Carleton, Downame, Abp. Ussher, above cited, wrote in the xviith century. Even lately, in the pleadings of the Gorham judgment, the mistakes made by the older writers ran through the argument for the defence [o];

places cited.) The phrase is very clearly explained by Estius in iv. d. 1. § 7. Le Blanc (a reformed writer) owns the explanation to be accurate. Thes. Theol. de usu et effic. Sacr. N. T. § 23. sqq.

[n] Dr. Bayford quoted Bp. Burnet in his speech, p. 61. Bucer, p. 115. Becon, p. 152. Turner [i. e. Urbanus Regius, a Lutheran, whose work he translated], p. 156. Davenant, p. 162. Whitaker, p. 164. Abp. Usher, p. 175. Downame, p. 182. Hopkins, p. 186. Cooper, p. 187.

[o] Mr Badeley's speech, p. 66. "The whole service of Baptism goes on the presumption that the infant is in original sin; has had no prevenient grace; is in a state of nature; and that it is brought to the Church in order to be put into a state of grace." Lord Campbell. "Which takes place by Baptism alone?" Mr. B. "Which state is produced by Baptism alone." Lord C. "I do not mean in the slightest degree to interrupt your argument, but I should be very glad to hear by-and-by, what is the distinction between that and the 'opus operatum' of the Roman Catholic Church." Mr. Badeley explained the current mistakes on that subject, p. 67, 8.

and a Counsel was asked, how the doctrine of the Church on Infant Baptism was to be "distinguished from the 'opus operatum' of the Church of Rome."

. The revisers of the Articles of 1562 were better instructed than those who had drawn up the unsanctioned Articles of 1552. The truth, contained under the words "ex opere operato," had been as clearly explained before 1552, as afterwards. But in 1552, those had the chief influence who lowered the whole doctrine of the Sacrament; in 1562, Abp. Parker, whom, for his belief in the Sacraments, his adversaries called "Lutheran, or Semi-Papist," was, both from his character and position, chief in authority and influence. There needs, then, no further explanation of the difference of the two sets of Articles, than the difference of belief in the leading minds of the two periods.

. Even apart from this, since it needed but an unprejudiced study of any of the Schoolmen, to understand what they meant by the "opus operatum," it is an historical paradox to attribute the change to an obscure national Council in Poland [p], which neither Ecclesiastical historians nor collectors of Councils have thought worthy of notice [q]. Synods, as well as Diets, had been often held at Piotrkow, or Petrikow, just as Parliaments and Convocations met simultaneously at Westminster.

[p] Referred to by Mr. Jenkins, p. 4. See further, App. ii. at the end.

[q] No Synod of Petricow is found in the latest edition of Councils by Colet, or in the supplements of Mansi. No mention is made of it in Raynald, or Natalis Alexander, or Du Pin, or Spondanus, or the continuation of Fleuri. Even Neugebauer, writing a history of Poland, only mentions what I have stated below.

But the chief Synods had been those of Gnesna. Poland was, at this time, full of Religious division. The great nobles were, over and above, at variance with the Bishops about jurisdiction in cases of heresy. The Clergy were, in numbers, very inadequate to the needs of the people. In 1542, the Archbishop of Gnesna had decided to convene a Synod[r], to consider how the state of the Church might be amended, and the new opinions checked. Councils were held at Petrikow in 1551, 1552, and 1553; but none of them were of any account[s].

Even a National Council of eminence could have had no weight then, beyond the boundaries of Poland. For the Council of Trent was now sitting, representing (although unequally) the different national Churches of the Roman Communion. Had a national Council in the Roman Communion, at that time, decreed any thing on any matter of doc-

---

[r] Raynald, 1542. § 48.

[s] That of 1551 confirmed the excommunication of Okski a Canon of Premislau, who had married contrary to his vow; added a new oath to that taken by the Bishops, and levied money from the Ecclesiastics, for the suppression of heresy. The struggle about jurisdiction was continued in the Diet of 1552, where the Bishops were present. (Neugebauer Hist. rer. Pol. L. 8.) The Summary in the "Universal-Lexicon" exhibits these Councils, as of less weight than others, before and after. "In 1412, the Polish Prelates held a Council there, in which they decided to collect in one volume all the ordinances of the old Synods at Gnesna, which collection was confirmed by Martin V. The acts of those held at Petrikow in 1539, 40, and 42 are extant. In 1551, 52, 53, Synods were also held there, and again in 1578. In 1621, there was a celebrated Synod held there, whose Ordinances Gregory XV. approved; and in 1628 a Provincial Assembly." (Sub v. T. 27. ed. fol.)

trine, its authority, if it had been confirmed by the Council of Trent, would have been merged in that of the larger Council; if unconfirmed, it would have been of no account whatever.

In 1555, Paul IV. wrote to the Archbishop of Gnesna, disapproving of any attempt on the part of the National Church to decide on doctrine[t].

"We could in no wise approve of what had been proposed, that a Council of the Bishops of your nation should be held to settle controversies as to faith and religion. For neither the laws of our forefathers, nor the principles of right and the decrees of the sacred Canons, allow that any matter of the Catholic faith and religion should be discussed or enacted in any Provincial or National Councils. For these things must be handled in Œcumenical or General Councils, in order that what appertains to all may be approved by all."

Paul IV. must have been speaking of later practice. For all the early heresies, except that of Nestorius, were first condemned in Provincial Councils. His statement, however, shews how little the decision of a natural Council would have been regarded, at that time, as the decision of the Church.

It is strange, in a discussion on the meaning of the English Articles, to have to turn aside to a Polish Synod, which, probably, has never until now, been noticed by any English writer. But since it has been put forward, as an element in the exposition of our English Articles, and in justification of the decision at Bath, it seemed necessary to say how little entitled it was to any such claim.

<hr>

[t] Raynald, A. 1555. § 61.

The revisers of the Articles in 1562, omitted·no doubt the condemnation of the term "opus operatum," because (although the prejudice against the term. yet continued) the leading minds among them knew that it had been wrongly censured. The revisers, omitting the term, condemned the error, which was intended to be condemned under·it,—an error, not of the Schoolmen, but of human nature, whether unregenerate or depraved.

The xxvth Article, "of the Sacraments," condemns this error, as to the Sacraments generally;

"In such only as worthily receive the same, they have a wholesome effect and operation; but they that receive them unworthily, purchase to themselves damnation, as S. Paul saith."

Although expressed thus generally in the plural, probably the one Sacrament of the Lord's Supper is intended. For the Article had just spoken of this Sacrament, although equally using the plural;

"The Sacraments were not ordained of Christ to be gazed upon, or to be carried about, but that we should duly use them;"

and St. Paul's words belong to the Holy Eucharist only.

The xxviiith Article having stated· the beneficial effects of the Holy Eucharist to "such as rightly, worthily, and with faith, receive the same," the xxixth rejects this same error, in special and distinct reference to the Holy Eucharist; nor can it, by any honest interpretation of the words, be made to oppose any thing beyond that error.

The body of the Article states that

" The wicked and such as be void of a lively faith, although they do carnally and visibly press with their teeth, as S. Augustine saith, the Sacrament of the Body and Blood of Christ, yet in no wise are they *partakers of Christ."*

The heading is,

" Of the wicked, which *eat not the Body of Christ* in the use of the Lord's Supper."

Both these phrases, " to be partakers of Christ," and to " eat the Body of Christ," are phrases of Holy Scripture. In Articles so based on Holy Scripture, and impregnated with its language, as our's are, we are especially bound to take their Scriptural language, in what is confessedly its Scriptural meaning. Now, apart from people's prejudices as to this Article, no one, however strong his bias, can differ as to the words " partakers of Christ," as they occur in Holy Scripture. And whether or no, any interpret our Lord's words in St. John, " eateth My Flesh, &c.," of the Holy Eucharist, he can interpret them, as they stand there, in no other sense, than, " eateth " in such a way, that a man should thereby " dwell in Christ, and Christ in him."

The words " partakers of Christ," occur in S. Paul's Epistle to the Hebrews, " [u] We are made *partakers of Christ,* if we hold the beginning of our confidence, stedfast unto the end." The same word is used of our relation to " God the Holy Ghost," soon afterwards in the same Epistle ; " and [v] were made partakers of the Holy Ghost."

No explanation can make the words " partakers of " plainer than they are. Nor can there be any

[u] iii. 14.　　　　　[v] vi. 4.

disagreement about their meaning. No one, of whatever school he may be, can assign a different primary meaning to them. "To be partaker of the Holy Ghost," is to have a share of *Him* Who is "the Gift of God," shed abroad in the hearts of all those who are Christ's. To be "partakers of Christ" is to have a share of *Him* Who dwells in the hearts of all those who are His, by the Spirit; as He has said, "We will come unto him, and make our abode in him." "What is this," says S. Chrysostome[w], "'we have been made partakers of Christ?' We partake of Him, He saith; He and we have become one;-inasmuch as He is the Head, we, the body; fellow-heirs, and concorporate. 'We are one body,' He saith, 'of His Flesh and of His bones.'" Let people paraphrase the full deep words, "partakers of Christ," how they will, and best can, in order to express, on different sides and aspects, the fulness and depth of that union with Christ, which is beyond expression or thought, there can be but one central meaning. It is, to "partake of Christ Himself."

These words of Holy Scripture the Article has retained. It does not say, that the wicked "cannot be partakers *of the Body and Blood of Christ.*" It says "are in no wise *partakers of Christ.*" Plainly, the wicked and such as be void of a lively faith, so long as they remain such, are not, and cannot be, "partakers of Christ." Rather, Holy Scripture says, "they are the enemies of the Cross of Christ;" they reject Christ; they "crucify the Son of God afresh,

---

[w] Ad loc. Hom. vi. § 2. T. xii. p. 64.

and put Him to an open shame." No Christian may doubt, that the wicked, while they are such, cannot be " partakers of Christ." But they themselves often think that they can be, and that they are. So there may be too much occasion, at all times, to lay down, that they cannot, and to warn them that it is useless to draw nigh with the body, or " carnally and visibly to press with their teeth the Sacrament of the Body and Blood of Christ." They cannot be " partakers of Christ."

I have remarked already[x], that, in the pacifications between the Zwinglians and Luther, even the Zwinglians were satisfied with this explanation that Luther " denied not that *our Lord Jesus Christ* (when in the assembly of the Church, the holy Supper is duly celebrated and distributed according to His institution), is only truly apprehended, participated, and perceived by a faithful mind."

The Church of England has practically accepted the sensible " declaration " affixed to the Articles, that " no man shall put his own sense or comment to be the meaning of the Article, but shall take it in its literal and grammatical sense." Much more must this be a duty in a judicial question. Whatever lies beyond the " literal, grammatical sense " of any Article, may not be obtruded by any of us upon the Article, or upon one another, as the meaning of that Article. Now no one can draw the words, " partakers of Christ," to any other meaning, than that which they have in Holy Scripture. No person, whatever his opinion may be as to the Holy Eucha-

---

[x] See above, p. 95.

rist, can force any meaning into these words, which will not be accepted by those, who believe that the wicked receive, to their own condemnation, that Body of the Lord which they do not discern.

This then would be sufficient as to the Article. For, plainly, no heading or table of contents, can make the body of a document mean what cannot be forced into the language of that document. The heading of an Article, of a Canon, of an Act of Parliament may, in any doubtful case, interpret the meaning of an expression, or a whole clause, in such Article, Canon, or Act. It may not lawfully be employed to introduce into the main substance of the Article, or Canon, or Act, a meaning which the grammatical structure of the words of such Article, Canon, or Act, refuses to admit.

Nor can the heading of the Article stand *per se*, as a substantive proposition, apart and distinct from the meaning of the body of the Article. For this would be to make the heading of the Article, a 40th Article; which no one would allow to be right.

Yet it is probable that the heading and the Article have one and the same meaning. Since then the meaning, attached by some to the heading, cannot be forced into the Article, it is obvious to think, whether the heading and the Article are not to be brought into harmony, by taking the heading in the only sense of which the Article admits. And this will result, if we take the two Scriptural phrases in their Scriptural sense.

There can be no question, that the phrase " eat not the Body of Christ," is taken from the 6th Chapter of St. John ; nor that, in that Chapter, it is always used of such eating, whereby a man dwelleth in Christ, and Christ in him; whereby he shall live for ever; whereby he hath eternal life, and liveth by Christ, as Christ liveth by the Father. To transcribe the places, once more[y]. "This is the Bread which cometh down from Heaven, that a man may eat thereof and not die." "I am the living Bread which came down from heaven." "If any man eat of this Bread, he shall live for ever; and the Bread which I will give is My Flesh which I will give for the life of the world." . . . "Verily, verily, I say unto you, Except ye eat the Flesh of the Son of Man, and drink His Blood, ye have no life in you." "Whoso eateth My Flesh, and drink-eth My Blood, hath eternal life." . . . . "He that eateth My Flesh, and drinketh My Blood, dwelleth in Me, and I in him. As the living Father hath sent Me, and I live by the Father: so he that eateth Me, even he shall live by Me." "He that eateth of this Bread shall live for ever."

So then the words, to "eat the Body of Christ and to drink His Blood," understood, as our Lord spake them, is, *so* to eat them as to dwell in Christ. But this is the same as to be "partakers of Christ." So then, understood in the only sense which the two phrases have in Holy Scripture, the body of the Article denies, that "the wicked, though they do carnally and visibly press with their teeth the Sacrament of the Body and Blood of Christ," are "partakers of Christ;" the heading denies, in the Scriptural sense of the words, that they so eat the Body

[y] S. John vi. 50, 51. 53, 54. 56-58. See Letter to Bp. of London, p. 61.

of Christ, as to dwell in Christ." He who does not *so* eat the Flesh of Christ and drink His Blood, that he should dwell in Christ and Christ in him, does not eat or drink them at all, *for any purpose or effect for which Christ gave them.* And so God, in Holy Scripture, frequently speaks of that which is not done according to His will, as if it had not been done at all. Thus, He says that " Israel sacrificed to devils, *not to God*[z]," and denies that, during the forty years in the wilderness, they sacrificed to Him [a], while yet the fact that the live coals were on the altar [b], shews, that sacrifices were actually offered. But since they sacrificed to devils also, He regarded them as no sacrifices at all. It is even a familiar phrase among ourselves, that a person "to all intents and purposes" did not do a thing, if he did not do it, so as to gain the end designed by it. If then, we take the two Scriptural phrases each in the sense of Holy Scripture, they mean precisely the same thing; but they only state, in different terms, that the wicked are not "partakers of Christ," that they do not, in the true intent of the words, " eat His Flesh and drink His Blood." They do not touch the question, what the wicked do receive, in the Lord's Supper, to their condemnation.

At this result as to the meaning of the Article, I arrived many years ago, from the consideration of the Article itself, at a time when I was under no personal bias. For the controversy on this subject had not begun, and I myself had arrived at no

[z] Deut. xxxii. 17. [a] Am. v. 25, 6. Acts vii. 42, 3.
[b] Num. xvi. 46.

definite conclusion as to what the wicked received, but, deferring to the apparent meaning of S. Augustine, and feeling the difficulty of the subject, I left it as a mystery[c].

Such would be the result of taking the words in the sense which they have in Holy Scripture, in which sense also alone are they in harmony with one another. But now, over and above, we know that the framer of the Article meant to express no more. It appears from a letter of Abp. Parker to Lord Burleigh, that Lord Burleigh had raised a question as to the meaning of the passage of S. Augustine, quoted in the Article. Abp. Parker's answer

---

[c] I expressed this in my "Letter to the Bishop of London," 1851, p. 58-62, ed. 8vo. Mr. Goode says of me, "The doctrine of Dr P. is precisely the same as that of Archdeacon Denison. He has, indeed, *cautiously abstained* from following it out to the conclusion so boldly advanced by both the Archdeacons, in open defiance of the 29th Article, namely, that the 'wicked eat and drink the Body and Blood of Christ in the Lord's Supper as well as the faithful;' but he has distinctly maintained, that, by consecration, that effect is produced upon the Bread and Wine, from which this conclusion clearly follows." (Nature of Christ's Presence p. 20, 1.) Certainly, it does follow from the doctrine of the Real, objective, Presence, that, *unless Almighty God interfere*, the wicked would receive Sacramentally the Body and Blood of Christ, although they cannot receive Christ to dwell in their souls, or be "partakers of Christ." But this was the very point on which I did not venture to decide. Mr. Palmer, on whose statement I was commenting, assumed that God *did* interfere, and that that Sacred Presence was withdrawn. I did not venture to do this, and left it (as I said) as a mystery, *what* the wicked received to their condemnation. I hope that Mr. Goode, when he says that I "*cautiously abstained* from following out the doctrine to this conclusion," meant that I was "cautious in making up my mind," not "cautious" as to expressing what I believe.

is still preserved in his own letter. "[d] Sir, I have considered what your honour said to me this morning concerning S. Augustine's authority in the Article, in the first original agreed upon, and I am still advisedly in mine opinion, *concerning so much wherefore they be alleged in the Article.*"

But the very expression of the Archbishop implies, that the words might have been alleged for more. No one, in writing English, would say of certain words, " concerning *so much*, wherefore they be alleged in the Article," unless there were something more, for which they could bave been alleged, and were not. Now there are only two points, for which the words *could* be alleged. 1) The denial that the wicked *partake of the Body and Blood of Christ.* 2) The denial that they are *partakers of Christ.* That, for which S. Augustine's authority is alleged in the Article, does, in the grammatical and idiomatic and Scriptural meaning of the words, stop short of a further point. And Abp. Parker, by saying, that he alleged that authority, only " for so much," says in fact, that he did stop short of alleging it for more. So then, we have clearly Abp. Parker's own authority, for taking the words " are not partakers of Christ," in their natural and Scriptural sense, and not stretching them to any other meaning, which lies beyond, and which, if intended to be conveyed, ought, of course, to have been conveyed in plain, definite English. And in this his judgment as to S. Augustine, I doubt not that Abp. Parker was

[d] Strype's life of Parker, p. 332. Parker's Correspondence, p. 318. P. S. quoted by Mr. Goode, p. 663.

right; and that, learned as he was, he saw that S. Augustine denied *so much* only, that the wicked are "partakers of Christ." For S. Augustine himself does often unmistakeably assert, that the wicked *do* eat the Body and Blood of Christ; that they eat the very same as the good. Nor can it be said rightly, that S. Augustine changed his belief in this respect, in his later years. For his assertions that the wicked receive the Body and Blood of Christ, occur up and down his works, at different dates; and not only so, but in the very treatises in which S. Augustine is thought to deny, that the wicked receive the Body and Blood of Christ, there occur also other passages in which he explicitly asserts that they do receive It.

We are told [e];

"It is known to almost every one, that very many of the earlier views of S. Augustine were altered in his later years, and that to his candour in admitting previous errors, we owe his 'Retractations,' one of the most valuable of his works. The argument of Mr. Grueber, from the other writings of S. Augustine, has therefore the less weight from the known modifications which the doctrine of that Father underwent."

The argument from S. Augustine's Retractations tells exactly the opposite way. A single glance at any chapter of that book, will shew to any one, how very minute the alterations are, which S. Augustine made in his books. It matters not, how slight the things were, in which he came to think, that an argument which he had used from Holy Scripture

[c] Mr. Jenkin's Strictures, p. 15.

was not valid, or that he had employed an incorrect expression, or had made a wrong assertion, or had explained Scripture wrongly, or had been misled by not referring to the Greek text; whatever of this sort he discovered, he corrected in his Retractations. He even notes down, when he supposes that he might be misunderstood, even although his own meaning was right[f]. Now it is utterly incon-

[f] Thus, Retract. ii. 12, he mentions that he had been misled by his MSS. of the Gospels to set " two " for " twelve disciples," S. Matthew xx. 17; in c. 14, that he had used " animas," " souls," for the Angels who fell, whereas he should have said " spirits;" c. 16, that he had said, " from Abraham began the race of the Hebrews, whereas it was truer to say that the name came from Eber; he had also confused Nathan, the son of David, with Nathan, the prophet;" c. 17, he had interpreted " malum " as a neuter, " put away *evil* from among you," whereas it appeared from the Greek, that it was " the evil man." So also c. 24, he had quoted Gal. iii. 19, " of the seed, to whom the promise was made ; *which* (*quod*, viz. " the seèd") was ordained, &c.," whereas he found that in the Greek and better MSS. it was *(quæ)* and to be understood of the law. There he explains, too, that his words " Adam, by sin, lost the image of God, after which he was made," " are not so to be taken, as if no image at all remained in him, but that it was so deformed that it needed to be reformed." c. 18, that he ought not to have cited the dying thief, as an instance that " suffering might supply the place of Baptism, since he *might* have been baptized." c. 22. he corrects his saying, " out of this obedience, father Abraham, who was not without a wife, prepared to be without an only son, and him, too, slain by himself;" " for, according to the Epistle to the Hebrews, we must rather believe that he believed, that if his son should be slain, he would be presently brought to life again, and so restored to him."

The graver alterations in this 2nd book, which reviews the works which he wrote as Bishop, are that, c. 1, he understands Rom. vii. 8, of the " spiritual man under grace," not of the unregenerate " under the law;" and that, c. 18, on the books of Bap-

ceivable, that, if his belief as to the reception of the Body and Blood of Christ by the wicked had changed, he, who so carefully corrected the slightest errors, which do not affect doctrine, would not have corrected this, which bears upon important doctrine, and the awful condition of impenitent Communicants.

S. Augustine, in his Retractations, reviews books of his own, in which he had asserted that the wicked received the Body of Christ. He either found nothing in them to correct, or corrected some slight thing; but he makes no mention of any change in his belief as to the reception of the Body and Blood of Christ by the wicked. No one can read his conscientious preface to the Retractations, and then glance ever so cursorily over the sort of changes which he *does* make, in reviewing his books, and not be absolutely certain, that if S. Augustine had changed his belief as to that which the wicked receive, he would have stated it. Indeed, no one change in this 2nd Book of Retractations relates to any matter of belief. S. Augustine, when he became Bishop, was too well instructed in the doctrine of the Church, to require any such change. Whatever, then, be the solution of these apparent

tism against the Donatists, he says that the words, " The Church, not having spot or wrinkle, is not to be understood as though it now were so, but because it is being prepared to be so, when it shall appear in glory."

The account of these changes must set vividly before the eyes, how certain it is, that had S. Augustine changed his belief as to the reception of the Body and Blood of Christ by the wicked, he must have mentioned it.

contradictions in S. Augustine, it certainly is *not*, that S. Augustine changed his belief.

Yet S. Augustine's statements that the wicked do receive the Body of Christ, are very distinct. I will take only such as are quite explicit.

"[g] The Lord Himself endureth Judas, a devil, a thief, and His betrayer: He allows him to receive, among the innocent disciples, What the faithful know to be our Ransom."

"[h] The rich upon earth, in this place, (Ps. xxii. 29) are to be understood as the proud. For it is not in vain that they have been so distinguished, that it should be said above, concerning the poor, 'The poor shall eat and be satisfied;' but in this place, 'All such as be rich upon earth have eaten and worshipped.' For they, too, have been brought to the Table of Christ, and receive of His Body and Blood: but they worship only; they are not satisfied, because they do not imitate. For eating Him, Who is poor, they disdain to be poor; since ' Christ suffered for us, leaving us an example that we should follow His steps.' "

"[i] But what is to be done with them, if they fear to take out their [Heathenish] earrings, and fear not, with the mark of the devil, to receive the Body of Christ ?"

"[k] Ye remember of *What* it is written, ' Whoso shall eat the bread or drink the cup of the Lord unworthily, shall be guilty of the Body and Blood of the Lord?' " And when the Apostle said this, the discourse was upon the subject of those who treating the Lord's Body like any other food, took it in an undiscriminating and negligent way. If, then, this man is rebuked, who does not discriminate, that is, see the difference of the Lord's Body

[g] Ep. 43. ad Glor. Eleus. § 23. See Real Presence, p. 503, add 510, 515, 524, 538.   [h] Ep. 140. ad Honorat. § 66. Ib. 507.
[i] Ep. ad Poss. 24. § 2. Ib. 508.   [k] Hom. lxii. in S. John. Ib. 516.

from other meats, how must he be damned, who, feigning himself a friend, comes to His Table a foe ! "

" [l] It was not *then*, as some think, who read negligently, that Judas received Christ's Body. For it is to be understood that the Lord had already distributed the Sacrament of His Body and Blood to them all, among whom was Judas also, as St. Luke most evidently relates the matter."

" [m] Those sacrifices, then, as being but expressions of a promise, have been abrogated. What is that which has been given as its fulfilment ? That *Body*, which ye know ; which ye do not all of you know ; which, of you who do know it, I pray God none may know it unto condemnation."

" [n] The signs that convey the promise are done away, because the substance that was promised is come. We are in this Body. We are partakers of this Body. We know That which we ourselves receive ; and ye who know not yet, will know It by and by ; and when ye come to know It, I pray ye may not receive It unto condemnation. 'For he that eateth and drinketh unworthily, eateth and drinketh damnation unto himself.' 'A Body' hath been 'perfected' for us ; let us be made perfect in the Body."

" [o] They are, then, great Sacraments, yea, very great. Would ye know how their greatness is set forth ? The Apostle saith, 'Whoso eateth the Body of Christ, or drinketh the Cup of the Lord unworthily shall be guilty of the Body and Blood of the Lord.' What is to 'receive unworthily ?' To receive disdainfully, to receive with contempt."

" [p] Let them who already eat the Flesh of the Lord and drink His Blood, think *what* it is they eat and drink, lest, as the Apostle says, 'They eat and drink judgment to themselves.'"

" [q] Let such a sentence issue from the mind itself, that

<hr>

[l] Ib. § 3. Ib.   [m] In Ps. xl. n. 12. Ib. p. 520.   [n] Ib.
   [o] Serm. 227 in d. Pasch. iv. p. 974. See the beginning of the Sermon in Real Pres. p. 528.
   [p] Serm. 82. [132] § 1. Ib. 527.   [q] Serm. 351 § 7. Ib. 531.

a person judge himself unworthy to partake of the Body
and Blood of the Lord, so that he who dreads lest, by the
final sentence of the Supreme Judge, he be severed from
the Kingdom of Heaven, be, by the ecclesiastical discipline,
severed for the time from the Sacrament of the heavenly
Bread."

" [r] As Judas, to whom our Lord offered the sop, not by
receiving what was evil, but by receiving evilly, made room
in himself for the devil, so any one who unworthily receives
the Sacrament of the Lord, does not, because he is evil
himself, cause it to be evil; nor, because he receives not
unto salvation, has he received nothing. For that was
no less the Body and Blood of the Lord, to those also, to
whom the Apostle said, 'He that eateth and drinketh unworthily, eateth and drinketh damnation to himself.' "

" [s] What of the very Body and Blood of Christ, the only
Sacrifice for our salvation, although the Lord Himself saith,
'Except a man eat My Flesh and drink My Blood, he
shall have no life in him;' doth not the same Apostle teach us,
that this too becomes harmful to those who use It ill? For
he says, 'Whosoever shall eat this Bread or drink this Cup
of the Lord unworthily, shall be guilty of the Body and
Blood of the Lord,' "

" [t] He had said, 'Bind him hand and foot, and cast him
into outer darkness; there shall be weeping and gnashing
of teeth.' He immediately added, 'For many are called,
but few chosen.' How is this true, since rather one out
of many was cast into outer darkness, unless in that one
was prefigured the vast body of all wicked men, who before
the judgment of the Lord shall be mingled together at
the Feast of the Lord? From whom the good, meanwhile,
separate themselves in heart and life, while together with
them, they eat and drink the Body and Blood of Christ,
but with a great distinction. For *these*, in honour of the

---

[r] De Bapt. c. Donat. v. c. 8. Ib. p. 537. add c. lit. Petil. § 110. Ib.
[s] c. Cresc. i. § 30. Ib. 538. add ad Don. post Coll. c. 7. lb. 539.
[t] Ad Don. p. Coll. c. 27. Ib. 539.

Bridegroom, are clad in the wedding garment, ' seeking not their own, but the things which are of Jesus Christ;' but *those* have not the wedding garment, that is, a most faithful love of the Bridegroom, since they seek their own, not the things which are of Jesus Christ. And hereby, although at one and the same feast, these eat mercy, those judgment : for the Psalm of the feast itself is, as also I have said above, ' I will sing to Thee of mercy and judgment, O Lord.' "

Now, to put together in brief, what S. Augustine teaches in these his many works, he tells us explicitly that Judas " received Christ's Body," received " what the faithful know to be our Ransom ; " that people, " with the mark of the devil, receive the Body of Christ; " " the proud rich receive of His Body and Blood," " eat Him Who is poor ; " that " good and bad together eat and drink the Body and Blood of Christ; " that *they* too receive It, "who treat the Lord's Body like any other food," " do not see any difference between It and any other meat," who come to the Lord's table in hypocrisy; that " the very Body and Blood of Christ, the only Sacrifice for our Salvation, become harmful to those who use it ill," i. e. " who eat this Bread, and drink this Cup of the Lord unworthily ; " that " men receive It to their own condemnation; " " eat and drink judgment to themselves, when they eat this Flesh, and drink this Blood ; " that " It is no less His Body and Blood to those who eat and drink unworthily."

Nay, so persuaded was S. Augustine that the wicked do eat the Body and Blood of Christ, that (as has been observed [u]) he quotes S. Paul's words in the

---

[u] Mr. Grueber, " Summary of the Formularies of the Church of England," p. 32, marg.

way of paraphrase [v], " Whoso eateth *the Body of Christ.*"

One, moreover, of these passages is taken from the very same homilies on St. John, as the passage quoted in the Article. The Books against the Donatists, in which others occur, were written, some when he was about forty-six; others, at fifty-two, or fifty-eight. At that mature period of life, no one, probably, will suppose that S. Augustine changed his belief. But, in truth, there is no ground to suppose that S. Augustine contradicts himself. He explains himself. He distinguishes two ways of "receiving the Body and Blood of Christ," accordingly as the communicant does, or does not, "dwell in Christ and Christ in him." He lays down distinctly, that to "eat Christ" is "[w] not *only* to receive His Body in the Sacrament; for many unworthy receive." And he says also, positively, "[x] that there is *a certain manner* of eating that Flesh and drinking that Blood in which whosoever eateth and drinketh, dwelleth in Christ, and Christ in him;" that "*he* doth not dwell in 'Christ and Christ in him,' who eateth the Flesh and drinketh the Blood of Christ *in any manner whatsoever*, but *only in some certain manner.*" The very point too which S. Augustine is illustrating in this last place, makes his meaning the more clear. He is explaining a difficulty, that St. Mark hath the words, " Whoso blasphemeth against the Holy Ghost, shall never be forgiven." Whence some argued, that any blas-

[v] See ab. p. 263.   [w] In Mai Bibl. Nov. Patr. T. i. S. 129. see Doctr. of Real Pres. p. 542.

[x] Serm. 71. [21] n. 17. p. 178. O. T. in Real Pres. p. 524, 5.

phemy whatsoever against God the Holy Ghost, is the unpardonable sin. S. Augustine answers; that Holy Scripture sometimes speaks absolutely, what yet must be understood in a qualified sense. Thus, 1) "God doth not tempt any one," we must understand he says, "so as to lead him into sin." For God "did tempt Abraham" in the way of trying his faith. 2) Our Lord says, "Whoso believeth and is baptized shall be saved." "Yet we do not understand, one who believes in such wise, as 'the devils believe and tremble;'" nor those baptized, such as Simon; but those who have that "faith which worketh by love." 3) Our Lord saith "Whoso eateth My Flesh and drinketh My Blood, dwelleth in Me and I in him." Plainly, He says, not one who eateth and drinketh that Body and Blood any how; for some eat and drink It to their condemnation. His whole argument requires, what He repeatedly states in the course of it, that we should believe that such *do* eat His Body and Blood, but not in that way to which our Lord promised His blessing.

"ʸ Those words of His, 'He that eateth My Flesh, and drinketh My Blood, dwelleth in Me, and I in him,' how must we understand? Can we conclude in these words those too, of whom the Apostle says, 'that they eat and drink judgment to themselves,' when they eat that very Flesh and drink that very Blood? What! did Judas the impious seller and betrayer of his Master (though as Luke the Evangelist declares more plainly, he ate and drank with the rest of His disciples this first Sacrament of His Body and Blood, consecrated by the Lord's hands), did he 'dwell in Christ and Christ in him?' Do so many, in fine, who either in hypocrisy eat that Flesh and drink that Blood, or who, after they have eaten and drunk, become apostate, do they 'dwell in Christ or Christ in them?' Yet assuredly there is *a certain manner of* eating that Flesh and drinking that Blood, in which whosoever eateth and drinketh, 'he dwelleth in Christ and Christ in him.' As then he doth not 'dwell in Christ and Christ in him,' who 'eateth the Flesh and drinketh the Blood of Christ' in any manner whatsoever, but only in some certain manner, to which He doubtless had regard when He spake these words; so also," [he applies the illustration as he had the rest] "in that too which He said, 'Whoso blasphemeth against the Holy Ghost hath never forgiveness,' He doth not mean, 'Whoso shall blaspheme in any way whatever, is guilty of this unpardonable sin, but whoso doth so *in a certain way*,' which He who pronounced this true and terrible sentence, willed us to enquire and understand."

The "blasphemy against the Holy Ghost," which yet does not come up to the fulness of the unpardonable sin, was still real blasphemy. The belief, wherewith the devils believed and trembled, was a real belief, although without love. The Baptism wherewith Simon Magus was baptized, was real, valid, Baptism. So too, S. Augustine's argument required, that the wicked really ate the Body and drank the Blood of Christ, although, receiving It without saving faith, or love, or obedience, they ate and drank It to their condemnation.

The other passage in which S. Augustine says, that to "eat Christ" is "not *only* to receive His Body in the Sacrament," shows how well Abp. Parker understood S. Augustine, when he adopted the words "partakers of Christ" as expressing S. Augustine's mind. He says, that they who dwell not in Christ, nor Christ in them, receive the Sacrament, and, receiving It, " receive His Body in the Sacrament," but receive It to their condemnation. They receive the Body of Christ but do not " eat Christ," because, he says, Christ does not and will not dwell in their souls. To " eat Christ " then, is, in his mind, to be " partaker of Christ."

[z] " What is to *eat Christ?* It is *not only to receive His Body in the Sacrament.* For many unworthy receive [viz. His Body in the Sacrament] for whom the Apostle saith, ' Whoso eateth the Bread and drinketh the Cup of the Lord unworthily, eateth and drinketh judgment to himself.' "

S. Augustine goes on to say, that *he* " eateth Christ who abideth in Christ; " and *he* " abideth in Christ," as Himself says, " who keeps His commandments." So, then, according to S. Augustine, *he* who communicates, being in a state of grace, " eats Christ ;" he who communicates, being unworthy, not in a state of grace, " receives His Body in the Sacrament," but therewith, eateth and drinketh judgment to himself and " getteth great torment."

It is the same distinction when he says of the eleven Apostles, in contrast with Judas, " [a] They ate the Bread, the Lord ; he, the bread of the Lord, against the Lord." He did not say [b], Judas ate the Bread, the Lord, against the Lord, because this would have expressed, that he partook of Christ Himself.

And so, in the passage quoted in the Articles. Bede, who so thoroughly studied S. Augustine, that

[z] Real Pres. p. 542.
[a] Hom. 59. in S. Joh. p. 737. O. T. Real Pres. p. 515.
[b] As Mr. Jenkins suggests that he would, p. 20.

his commentaries, to a certain extent, replace lost works of S. Augustine, filled up the words of S. Augustine according to his mind, and with words which S. Augustine had used elsewhere.

S. Augustine is arguing from the same words of Our Lord; "He that eateth My Flesh and drinketh My Blood, dwelleth in Me and I in him." "[c] This then it is to eat that meat, and drink that drink; to dwell in Christ and to have Christ dwelling in him." Such is the end of the Sacraments. Such is the fruit, the object of the Sacrament. To receive the Sacrament without this is to fail of all, for which the Sacrament was given. Since therefore, the whole object of eating the Flesh of Christ, and drinking His Blood, is union with Himself, S. Augustine goes on; "And, therefore, who dwelleth not in Christ, and in whom Christ dwelleth not, without doubt doth neither [spiritually] eat His Flesh nor drink His Blood, [albeit carnally and visibly he press with his teeth the Sacrament of the Body and Blood of Christ] but rather doth unto judgment to himself, eat and drink the Sacrament of so great a thing."

The words inserted by Bede are words which S. Augustine uses elsewhere on this very subject, and so they fill up what he says more concisely here.

"[d] It was not that the sop of the Lord was poison to Judas. And yet he received; and when he received, the enemy entered into him: not that he received an evil thing, but that he, being evil, did, in evil wise, *receive what was good.* Look to it

[c] Real Pres. p. 512.
[d] In S. John. 'Hom. 26. § 11, p. 407. Real Pr. p. 510.

then, brethren; eat ye *spiritually* the heavenly Bread, bring innocence to the Altar."

" [e] This, then, is the Bread which cometh down from Heaven, that whoso eateth thereof may not die. But this, in regard of the virtue of the Sacrament, not in regard of the visible Sacrament; of him who eateth inwardly, not outwardly; who eateth in the heart, not who presseth with his teeth."

S. Augustine, thus understood, is in harmony with himself. He believed that the wicked received the Body and Blood of Christ in the Sacrament; but that they did not, and could not, receive Christ in their hearts. "There is *a certain manner*," he said [f], " of eating that Flesh and drinking that Blood, in which whosoever eateth and drinketh, he dwelleth in Christ, and Christ in him." They, then, who did not eat the Flesh and drink that Blood *in that certain manner*, i. e. with living faith, did, in his belief, really eat that Flesh and drink that Blood, but had no fruit of the Sacrament. They did not " spiritually " eat it, because they did not eat it with their spirit, and so that Christ could dwell in their spirit.

S. Augustine, indeed, in one place, goes beyond this, and expresses his belief, that they who do not persevere to the end, have never really so received the Sacrament, that Christ ever dwelt in them, or they in Christ. So that, if he were understood to mean, that they never received the inward part of the Sacrament, this would involve, that none but those who persevered to the end, ever received any thing but the shell of the Sacrament. It is in the

[e] § 12, p. 409. Ib.   [f] Serm. 71, quoted above.

same homilies on S. John, in which he also speaks of the wicked receiving the Body and Blood of Christ.

"[g] It relates to the Body of the Lord, which He said that He giveth to be eaten for eternal life He expounded the manner of this bestowing and of His gift, how He would give men His Flesh to eat, when He said, 'He that eateth My Flesh and drinketh My Blood, dwelleth in Me, and I in him.' The sign which shews that one hath eaten and drunk is this, if he dwelleth and is dwelt in, if he inhabiteth and is inhabited, if he cleaveth that he be not abandoned. This then it is, that He hath taught and admonished us in mystical words, that we be in His Body, under Himself the Head in His members, eating His Flesh, not forsaking the Unity of Him."

S. Augustine, in thus speaking, is in fact explaining our Lord's words, what *He* meant, when He used the words, "Whoso eateth My Flesh and drinketh My Blood, dwelleth in Me, and I in Him." S. Augustine also (it must be remembered), had to do with a class of persons, of whom Cain was the first instance,—people who think that it will be well with them, if they in any way draw near to God, while their hearts are far from Him. These perverted our Lord's words, "If any man eat of this bread, he shall live for ever," and maintained that all the baptized, "who had become partakers of His Body, howsoever they may have lived, in whatever heresy and impiety, must, of necessity," by virtue of that promise of Christ, "be somehow brought to life eternal." Another class confined this hope to Catholics[h]. Since this is a manifest perversion

---

[g] On vi. 57. Hom. xxvii. § 1. Real Pr. p. 513.

[h] De Civ. D. xxi. 19. 20. see in the Real Pres. p. 532.

of our Lord's words, and contradicts the whole tenour of Holy Scripture, there must be some other way of understanding those words. And this, S. Augustine says, our Lord's words themselves furnish. For He speaks of an eating and drinking, whereby a man dwelleth in Him and He in that man. And since He will not dwell in the soul, which is given up to sin, *their* eating and drinking cannot be of that sort, to which our Lord attached the promise, that those who so ate and so drank, should have eternal life.

S. Augustine then, in these places, is not contradicting what he so often says, that the wicked do receive the Body and Blood of Christ in the Sacrament. He is meeting an actual evil, such as has always existed and always will exist, that men think that they may be saved by Christ, without obeying Him or loving Him. He cuts at the root of their delusion, by shewing that they had not "the reality of the Sacrament;" viz. Christ Himself, dwelling in the souls of those, who, in the Sacrament of His Body and Blood, with living faith, eat His Flesh and drink His Blood. And this he shews, by shewing them the true meaning of our Saviour's words, which they had also distorted.

This also accounts for the stress which S. Augustine lays on the very word, by which our Lord's word, ὁ τρώγων, was expressed in the Latin translation of St. John's Gospel. What S. Augustine denies of the wicked, he always expresses in the very words of St. John's Gospel[1]. He does not deny,

---

[1] Nec manducat carnem ejus, nec bibit ejus sanguinem. (in Joh. Tr. 27. § 18.) Signum, quia manducavit et bibit. (Ib. Tr. 27. § 1.)

he even affirms, that "those who eat and drink unworthily, *receive* the Body of Christ in the Sacrament." But he affirms that they do not *eat Christ*, unless they dwell in Christ, and Christ in them.

"[h] What is, to *eat Christ?* It is *not only to receive His Body* in the Sacrament. For *many unworthy receive*, of whom the Apostle saith, 'Whoso eateth the Bread and drinketh the Cup of the Lord unworthily, eateth and drinketh judgment to himself.' But how is Christ to be *eaten?* How, He Himself says: 'He that eateth My Flesh, and drinketh My Blood, abideth in Me, and I in him.' If he abideth in Me, and I in him, then he eateth, then he drinketh."

This same word of St. John's Gospel, which S. Augustine always uses, when he speaks of that mode of eating, whereby Christ dwelleth in the soul of the Communicant, is also the word which is employed

Carnem illam manducant, et sanguinem bibunt. (Serm. 71. § 11.) Est quidam modus manducandi illam carnem et bibendi illum sanguinem. [Ib.] Ipse *vere* dicendus est manducare corpus Christi et bibere sanguinem Christi. (de Civ. D. xxi. 25. 2.) Non dicendum esse eum manducare Corpus Christi. (§. 4.) Nec ergo dicendi sunt manducare carnem Christi. (§ 4.) Quid sit, non sacramento tenus, sed re vera corpus Christi manducare, ejus sanguinem bibere. (Ib.) Non se dicat aut existimet manducare corpus meum aut bibere sanguinem meum. (Ib.)

[h] " Quid est Christum *manducare?* Non hoc est solum, in Sacramento Corpus Ejus *accipere;* multi enim *accipiunt* indigni, de quibus dicit Apostolus: qui manducat panem et bibit calicem Domini indigne, judicium sibi manducat et bibit. Sed quomodo manducandus est Christus? quomodo Ipse dicit: qui manducat Carnem Meam et bibit Sanguinem Meum, in Me manet et Ego in illo. Si in Me manet, et Ego in illo, tunc *manducat*, tunc bibit." See Real Presence, p. 542. This passage is quoted by Gratian from S. Aug. (de Cons. d. ii. c. 46.)

in the heading of our Article. "ⁱImpii non *manducant*
Corpus Christi in usu cœnæ." "ᵏ De *manducatione*
Corporis Christi, et impios illud non *manducare.*"

The two sentences of Prosper, which Abp. Parker
quoted, are almost verbally S. Augustine's ; and it
illustrates Abp. Parker's meaning, that the first
which he quotes, says only what sort of men we must
be, that the Flesh of Christ may be *our life.*

"ˡThe Flesh of Christ is the life of the faithful, if they
neglect not to be His Body. Let them then become the
Body of Christ, if they wish to live from the Spirit of Christ;
from which none liveth but the Body of Christ."

This sentence of S. Prosper would absolutely
have no bearing whatever upon the 29th Article,
unless the meaning of the Article were confined to
the simple tenour of its words, " are in no wise partakers of Christ." Abp. Parker alleges that S. Augustine, " in other places, and Prosper, in his 'Sentences' wrote of S. Austin (Sent. 338, 339), doth
plainly affirm our opinion in the Article to be most
true." Now the opinion which the above sentence
of S. Prosper " doth affirm to be true," is, that " the
Flesh of Christ is *the life* of" those only who are
members of His mystical Body. Since then Abp.
Parker says, that this passage " affirms *our* opinion
in the Article to be most true," that " opinion in the
Article" can be no other than, that the Flesh of

ⁱ Heading of Art. xxix. as accepted by the Convocation of
1562. See Dr. Lamb, Articuli e. MS. cui Tit. Synodal. p. 13.

ᵏ Heading of Art. xxix. in the edition of Joh. Day, 1571, p. 11,
and retained until now.

ˡ 342. al. 340. ante, 338. p. 318.

Christ profiteth not the wicked; Christ is not their life; because "they are in no wise partakers of Christ." There is no ambiguity; no question can be raised upon it. The Article affirms nothing else of the wicked or those void of faith, than that they are not, in the Sacrament, "partakers of Christ;" the sentence of Prosper affirms only, that to those who, by sin or faithlessness, are severed from the body of Christ, to them, in the Sacrament, "the Flesh of Christ is" not "life." The two passages agree perfectly together. But the sentence of Prosper could not in any way have "affirmed the opinion" of Abp. Parker, had he had any other meaning than that expressed in the grammatical sense of the Articles. He could not, in such case, have alleged it.

The other passage of Prosper begins in the very same way [m];

"*He* receiveth the Food of life and drinketh the Cup of eternity, who abideth in Christ, and whose Indweller Christ is."

This is the condition, on which S. Augustine repeatedly insists, as being embodied in our Lord's words, that he only who dwelleth in Christ, and in whom Christ dwelleth, *really* eateth the Flesh of Christ and drinketh His Blood, as Christ gave them to be eaten and drunken. But Prosper explains S. Augustine's words, by the addition "receiveth the Food *of life* and drinketh the Cup *of eternity.*" And so he draws out S. Augustine's meaning, that *he* too is speaking of *such* reception, whereby a man hath life from Christ, and that for ever.

[m] 343, al. 341; ante, 339.

The rest of the sentence of S. Prosper is contracted from the passage of S. Augustine, which is in part cited in our Article.

"For he who is discordant from Christ, neither eateth His Flesh, nor drinketh His Blood, although he daily indiscriminately receive, to the condemnation of his own presumption, the Sacrament of so great a thing."

The passage adds nothing to that of S. Augustine, of which it is a compendium, because it is one and the same with it. But on the other hand it may be observed, that 1) the sentence which Prosper prefixed to it, is a comment upon it. For Prosper does not simply set the two statements, side by side; but he alleges the second, as the ground of the first. This he marks by the word "For." "He, *and he only*" (he must mean) "who dwelleth in Christ and whose Indweller Christ is, receiveth the Food of life, and drinketh the Cup of eternity. *For* he who is discordant from Christ, neither eateth His Flesh, nor drinketh His Blood:" plainly in the same sense as before, so that it should be "Food of life," "the Cup of eternity."

2) Gratian must have understood this passage, as only speaking of the reception of the Body and Blood of Christ, *unto life.* For he quotes it[n] together with passages in which S. Augustine asserts, that the wicked do receive the Body and Blood of Christ. Within twelve lines of this passage follows a heading, "[o]he too who receiveth unworthily, receiveth the Body of Christ." The passage, which Gratian thus headed, is the very explicit passage of S. Augustine

---

[n] De cons. d. ii. c. 65.   [o] c. 68.

against the Donatists, in which Gratian also includes these words;

"For it was, *none the less, the Body of the Lord and the Blood of the Lord to those* also, to whom the Apostle said, 'Whoso eateth and drinketh unworthily, eateth and drinketh damnation to himself.'"

Gratian has carefully digested his extracts from the Fathers, although, obviously, he could not help admitting passages which he did not know to be spurious. He could not mean to contradict himself. When then he put, as neighbouring headings,

"[p] He receiveth the Sacrament, not the verity of Christ's Body, who is discordant from Him."

"[q] He too, who receiveth unworthily, receiveth the Body of Christ;"

by the words "the verity of Christ's Body" he must have meant, "receive It not, as Christ gave It to be received, so that Christ Himself should dwell in him who receiveth it."

He too must have understood S. Augustine, as not contradicting himself, but as speaking, in the one set of passages, of receiving the Body and Blood of Christ to condemnation; in the other, of receiving them so as to receive Christ Himself, as an In-dweller.

So understood, as believing that the wicked do receive the Body and Blood of Christ, yet not spiritually, so that Christ should dwell in them, or they in Him, S. Augustine agrees with the great body of the Fathers, in the East and West.

[p] c. 65.   [q] c. 58.

Tertullian[r] speaks with indignation against the makers of idols, that they "should approach those hands to the Body of the Lord, which bestowed bodies on demons;" "receive from other's hands That which they defile;" that they should "assault His Body," "offend the Body of the Lord."

Origen[s] speaks of people, "oppressed with the disease of sins," "approaching the Eucharist to communicate of the Body of Christ, as though clean and pure, and there were nothing in them unworthy." He says that "Judas betrayed his Master the Saviour, together with the Food of the Divine Table and the Cup;" and that "such are all in the Church, who plot against their brethren, with whom they have been together frequently at the same Table of the Body of Christ and at the same draught of His Blood." On the passage itself of St. Paul he says, "Not unpersuasively might it be said on this passage, that 'he that eateth

[r] Real Pres. p. 332.

[s] See Real Pres. p. 345-7. Mr. Jenkins quotes, on the other side, a passage of Origen, which Origen prefaces by saying that he is going to apply our Lord's words of consecration *unsacramentally.* "And that which he says 'Jesus taking bread' and in like way, 'taking the Cup,' he who is a babe in Christ and who in Christ is yet carnal, *understands in the ordinary way*" [i. e. as the words sound, of the Sacrament]. "But let him who is wise enquire, from whom Jesus receiving, [doth this,] For God giving, He receiveth and giveth to them who are worthy to receive from God, bread and cup." The interpretation which follows is mystical, since Origen contrasts it with the common or literal. If Origen's words were to be applied sacramentally, they would still only contain the simple truth, that without Christ we cannot be partakers of Him. "He who said, when He took the Cup, 'drink ye all of this,' doth not depart from us when we drink, but Himself drinketh it with us, inasmuch as He is in each of us; for alone and without Him, we cannot either eat of that bread or drink of that fruit of the vine" (in Matt. Comm. Ser. § 86. T. iii. p. 899). S. Jerome imitates the passage, applying it to Sacramental Communion and participation of Christ Himself. Ep. 120. ad Hedib. See Real Pres. p. 472, 3.

the Bread of the Lord or drinketh His Cup unworthily, eateth and drinketh damnation to himself;' one and the same excellent Power in the Bread and in the Cup, inworking good in a good disposition which receives It, implanting damnation in the evil. So the sop from Jesus was of a like nature with that which was given to the rest of the Apostles with the words 'Take, eat,' but to the one for salvation; to Judas for damnation, since after the sop Satan entered into him."

Another place of *Origen,* which has been alleged in proof that he did not believe, that the wicked receive the Body and Blood of Christ, shews rather, that he made the same distinction as S. Augustine, that they *do* receive the Body and Blood, but are not "partakers of Christ" Himself. Origen says (in a passage which I have already quoted, in proof that he believed the natural substances to remain),—

"[t] not the matter of the bread, but the words spoken over it, is that which benefiteth him who eateth it not unworthily of the Lord."

To this he subjoins;

"But many things might be said concerning the Word Himself *also,* Who became Flesh and true Food, which whoso eateth shall surely live for ever, no wicked man being able to eat It. For if it were possible that one, still remaining wicked, should eat Him Who became Flesh, being the Word and the living Bread, it would not have been written, that every one who eateth this bread shall live for ever."

The word *also,* (concerning the Word Himself *also,*") shews that Origen is speaking of something

[t] Quoted in Real Pres. p. 149, by Mr. Goode, p. 365, 6.

distinct from the reception of the Body and Blood of Christ, of which He had just spoken.   He *does* go on to speak, not of the Holy Eucharist, but of Christ Himself, of whom, beyond question, the wicked cannot be "partakers."   But Origen (in that, in contrast with the Body of Christ in the Holy Eucharist, he says, that of *Christ Himself* the wicked cannot be partakers) implies here, what he elsewhere asserts, that they *can* receive His Body and Blood in the Holy Eucharist, although to their hurt[u].

[u] Mr. Goode quotes, p. **336**, in addition, 1) " No *wicked* soul can eat the holy flesh of the Word of God " (in Lev. Hom. iv. § 8. Opp. ii. 203).   This is a mistranslation; and the context is not of the Holy Eucharist, but of understanding mysteries.   The passage is an allegorical interpretation of Lev. vi. 19.   " All the males among the children of Aaron shall eat of it."   " He too touches the flesh of the Word of God, who understands its inward meaning, and can explain hidden mysteries."—" No woman, nor any remiss or relaxed [dissolute] soul can eat the holy flesh of the word of God."

2) " He who has eaten *these* first fruits [Christ] and tasted the Bread Who came down from heaven, shall not die, but abideth unto life eternal.   For He is the Bread, Who, being ever eaten, ever abideth, yea, always increaseth.   He is then, as the Apostle says, spiritual Food, which the more it is consumed, the more it increaseth.   For the more thou takest the word of God, the more earnestly thou eatest that Food, the more abundantly it will abide in you " (in Num. Hom. xi. § 6. p. 309).   Undoubtedly, such is the course of the Christian soul; the more it hungers after Christ, the more it feeds upon Him, the more it is satisfied.   But Origen is speaking of what is the course of grace; not affirming that none fall away from grace, or that no one ever perished, who ever, once in his life, fed on Christ.

3) " We ought to understand, that they who are occupied in feastings and worldly anxieties, do not ascend into that upper chamber, nor see its quietness, nor consider how it is furnished and adorned.   Wherefore neither do they celebrate the Passover

S. Cyprian[v] complains of those priests who, to such as had denied Christ and had not shown full repentance, " dared to give the Eucharist, that is, to profane the sacred Body of the Lord, though it is written, ' Whosoever shall eat this bread &c.' " He condemned those who, " fresh from the deadly infection " of apostasy, " invade the Body of the Lord," " offering violence to His Body and Blood; " and so, " sinning more against the Lord with hand and mouth, than when they were denying Him." He speaks of those " impiously wrathful against the Priests, because not permitted to take the Lord's Body in defiled hands, and drink His Blood with polluted mouth."

S. Firmilian[w] says; " How great is the sin of those who, their sins not laid aside, in communion rashly granted, touch the Body and Blood of the Lord, whereas it is written ' Whosoever shall eat &c.' "

Eusebius[x]; " Judas did not eat with Him [the Saviour] only common bread, but was permitted to eat of that which nourisheth the soul, of which the Saviour said, ' I am the Bread of life.' "

with Jesus, nor receive the bread of benediction from Him, nor the Cup of the New Testament " (Comment. Ser. in S. Matt. § 79. Opp. iii. 896). Origen's allegorical interpretation of S. Mark, xiv. 13—15, relates, again, to the understanding of mysteries. There is no reference to the Holy Eucharist. If there were, the words would mean, that those " occupied in feastings and worldly cares " would not come to the Holy Eucharist at all. Nor is it again a question as to the wicked.

4.) " He who is still instructed [παιδευόμενο, Mr. G. renders " nourished "] by that bread, may reasonably suffer death; but he who cometh to the Bread after it, and eateth It, shall live for ever " [in Joann. T. vi. § 26. Opp. iv. 145]. Again, there is no mention of the Holy Eucharist; nor can it be supposed that Origen meant, that one who *once* came to Christ, necessarily persevered to the end. The passage relates, in any case, to those who are " partakers of Christ Himself," which no one supposes the wicked to be.

[v] R. P. 355, 8, 9.   [w] Ib. p. 348.   [x] Ib. p. 367, 8.

S. James of Nisibis exhorts; "[y] Abstain thou from all uncleanness, and then receive the Body and Blood of Christ, and carefully guard thy mouth through which the King hath entered; nor mayest thou, O man, any more bring forth through thy mouth words of uncleanness. Attend to what the Lord, our Life, hath said, 'that which entereth into a man &c.'"

S. Athanasius exhorts; "[z] See that thou give not to the unworthy the purple of the sinless Body."

S. Hilary says; [a] "In this our bodily life, our soul is to be

[y] p. 370. [z] Ib. p. 376.

[a] Ib. p. 398, Mr. Jenkins (p. 29) quotes, on the other side, a passage in which S. Hilary is speaking of Judas quitting before the Communion. "After which, Judas the traitor is made manifest; without whom the Passover is celebrated, the cup being drunken and the bread broken. For he was not worthy of the communion of the everlasting Sacraments. For, that he departed at once, appears from his returning with the multitudes. Nor could he in truth drink *with Him*, who was not about to drink in Heaven" (in S. Matt. c. 30). The emphasis, in S. Hilary, is on the drinking It *with our Lord* Himself, Who had promised to drink It new *with them* in His Father's kingdom. It is a moral unfitness of which S. Hilary speaks, not a physical impossibility. S. Hilary moreover is speaking of the reception of the *Sacrament*, which Mr Jenkins also would allow, that all, bad as well as good, might receive. Mr. Jenkins comments, "In the very early controversy, whether Judas was present at the institution of the Supper, there appear many traces of the same doctrine. The unworthiness of the false disciple was held by those who denied that he was then present, to preclude the possibility of his reception of it [the Supper], the reality of the Presence being always, in their apprehension, to life." I know not that any early writer supposes Judas to have gone out before the institution of the Holy Eucharist, except S. Hilary, and the author of the Constitutions, v. 14. For Pseudo-Dionysius, who has been so interpreted (de Eccl. Hier. iii. 3. 1), manifestly says the contrary. St. Luke (xxii. 14-21) so very plainly declares that he was present. But no one could argue that Judas could not have been present, because he was finally lost, unless he believed that all communicants were saved.

nourished, obtaining the Living Bread, the Heavenly Bread from Him who said, ' I am the living Bread from Heaven,' which, according to the Apostle's law, whoso receiveth unworthily, bringeth judgment on himself."

Hilary the Deacon, commenting on 1 Cor. xi. 30, " [b] That he may prove it to be true, that there will be a trial of those who *receive the Body of the Lord*, he already shews here the semblance of judgment upon them who had received *carelessly the Body of the Lord*—that the rest might amend, knowing that the negligent *reception of the Body* of the Lord is not unavenged."

S. Pacian, of those who came impenitent to communion; " [c] Doth he escape, who violates the Body of the Lord ? "

S. Ephrem; " The[d] righteous, with sinners, fill themselves with the Living Body which is on the Altar."

S. Basil asks, " [e] Is it safe for a man who purifieth not himself 'from all defilement of flesh and spirit,' to eat the Body of the Lord, and to drink His Blood ?" He answers, " By how much there is here, That which is ' greater than the temple,' according to the Lord's words, by so much the

Mr. Goode (p. 370) alleges the passage, of S. Hilary, so often quoted by Melanchthon of the benefits of the Holy Eucharist; " These [the Body and Blood of Christ] received and drunken, cause that both we are in Christ, and Christ in us " (quoted Real Presence, p. 395). Mr. Goode subjoins; ' This certainly cannot be said of the wicked, and therefore according to this, they do not receive our Lord's Flesh and Blood." This begs the whole question. S. Hilary, following our Lord Himself, says that through the Holy Eucharist, Christ comes to dwell in us [i. e. in the faithful] and we in Him. He does not allude to the wicked. The prayer of the wicked is " turned into sin." They do then pray. Yet if Mr. Goode's argument were valid, it might equally be inferred from the words " Thou that hearest prayer," " this cannot be said of the prayer of the wicked; and therefore, according to this, they do not pray." The prayer of the wicked, and the communion of the wicked, being both contrary to the will of God, bring evil instead of good.

[b] p. 401.　　　[c] p. 411.　　　[d] p. 414.　　　[e] p. 429.

more dreadful and fearful is it, in defilement of soul, to dare to touch the Body of Christ, than to touch rams or bulls, as the Apostle says, 'Whosoever shall eat this Bread, or drink this Cup of the Lord unworthily, shall be guilty of the Body and Blood of the Lord.'"

S. Gregory of Nyssa, exhorts "'when we receive that gift of the Body, not to receive it in defiled linen of our conscience, nor to lay it in the tomb of our heart, while stinking from dead bones and all uncleanness. But as the Apostle saith, 'Let a man examine himself,' that the grace be not condemnation to him who receiveth the grace unworthily."

S. Gregory of Nazianzum addresses those who, out of covetousness, disturbed graves;

"[g] And thou, wretched man, wilt thou boldly receive in thy palms the Mystic Food, or God embrace with hands, wherewith thou hast dug up my grave?"

S. Cæsarius, his brother,

"[h] He trampleth under foot God the Word, the Son of God, who, in covetous hands lifted up against his neighbour, receiveth fearlessly the Sacramental Elements, accounting them like *common* bread and wine, which in the eyes of the faithful mind are contemplated, God."

S. Esaias Abbas; "Woe[i] to us who, when the Apostle saith, ' he who eateth and drinketh unworthily, eateth and drinketh damnation to himself, not discerning the Lord's Body,' defiled by our uncleannesses, approach to the aweful and fearful mysteries of God. For he who hath neither pure thoughts, nor chaste eyes, nor undefiled body, nor clean soul, and sits down by God (assidet Deo), will incur eternal torments and boundless shame."

" If thou willest to take the Body of Christ, take heed that there be no anger or hatred in thy heart against any one."

Eusebius of Alexandria pictures[j] our Saviour saying to the unmerciful, in the day of judgment; "'Depart from Me,

p. 435.   [g] p. 438.   [h] p. 439.   [i] p. 443.   [j] p. 453.

I know you not.' Why do ye call upon Me, saying, 'Lord, why dost Thou send us from Thee? have we not the seal of thy Body?'"

S. Ambrose[k] bids the priests, "Touch not with feverish hand the Body of Christ. First be cured, then thou mayest be able to minister." And to the Emperor Theodosius, stained with the massacre of Thessalonica; 'How in such hands wilt thou receive the all-holy Body of the Lord? how wilt thou bear to thy mouth the Precious Blood, having in thine anger unlawfully shed so much blood?"

S. Jerome says; "[1]We pollute Bread, that is, the Body of Christ, when, being unworthy, we approach the Altar, and being impure, drink pure Blood, and say, the Table of the Lord is contemptible;" and, "In the Mysteries, one is the sanctification of lord and servant, noble and ignoble, king and soldier, although, according to the deserts of the recipients, that becometh diverse, which is one. For whosoever shall 'eat and drink unworthily, shall be guilty of the Body and Blood of Christ.' Or, because even Judas

---

[k] p. 463, 466. Mr Goode (p. 367, 8) quotes four passages from S. Ambrose, in proof that the wicked do not receive the Body and Blood of Christ. Three of these, which relate to the Holy Eucharist, I have quoted in the Doctrine of the Real Presence, p. 457, 460, 291. They are simply passages in which S. Ambrose speaks of the fruits of *right* reception. "Whoso receiveth shall not die the sinner's death; for this Bread is the remission of sins." "This is the Bread of life; whoso then eateth Life, cannot die." "Whosoever shall eat this, shall never die; and it is the Body of Christ." Such passages are irrelevant to the question as to the reception by the wicked. See above, p. 280, 1, 4.

The fourth passage (Ep. 70. ad Horont. § 13. Opp. ii. 1065) relates to the reception of Christ Himself, Whom none believe the wicked to receive. "Every soul therefore, which receiveth that Bread which cometh down from heaven, is the house of bread, i. e. the Bread Christ, and is nourished by the strengthening of the heavenly Bread dwelling in it, and 'is strengthened in heart.'"   [1] p. 481, 477.

drank of the same Cup as the other Apostles, were his deserts therefore the same as theirs ? "

S. Jerome, like S. Augustine, so identified the reception of the Body and Blood of Christ with the reception of the Sacrament, that he even substitutes the words, " the Body and Blood," when quoting the Apostle, "[m]Whence the Apostle too says, ' Let a man examine himself, and so let him approach the Body and Blood of the Lord.'" And this he does as to the passage in which St. Paul is speaking of " eating and drinking damnation " to themselves.

Jerome of Jerusalem[n]; " Not to make the sign of the Cross,

[m] p. 479.

[n] p. 486. S. Jerome has *one* passage which seems to deny the reception by the wicked, in commenting on Is. lxvi. 17 (quoted Real Presence, p. 478-9). But the context shews that he, like S. Augustine, is speaking only of such eating, whereby men become " partakers of Christ Himself." " Since they are not holy in body and spirit, they neither eat the Flesh of Jesus, nor drink His Blood, whereof Himself saith ' Whoso eateth My Flesh and drinketh My Blood hath eternal life.' '*For* Christ our passover is sacrificed,' *Who* is not eaten without, but in one house and within."

In the other passage alleged by Mr. Goode (p. 369) he, like S. Augustine, denies that *heretics* have the Sacraments: " The Apostle teacheth, that there is one Altar in the Church, and one faith, and one baptism, which the heretics forsaking, have made unto themselves altars, not in order to propitiate God, but for the multitude of their transgressions. Wherefore they attain not, to receive the laws of God, seeing that they had already despised those which they had received. And if they say aught respecting the Scriptures, it is no wise to be compared with the Divine words, but with the mind of the Gentiles. These offer many sacrifices and eat their flesh, forsaking the one Sacrifice of Christ: and not eating *His* Flesh, Whose Flesh is the Food of believers. Whatsoever they do, aping the order and mode of sacrifices, whether they give alms, or promise chastity, or ape humility, and deceive the simple with feigned allurements, the Lord will accept nought of sacrifice of this sort " (in Os. L. ii. c. viii. 12. T. vi. p. 88, 9. ed. Vall.). The question as to *heretical* sacraments is distinct from that as to the wicked. S. Jerome also is denying

nor to partake of the Body of Christ, are the signs of the true Christian. For perhaps unbelievers too, and heretics partake of it, and all which we do, they do."

S. Gaudentius; "We[o] ought, by the command of God, first to mortify the lusts of the flesh, and so to receive the Body of Christ who was slain for us. 'Wherefore let a man examine himself,' saith the Apostle, 'and so let him eat of that Bread and drink of that Cup.' But when he says, we must 'eat it in haste,' he teaches that we receive not the Sacrament of the Lord's Body and Blood with sluggish hearts and languid lips."

S. Chrysostome teaches the same doctrine very often. "[p]Approach not then this Table with stubble or wood or hay, lest thou increase the conflagration, and *consume the soul which* partaketh." "[q]He who is guilty and unclean would not be meet, even in a feast, to partake of that holy and awful Flesh." "[r]This is the Body, which thou, O Judas, didst sell for thirty pieces of silver: this is the Blood, for which, a little before, thou madest that shameless compact with the reckless Pharisees. O the love of Christ for man! O the frenzy, the madness of Judas! for Judas sold Him for thirty pieces of silver; but Christ, even after this, refused not to give the very Blood which was sold, for the remission of sins, to him who sold it, if he willed." "[s]We have lately read to you Paul's law concerning the participation in the Mysteries, laid down for all the initiated. The law was this (for there is no reason that I should not now read it to you again), 'let each examine himself, and so let him eat of that Bread and drink of that Cup.' They who are initiated in the mysteries know what we say, and what that Bread is, what that

that the heretics have any thing whatever of Christ, since they seek Him not, where He is to be found. They have, he says in allusion to the words of Hosea, neither the Laws of God, nor the words of God, nor the Sacrifice of Christ, which they forsake, nor His Sacraments.

[o] p. 488 [p] p. 550. [q] p. 552. [r] p. 555. [s] p. 558.

Cup. For he saith, 'Whoso eateth and drinketh unworthily of the Lord, he shall be guilty of the Body and Blood of the Lord.' This law we have rehearsed to you; and we have explained the meaning of the words. I have said what it means, 'He shall be guilty of the Body and Blood of the Lord.' It is, that he shall undergo the same punishment as they shall endure who crucified Christ. For he says, 'As they, the murderers, were guilty of the Blood, so those also who partake unworthily of the mysteries.' For this is, 'He shall be guilty of the Body and Blood of the Lord.' What I said seemed to be excessive, and the threat unendurable. I add a ground from an instance, which has much analogy. For, as I said, if any tear the Royal Purple, or defile it with mire, he in like way insults the king who is clad with it; so also here. They who slew the Lord's Body, and they who receive with an unclean mind, equally insult the royal raiment. The Jews rent it by the Cross, but he who receiveth It in an impure soul, defileth It. So that though the transgression is different, the insult is the same."

"[t]Wherefore I too now cry with a loud voice, and protest and entreat and implore, that you would not approach this Holy Table with an evil conscience; for this would not be approach, or Communion, though we were countless times to touch that Holy Body, but condemnation and chastisement, and increase of punishment. Let no sinner then approach; nay rather, I say not, no sinner, since then I should first exclude myself from the Holy Table, but let no one approach who persevereth in sin."

"[u]But take heed that thou be not like Herod, and say, 'that I may come and worship Him,' and when thou art come, be minded to slay Him. For him do they resemble, who partake of the Mysteries unworthily; it being said, that such an one 'shall be guilty of the Body and Blood of the Lord.'"

"[v]Satan entered into him (Judas), not as despising the

[t] p. 564.   [u] p. 565.   [v] p. 569.

Lord's Body, but thenceforth laughing to scorn the traitor's shamelessness."

" [w] Look therefore, lest thou also thyself become guilty of the Body and Blood of Christ. They slaughtered the All-Holy Body ; but thou, after such great benefits, receivest It in a filthy soul."

" [x] Let no one communicate, who is not of the disciples. Let no Judas receive, lest he suffer the fate of Judas. This multitude also is Christ's body. Take heed, therefore, thou that ministerest at the Mysteries, lest thou provoke the Lord, not purging this body. Give not a sword instead of meat."

" [y] I would give up my life rather than impart of the Lord's Blood to the unworthy : and will shed my own blood rather than impart of such awful Blood contrary to what is meet."

" [z] Let us therefore wake ourselves up, and be filled with horror, and let us shew forth a reverence far beyond that of these Barbarians ; that we may not, by random and careless approaches, heap fire upon our own heads."

" [a] Whosoever shall eat this bread and drink this cup of the Lord unworthily, shall be guilty of the Body and Blood of the Lord. Why so ? Because he poured It out, and made the thing appear a slaughter, and no longer a sacrifice. Much therefore as they who then pierced Him, pierced Him not that they might drink, but that they might shed His blood: so likewise doth he that cometh for It unworthily, and reaps no profit thereby."

" [b] How shalt thou present thyself before the judgment-seat of Christ, thou who presumest upon His Body with polluted hands and lips ? Thou wouldest rather choose not to come at all, than come with soiled hands. And then, thus scrupulous as thou art in this little matter, dost thou come with soiled soul, and thus dare to touch It ? And yet the hands hold it but for a time, whereas into the soul It is received entirely."

" [c] It is not presumptuous to receive often, but to re-

<hr>

[w] p. 571. [x] p. 572. [y] p. 573. [z] p. 585. [a] p. 588.
[b] p. 591. [c] p. 595.

ceive unworthily, though but once in a whole life.   But
we are so miserably foolish, that, though we commit num-
berless offences in the course of a year, we are not anxious
to be absolved from them, but are satisfied that we do not
often make bold, impudently to insult the Body of Christ,
not remembering that they who crucified Him, crucified
Him but once.   Is the offence then the less, because committed but once?   Judas betrayed his Master but once.
What then?   Did that exempt him from punishment?"

"[d] They shed the Righteous blood, who drink the Blood
of the Lord, and are defiled with foul deeds."

[d] p. 597.   Other passages are quoted in the "Doctrine of the
Real Presence, p. 567, 575, 582, and S. Chrysostome's exposition
of 1 Cor. xi. 29. is given below.   Mr Goode omits all notice of
these passages and selects one, alleged in a Catena on S. John,
published from a very old MS. by Corderius.   The passage is
of no moment; for it simply asserts *a* fruit of the Holy Eucharist, in itself; of course to those who receive It aright.   "He that
hath partaken of this Food will be beyond the power of death."
But Mr. Goode goes on to suggest that the passage may have
been suppressed by Roman Catholic editors.   "The sentence, of
which these words form a part, does not appear in Chrysostome's
comment on S. John, *as printed in his Works;* but that fact is by
no means adverse to its genuineness, and only suggests the probability of there being here another instance of Romish suppression of Patristical testimony." p. 370.   Mr Goode forgot
that Corderius, who published the passage in the Catena, was a
Jesuit, and that Sir H. Savile, who, on his hypothesis, would have
been party to its "suppression" (since the passage is not in his
edition), was a learned member of the English Church.   Savile
diligently collated valuable and ancient MSS.   The passage does
not occur in two Bodleian MSS. of the 11th cent., nor in a Christ
Church MS. of the same date, nor in a MS. at the close of the
11th cent. in that of Magdalene Coll.
    On the other hand, the author of this Catena, published by
Corderius, did (as almost all do) make several mistakes as to the
authors whom he cited.   It would be very unsafe to assert any
passage to belong to an author on the authority of one MS. of *one*
Catena, against other testimony.   The passage *may* however, be

S. Cyril of Alexandria. " ᵉ They then who are yet un-circumcised, i. e. unclean, ought not to touch the Holy Body."

S. Isidore of Pelusium. " ᶠ He did not, as you suppose enter into him, despising the Lord's Body, but having dis-covered his wickedness, that he was incurably sick."

Theodoret. "He shall be guilty of the ' ᵍ Body and Blood,' showeth this, that, like as Judas betrayed Him and the Jews insulted Him, so they dishonour Him, who receive His

taken from some other work of S. Chrysostome; but does not bear upon the question.

ᵉ Ib. 644. Mr. Jenkins *infers* that S. Cyril held that the ungodly did not receive at all, because S. Cyril, commenting on our Lord's words, "Whoso eateth My Flesh and drinketh My Blood dwelleth in Me and I in him," says, "For as when melted wax, poured upon other wax, becomes one substance with it throughout, so when any one receives [lit. he who receives] the Body and Blood of the Lord, he becomes so united with Him, that Christ is found in him and he in Christ." Mr Jenkins *infers*, "It is manifest that in this passage, the unfaithful are excluded not only from the beneficial effects or *fructus* of the Sacrament, but from the reality of the presence also." p. 30, l. It is evident to any student of S. Cyril, that in such passages, he is speaking of the greatness of the union with Christ bestowed through the Holy Eucharist on the faithful Communicant, and not thinking of the unfaithful at all. It would be the same mode of argument if any were to say that because our Lord said, "Ask and ye shall receive," therefore there were none, who "asked and received not, because they asked amiss." The passages of S. Cyril referred to by Mr. J. are given more fully, Real Presence, p. 633. 639. Mr. Goode, p. 371, quotes one of these same passages, another, quoted in the Real Presence, p. 630, and two others of the same sort. If passages which speak of the benefit of the Holy Eucharist to pious Communicants, were to be evidence that the ungodly receive nothing at all, there would be an end of speaking freely of Christ's gifts to us, without the clause, "if we rightly, worthily, and with faith, receive the same, and if, after we have received, we persevere unto the end," inserted in every sentence.

ᶠ p. 667.   ᵍ p. 680.

All-Holy Body with impure hands, and bear It to their defiled mouth."

S. Peter Chrysologus. "[h] The apostle in such wise admonishes and bewails those who touch unworthily the Body of Christ, saying, 'whoso touches unworthily the Body of Christ, receives to himself judgment.'"

S. Proclus. "[i] Now that we are about to approach the Divine Mysteries, let us cast away all anger, let us cleanse ourselves from all malice; that our Lord, when He entereth our souls, may not find any full of hypocrisy, like Judas; but may find all pure."

Sedulius. "[k] After He had consecrated the two Gifts of His Body and Blood, and had given them as Food and Drink, through Whose perpetual supply faithful souls without spot might never hunger nor thirst, forthwith into Judas, where envy had its abode, that foulest spirit entered."

S. Leo the Great. "[l] When, in order to conceal their infidelity, they [the Manichees] ventured to be present at our assemblies, they so compromise with themselves in the Communion of the Sacrament, as sometimes, lest they should not be able entirely to escape notice, to receive with unworthy mouth the Body of Christ; but the Blood of our Redemption they altogether refuse to drink."

He apostrophises Judas; "[m] Why distrust His Goodness, Who repelled thee not from the Communion of His Own Body and Blood?"

[h] p. 684.   [i] p. 690.   [k] p. 694.   [l] p. 695.

[m] Ib. p. 696. Judas is the very type of unworthy Communicants, whom the Fathers so often compare with him. Yet S. Leo says, that the Lord allowed him to receive His own Body and Blood. Mr. Jenkins *infers* that S. Leo did not believe what he here shews that he did, that unworthy Communicants receive our Lord's Body and Blood, from another passage in which S. Leo argues from the Real objective Presence to unworthy Communicants also. S. Leo is arguing from the truth of the Real Presence to the truth of the Incarnation. "Since the Lord says, 'Except ye eat of the Flesh of the Son of Man,

This doctrine, so uniformly attested by Christian antiquity[n], is the obvious meaning of S. Paul's words. S. Paul, in order to bring the Corinthians to a sense of the greatness of their sin, sets before them

and drink His Blood, ye have no life in you,' ye ought so to communicate of the holy Table, as to doubt nothing of the truth of the Body and Blood of Christ. For by the mouth is that received which is by faith believed: and vainly is Amen answered by those, who dispute against what they receive." S. Leo means, " it is in vain to say Amen, i. e. it is true, when the Priest says to you, ' the Body of Christ,' if you deny (as the Eutychians did) that our Lord had a true human Body. You receive that which is the Object of our faith, the true Body and Blood of Christ. It is in vain to say of what you receive, that it is the Body of Christ, if you deny that Christ ever had a true Body." See The Doctrine of the Real Presence, p. 698, and similar arguments by other Fathers, Ib. p. 85, and indeed p. 75 sqq. On the use of the word Amen, see above, p. 174-7. add S. Aug. c. Faust. iii. 10. (Real Pres. p. 534.) " The Blood of Christ hath a loud voice on earth, when, on receiving It, all nations answer, Amen."

[n] Besides the passages of S. Augustine, there is no one from the Fathers, on the other side, which prevents any seeming difficulty. Burnet quotes one from " Zeno Bp. of Verona, who is believed to have lived near Origen's time " (on Art. 29). S. Zeno must have lived at the very end of the 4th century. (See Diss. i. Ballerin. c. iii. Opp. p. lxi-ix.) But the passage which Burnet and others have attributed to him, is not his, but belongs to Ratherius Bp. of Verona. (See L. ii. Tract xiv. p. 195. not. 32.) Ratherius lived in the 10th cent., at which time some believed the withdrawal of the Body and Blood of Christ, when the wicked attempt to receive them, as Aquinas attests.

Mr. Goode, besides the passages already noticed, cites only a passage of S. Macarius (quoted in the Real Presence, p. 448) on Christ's gifts to His own children; and one from S. Isidore of Seville (A. D. 595) (on Gen. xlix. 20), " ' Whose bread is made fat,' i. e. *His* Flesh, which is the Food of saints, which whoso shall have eaten, he shall not die eternally." These, again, are inferences as to the wicked, who forfeit the gift, from what is said as to the nature of the gift, in God's purpose of love.

our Lord's institution of the Sacrament, as it had been revealed to him by our Lord Himself;—how Jesus had said, "This is My Body which is broken for you." "This Cup is the New Testament in My Blood." To this he subjoins, "*Wherefore* whosoever shall eat this bread, and drink this Cup of the Lord unworthily, shall be guilty of the Body and Blood of the Lord." The Apostle connects this guilt with our Lord's words. Those, who ate that Bread and drank that Cup unworthily, did, in some very special way, sin against the Body and Blood of our Lord. S. Paul does not say, in a general way, that they sinned "against the Lord;" as he does say of those that were an occasion of sin to others, "when ye[o] sin so against the brethren, and wound their weak conscience, ye sin against Christ." The Corinthians, by eating and drinking unworthily, had contracted guilt, by which they were held bound[p], not against Christ only, but against "His Body and Blood."

The word "guilty of[q]" is used in the same way, in the Septuagint version of the Old Testament, of those with regard to whom a man contracts guilt. "[q]They who are guilty with regard to thee" [Jerusalem], i. e. by hostility to it. "[r]There shall be no one among you guilty as to blood," by shedding it. So in S. James[s], "he who breaketh one law is guilty of all" the law, in that, by wilfully breaking one law, he has despised the authority which gave them all. How then is one who receives the Holy Eucharist unworthily, guilty, as others are not, of

[o] 1 Cor. viii. 12. [p] ἔνοχος. [q] Is. liv. 17.
[r] Deut. xix. 10. [s] ii. 10.

the Body and Blood of our Lord?   On the ground of the Real Presence, it is obvious. He shews a dishonour to our Lord's Body and Blood, supernaturally and spiritually present there, in a way in which dishonour cannot, by any other human act, be shewn to that Body and Blood.

Yet one who comes to Holy Communion, without examining himself, does not mean any irreverence to our Lord's Body and Blood. Unless there is some special Presence, his act would be the same as that of one, who hears impenitently the history of our Lord's Passion, or, indeed, who hears His Sacred Word carelessly. It is the theory of the "Reformed," that the Word and the Sacraments are instruments in the same way, sealing the promises of God. If, as they say, the Holy Communion had been nothing more than eating and drinking mere bread and wine, in memory of our Lord's Passion, there would have been no more offensiveness in coming with uncleansed, impenitent consciences to this, than to any other act of devotion.

All Sacrifice foreshadowed our Lord's Death, till He came. Holy Scripture itself tells us, that the Paschal Lamb was an eminent type of Him. God Himself says, that " the sacrifice [t] of the wicked," i. e. one who persevered in his wickedness, " is an abomination to the Lord ; " that " his prayer shall be turned into sin."   The pouring out of the blood of the sacrifice pictured more vividly than the Holy Eucharist, the shedding of His Blood, the Innocent for the guilty. Jesus bore the name of " the Lamb without spot," " Christ our Passover." Yet one who came

---

[t] Prov. xv. 8. add xxi. 27, Is. i. 13, 14.

to the Passover or who offered sacrifice impenitently, although he thereby added to his sin, was not said to be guilty of the Body and Blood of the Lord, the symbols of whose Passion he abused.

Again, to pass from the shadows to the substance. In Baptism we are washed with His Blood [u]; "buried with Him," the Apostle says [v], "by Baptism into death, that we may also rise to newness of life." An adult who comes impenitently to Baptism, as Simon Magus, gains harm by it, and falls a readier prey to Satan. Yet one who receives Baptism unworthily is not said to be guilty of the Blood of Christ. Nor are such threatened with special punishment of the body too, as is said of the unworthy Communicant; "for this cause many are weak and sickly among you, and many sleep." It is not, even thus far, a natural interpretation, that unworthy Communicants are "guilty of the Body and Blood of the Lord," because they receive what, if His Body and Blood were not there, would be mere symbols of His Passion, and those, symbols not so vivid as the Paschal Lamb.

Again, S. Paul speaks to the Galatians of his own preaching, as setting forth Christ crucified vividly before their eyes. "[w] O foolish Galatians, who hath bewitched you, that ye should not obey the truth, before whose eyes Jesus Christ hath been evidently set forth, crucified, among you?"

They had had the Death and Passion of our Lord so vividly pictured before their eyes, that they had,

---

[u] 1 Cor. vi. 11. See passages of the Fathers, quoted by Bp. Jewell, Replie to Harding, p. 285, 7. &c.

[v] Rom. vi. 4.   [w] iii. 1.

through faith, seen Him, as it were, crucified, hanging on the Cross for them, in the midst of them, before their own eyes. "[x] By the eye of faith they had seen more distinctly," says S. Chrysostome, "than some who were present as spectators." "Him whom they had seen, for their sakes, stripped, naked, transfixed, nailed to the Cross, spit upon, mocked, fed with vinegar, upbraided by thieves, pierced with a spear (for all this is implied in the words, 'evidently set forth crucified'), Him had they left, and untouched by all these His sufferings had betaken themselves to the law." They had so fallen away, that they needed, as it were, a new birth, to restore them to life. "My little children, of whom I travail in birth again, until Christ be formed in you." Yet the Apostle nowhere says, that they were "guilty of His Body and Blood." Other sins have their own guilt and their own punishment. But the special sin of being "guilty of His Body and Blood" is assigned to those who "eat or drink unworthily that Bread and that Cup," of which alone it is said, "This is My Body, This is My Blood."

Neither, again, is it said generally, that those who "*go* to the Holy Communion, or to the Lord's Supper," or who "*receive* the Sacrament unworthily," are guilty as to the Body and Blood of Christ. No general terms are used; but, on the contrary, the terms are very specific. The sin is specified to consist in the act of "eating and drinking." Four times in four following verses, the Apostle repeats these emphatic words. "As often as ye eat this bread

---

[x] Ad loc. p. 49. O. T.

and drink this cup, ye do shew the Lord's death till He come."   "*Wherefore*, whosoever shall eat this bread, and drink this cup of the Lord unworthily, shall be guilty of the Body and Blood of the Lord."   "But let a man examine himself, and so let him eat of that bread, and drink of that cup." "*For* he that eateth and drinketh unworthily, eateth and drinketh damnation to himself, not discerning the Lord's Body."   This great emphasis on the act of eating and drinking is accounted for, on the belief of the Church, that there, under the outward elements, we do invisibly eat and drink the Body and Blood of Christ.   It is not accounted for, on any other theory.

Again, the Apostle says, that such an one eateth and drinketh damnation to himself, not *discerning the Lord's Body*.   He does not say, not reverencing the *symbols* of the Lord's Body," or "the *Sacrament* of the Lord's Body," but "not discerning," or distinguishing "the Lord's Body" from ordinary food. But since the special sin of the Corinthians was that they ate and drank irreverently as common food, what was the Body and Blood of Christ, that Body and Blood must have been present there.

"They did not distinguish the Lord's Body," says Cassian[y], "no way severing that heavenly food from the cheapness of common food, nor distinguishing it to be such that none may presume to receive it, save with pure mind and body."   And S. Chrysostome[z].   "*Not discerning the Lord's Body,*' i. e. not searching, not bearing in mind, as he ought, the greatness of the things set before him; not estimating the weight of the gift.   For if thou shouldest come

[y] Collat. xxii. 4.   [z] Ad loc. Hom. 28. § 2.

to know accurately, Who it is that lies before thee, and Who He is that gives Himself, and to whom, thou wilt need no other argument, but this is enough for thee to use all vigilance, unless thou shouldest be altogether fallen."

It has been argued, on the other side, that the wicked cannot, in any way, eat the Flesh of Christ and drink His Blood, because our Lord says, " Whoso eateth My Flesh, and drinketh My Blood, hath ever-lasting life," which the wicked have not.

The argument, if true, would go farther than most of those who use it, are prepared to follow it. For it would follow, that no one ever perished, who ever, in his life, really received the Body and Blood of Christ. And since those who use this argument, mostly apply the words to any feeding upon Christ by faith, it would follow, according to them, that no one ever perished who had ever once, at any moment in his life in which he was touched by the grace of God, spiritually fed upon Christ by faith. For im-mediately after the words, "Whoso eateth My Flesh, and drinketh My Blood, hath eternal life," our Lord adds, "and I will raise him up at the last day." Our Lord speaks not of a present blessing only in this life, but of one also which is beyond this life; and of both He speaks in the same way. " This is the Bread which cometh down from heaven, so that a man may eat thereof, and not die." " If any man eat of this bread, *He shall live* for ever." " As the living Father hath sent Me, and I live by the Father, so he that eateth Me even he *shall live by Me*." " *He* that eateth of this bread *shall live for ever*." The Gift in the Holy Eucharist, union with our Lord Himself through His Body and Blood, is a present

Gift, involving a future and further Gift, if we persevere, and aiding us to persevere.

But all God's gifts and promises imply a right condition on the part of the recipients. The promise, on God's part, is absolute; as we were taught as to our Baptism; "which promise, He, *for His part*, will most surely keep and perform." But every promise of His presupposes that we are of that character, to which He makes these promises. When He says, "He that believeth and is baptized shall be saved," He does not mean this of a faith without love, as the devils believe and tremble. When He says, "Whosoever shall call upon the Name of the Lord shall be saved," He does not mean those who say, "Lord, Lord, and do not the things which He saith;" to whom He will say in that day, "Depart from Me, I never knew you, all ye that work iniquity." He saith, "He that asketh, receiveth;" yet not they to whom S. James saith, "ye ask and receive not, because ye ask amiss." God saith to His people; "[a] Return to Me, and I will return to you:" but He meant it only of those who should return with their whole heart, not of those who, He says, "[b] turned unto Me, not with their whole heart, but feignedly." Our Lord says, "Come unto Me, *all ye* that labour and are heavy laden, and I will give you rest," but He means those who come to Him with a true heart.

S. John, following closely his Master's mode of speaking, says, "If[c] we confess our sins, He is faithful and just to forgive us our sins." Yet not all confes-

---

[a] Mal. iii. 7.   [b] Jer. xxiv. 7; iii. 10.

[c] 1 John i. 9; ii. 10; iv. 12; iii. 14.

sion of sins, but confession, with faith in Jesus and true contrition of heart, is so accepted. "He that loveth his brother, abideth in the light, and there is none occasion of stumbling in him." "If we love one another, God dwelleth in us, and His love is perfected in us." "We know that we have passed from death unto life, because we love the brethren." Now to "have passed from death unto life," to "abide in the light," and that God should "dwell in us," involve, or are, *present* spiritual states of being, which the Apostle affirms universally of all those, who "love the brethren," or "one another." They all involve, that the person of whom they are said, is in a state of grace; i. e. that he has God's Holy Spirit dwelling in him. S. John uses the very word, "if we love one another, God dwelleth in us," as our Lord says, "He that eateth My Flesh, and drinketh My Blood, dwelleth in Me, and I in him."

There is no ground then for a distinction which has been applied here, that

"[d] Promises as to the future are to be understood with a condition appendant, yet propositions at present are declarations of a thing in being, and suppose it actually existent. 'He that eateth My Flesh and drinketh My Blood hath eternal life,' is an affirmation of a thing in being, and therefore implies no other condition but the connection of the predicate with the subject, 'He that eats, hath life.'"

It is true, that, where the declaration relates to the future, there is a still farther condition im-

[d] Bp. Taylor, "the Real Presence," quoted by Mr. Goode, p. 98.

plied ;—perseverance in well-being to the end. But besides this, God, in speaking of His Gifts, has not seen it needful, on every occasion, to express, that He only promises those gifts to such as are qualified to receive them. The whole object of His dispensation towards us (as far as relates to us) is to renew His Image in us, and make us such as He can love, such as can love Him, eternally. All His institutions, appointments, commands, promises look towards this end. In all His promises therefore to us, connected with these institutions or appointments, whether sacrifice under the Old Testament, or Sacraments in the New, whether it be worship, or belief, or prayer, or repentance, or obedience, or love of our neighbour, God presupposes, so to speak, that we shall understand Him to speak of that which is done according to His Mind, not against it. He does not, as we do, jealously guard His sayings, nor does He speak, for the most part, of "*true* repentance," or "right faith," or "living faith," or of "love or works which are the fruits of faith," or of His Spirit; or of worship "*from the heart.*" He, the Fountain of all grace, has told us to whom, and what character of persons, He gives His grace. But then, He uses the words freely. He pronounces that they who "believe," "love," "ask," "seek," "come unto Him," "call upon His Name," "love the brethren," "love one another," have, or shall have, certain blessings; and, in so promising, He presupposes that the faith, love, prayer, will be of the right sort, the fruits of His Spirit, unhindered by any thing contrary to His Holy Will. The Holy God makes us holy, for unholy; He does not bestow His Gifts on the unholy. Having declared to us, that we "cannot serve God and Mammon," that there is "no concord of Christ with Belial," He, ordinarily, speaks to us, as knowing already that His gifts are for His own children, not for the children of the devil. This, then, all God's promises have in common. They who "draw nigh to God with their lips, while their hearts are far from Him," draw on themselves a curse, not a blessing. "You only have known," says God[e], "of all the families of the earth; *therefore* will I punish you for all your iniquities." And therefore God, as I said, takes it for granted that we know this, and speaks to us, as we ought to understand Him, not fettering His promises by explanations or limitations, which are presupposed by our whole relation to Him, and by His very Nature and Being.

If people abuse His promises, then He condescends to enforce what we ought to know already. Thus, in the Old Testament, He bids His people, "seek the Lord." "Seek ye My face." To "seek the Lord" was a well-known religious phrase. It is used, throughout the Old Testament, of seeking the Lord in the way that He may be found; seeking Him aright, with the heart. When the elders of Israel came to the Prophet to seek, through him, to know the Will of God, having "[f]set up their idols in their heart," God resents it indignantly, and says that those who *so* sought Him, He would cut off from the midst of His people.

In the New Testament, our Lord teaches absolutely, "Ask, and ye shall receive." S. James tells

[e] Am. iii. 2.
[f] Ezek. xiv. 2. 8.

us the conditions of acceptable prayer. Our Lord says, "He that believeth and is baptized, shall be saved." S. Peter inculcates the needs of "the answer of a good conscience towards God." S. Paul speaks largely on the province of faith; S. James explains more at large, what S. Paul also had said, that it must be "faith which worketh by love."

So then, as to eating and drinking our Lord's Body and Blood in the Holy Eucharist, our Lord tells us the blessing of eating and drinking It. When abuses came in among the Corinthians, S. Paul distinguishes between eating and drinking worthily and unworthily, and bids us, "Let a man examine himself, and so let him eat of that Bread, and drink of that Cup." He lays down a necessary preliminary, that we may *so* eat and drink it, as to become partakers of the benefits, which our Lord promised to those who eat and drink it. Our Lord tells us what the benefits of that gift are in itself; S. Paul tells us what we must do and be, in order to partake of them.

There is, then, nothing in our Lord's mode of speaking, from which we should infer, that none, *in any way*, "eat His Flesh and drink His Blood," save those who eat and drink them worthily, and persevere in so doing unto the end. He uses exactly the same mode of speaking, as the Beloved Disciple afterwards did, through His Spirit. As our Lord says, "He that eateth My Flesh and drinketh My Blood, dwelleth in Me, and I in him," so S. John says, "If we love one another, God dwelleth in us, and His love is perfected in us."

x

Yet S. John did not mean that they who had a mere natural love for one another, were, therefore, indwelt by God; but those only, who loved in a certain way, through that "love shed abroad in our hearts by the Holy Ghost which is given to us." Nor yet would S. John say, that those who do not love with a Divine, God-given, love, have *no sort of love* for one another, but only that they have not that love which is a grace, the fruit and proof of the in-dwelling of God. So then neither does it follow, that, because our Lord says, "He that eateth My Flesh, and drinketh My Blood, dwelleth in Me, and I in him," therefore whoso does not dwell in Christ, or Christ in him, does not, in any way, eat it. Our Lord is speaking of the benefits resulting from the due eating of His Flesh, and drinking of His Blood. There is no more ground for saying that those who do not dwell in Christ, do therefore, in no sense, eat His Flesh, than there is for arguing, that those who do not "receive," in no wise "ask" of God; or that those who do not "find," in no sense "seek;" or that those to whom it is not opened, in no sense "knock."

Our Lord, Who says, "Seek, and ye shall find," says also, "Many shall seek to enter in, and shall not be able." He, Who says, "Ask, and ye shall receive," says also, "Not every one that saith unto Me, Lord, Lord, shall enter into the kingdom of Heaven, but he that doeth the will of My Father which is in Heaven." He, Who says, "Knock, and it shall be opened," tells us also of those who shall knock too late, when the door is shut.

This being so, it is obviously more right to go to

S. Paul, and learn from his plain words what the wicked receive, than to deny that they receive any thing, on the ground of our own inferences from the words of our Lord. Our Lord is speaking to us of the blessings of devout Communion, and enlarging upon them; He is not saying any thing of those who profane His Gift. S. Paul is speaking directly of these who *do* profane that Gift, and that, not by *any* kind of profanation, but by " eating and drinking unworthily" *That*, of which our Lord says, " Take, eat, this is My Body; Drink ye all of this, This is My Blood of the New Testament." Of these he says, that " they eat and drink their own damnation, not discerning the Lord's Body;" surely, that same Body of which our Lord says, " Take, eat, This is My Body." Surely, then, the Body of our Lord, which they do not discern, is that Body which they eat unworthily, and eating which profanely, they eat, not life but death.

I was myself long in suspense about these words, partly deferring to the apparent authority of S. Augustine, partly withheld by the difficulty which S. Augustine states, that the wicked cannot "dwell in Christ, or Christ in them." I thought and said, " ᵍ But Christ dwelleth not in the soul in which Satan dwelleth. Nor yet can the Body and Blood of Christ be present without Him; for where His Body is, there is He. It is the very test of the reprobate, that the Spirit of Christ dwelleth not in them; and if the Spirit of Christ is not in them, they are none of His."

It did not occur to me, that Christ, although He

ᵍ See Letter to Bishop of London, p. 58, ed. 8vo.

could not dwell in their souls, could be present, as their Judge. God is present in Hell. Now, having seen more accurately, that S. Augustine does agree with that great body of Christian fathers, who believe that the wicked do receive His Body and Blood, I have yielded my belief to what before seemed to me the plainest meaning of S. Paul's words, that the wicked, while they " are in no ways partakers of Christ " Himself, yet receive within them, sacramentally, His Body and Blood, which they do not discern, nor discriminate [h].

This, then, I believe as certain truth, drawn from Holy Scripture, yet not as a matter of faith, because differences of opinion have been allowed by the Church; and the Church has not overruled the opinion, mentioned by Aquinas [i] as held by certain " ancients," that "the Body of Christ is not even sacramentally received by sinners, but the Body of Christ ceases to be under the sacramental kinds, so soon as touched by sinful lips."

The Church of England has, I believe, not thought it needful to lay down as matter of doctrine, what it is, which the wicked receive. Yet in different places, she speaks as if they received the *same thing* as those, who " rightly, worthily,

[h] I said before, " And yet it must, in some sense, be the Body and Blood of Christ, since the very ground why those who profaned the Lord's Supper, 'ate and drank damnation to themselves,' is, according to Holy Scripture, that 'they did not discern the Lord's Body.' " Ib. p. 59, 60.

[i] 3 p. q. 80, art. 3. " Some ancients erred, saying," &c., as in the text. Mr. Palmer held the withdrawal of the Body and Blood of Christ, in the case of unworthy Communicants.—On the Church, I. 529.

and with faith, receive it;" only, since they receive it profanely, to their harm.

The xxvth Article lays down as to Sacraments, that

" in such only as worthily receive the same, they have a wholesome effect or operation; but they that receive them unworthily, purchase to themselves damnation, as S. Paul saith."

The Article, although it uses the plural, "they," is plainly speaking of the Holy Eucharist alone. For of this only does S. Paul affirm that, for which the Article cites him; and to it alone belongs what the Article had just before affirmed; "The Sacraments were not ordained of Christ to be gazed upon, or to be carried about." But the Article contrasts those, who "worthily receive the same," and those "that receive them unworthily," and says that in the former only "they have a wholesome effect or operation." Now, assuredly, it is not the outward elements, but the " inward Presence," which "has a wholesome effect or operation." But by the very structure of the sentence, the wicked receive that, which has a wholesome effect on those who receive it worthily, i. e. the Body and Blood of Christ under the outward sign.

In like way, the first Exhortation in the Liturgy speaks of one and the same thing, as, "being so Divine and comfortable a thing to them who receive It worthily, and so dangerous to them who receive It unworthily." Now certainly the outward elements would not, of themselves be a " Divine thing." Yet it is that which, to those who receive It worthily, is a "Divine thing," which the

Exhortation says is "so dangerous to them who will presume to receive It unworthily."

Again, it warns men,

"If any be a blasphemer of God, an hinderer or slanderer of His Word, an adulterer, or be in malice, or envy, or in any other grievous crime, repent you of your sins, or else come not to that holy Table: lest after the taking of that holy Sacrament, the devil enter into you, as he entered into Judas, and fill you full of all iniquities, and bring you to destruction, both of body and soul."

Now, although some two or three ancient writers thought that Judas did not receive the Communion, yet all that believed that Judas received that "Holy Sacrament," believed also that he received the same as the rest of the Apostles, the Body and Blood of Christ.

Except, indeed, on the ground of a special Presence, no reason could be assigned, why this special peril of profaning the Sacrament should belong to the Holy Eucharist. Doubtless they who approach to God, in any way hypocritically, draw down His displeasure upon them. Still, it is not said, that they who are baptized unworthily, are washed with water to their own damnation. Of the Holy Eucharist alone, S. Paul gives this warning, that such "eat and drink their own damnation, *not discerning the Lord's Body:*" of the Holy Eucharist alone, the Church of England repeats it, and actual experience shews, that God punishes in a special manner the profanation of this Sacrament [k].

[k] The writer knew, long since, of two instances, in which suicide followed, on the night after the profanation of the Holy

The last Exhortation cast into a hortatory form the teaching of S. Paul, retaining his words. Whatever S. Paul means, that Exhortation means. But yet the contrast between those who receive It worthily, and those who receive It unworthily implies that the writer of the Exhortation, understood S. Paul's words, " not discerning the Lord's Body," of His Body truly present and received.

" As the benefit is great, if, with a true penitent heart, and lively faith, we receive that holy Sacrament,	" So is the danger great, if unworthily, we receive the same.
"For then we spiritually eat the Flesh of Christ, and drink His Blood.	"For then we are guilty of the Body and Blood of Christ our Saviour. We eat and drink our own damnation, not considering the Lord's Body."

Surely they cannot have meant otherwise, than that by one and the same act, only with opposite dispositions, the one ate the Flesh of Christ, and drank His Blood spiritually, i. e. to their souls' health; the other, by eating and drinking unworthily, became guilty of the Body and Blood of our Saviour Christ, present to them as to the others, but by them, unconsidered and so profaned.

The Church of England, then, while, as matter of belief, she holds that " the wicked are in no wise

Eucharist. In the one case, that of an unhappy sexton in Oxford, the Jury, contrary to their habit, brought in the verdict, " Felo de se." The verdict in the other case I do not know.

partakers of Christ," fully justifies the belief of those, who hold that the wicked receive, to their condemnation, the Body and Blood of Christ, against which they sin. She does not formally require this to be held; but practically, none could be warned more solemnly than the children of the Church of England, of the awful peril of being, through unworthy Communion, "guilty of the Body and Blood of Christ," their Redeemer.

It may be, that the conflict of belief on this point, prevented her from laying down any thing formally in her Articles, beyond the one warning that the wicked cannot be partakers of Christ. The Exhortations leave none unwarned.

II. The Church of England has maintained the same reserve, as to the practice of adoring our Lord present in the Holy Eucharist. The very structure of our Liturgy shews (what we know from other sources), that those who framed it, were intent upon making the Communion prominent. Masses for the departed had been multiplied; communions had become rare. The framers of our Prayer Book strove to bring back the communions, to insure greater frequency of communions, and a larger number of Communicants; and they made all the prayers to bear upon the Holy Communion, which we ourselves are about to receive. Hence, although the great act of Eucharistic Sacrifice remains in the Consecration itself, and it has been, all along, an object of belief in the Church of England, it is mentioned only, when we pray to God to " accept this our sacrifice of praise and thanksgiving." With regard to the Adoration, we are rather told that the Sacraments were not ordained of Christ, to be adored, but to be received.

" [1] The Sacraments were not ordained of Christ to be gazed upon, or to be carried about; but *that we should duly use them.*"

And, in the same sense,

" [m] The Sacrament of the Lord's Supper was not, by Christ's Ordinance, reserved, carried about, lifted up or worshipped."

The English Article is worded very carefully, and with remarkable moderation. Its framers were content with asserting what was necessary to justify our own practice, without condemning in others, the reservation for the express purpose of adoration, which they did not think right to retain for the Church in England. The statement in Art. xxv. only asserts that such was not the object, for which our Saviour Christ ordained the Sacraments. "They were not ordained of Christ," it says, " to be gazed upon or to be carried about." It does not even say, that this *may* not be done; only, that this was not *the* end for which it was ordained.

Such also is the meaning of the statement in the 28th Article, although grammatically it is cast in a different form. "The Sacrament of the Lord's Supper was not, by Christ's Ordinance, reserved " &c. The Article clearly did not mean to condemn all reservation of the Holy Eucharist, e. g. for the sick. For there is no instance, in which the Church of England has condemned any practice of the Primi-

[1] **Art. xxv.**   [m] **Art. xxviii.**

tive Church, which did unquestionably reserve the consecrated element, both for the communicant's own use[n], and for the sick[o]. Then also, the Church of Scotland clearly did not so understand the Articles, since she received them, and yet allows of reservation.

The words, "ordained by Christ to be," " were, by Christ's ordinance," were known theological phrases of that time, which express the object for which our Lord instituted the Sacrament, or the mode in which He instituted it. They occur, at the same time, in the Council of Trent, which concedes that the Sacrament "[p] was instituted by the Lord Christ in order to be received," although it lays down, that it is " not on that ground the less to be adored." [q] Again, it says that " the Lord Christ, in the last supper, *instituted* this venerable Sacrament in the species of bread and wine and so delivered it to the Apostles," but contends, " yet that *institution* and tradition do not tend thereunto, that all the faithful of Christ be bound by the statute of the Lord to receive both kinds."

Our Articles stop short with the assertion, that our Lord Jesus Christ did not institute the Holy Eucharist, for the purpose of being "reserved, carried about, lifted up, or worshipped," but that it should be duly received. She justified her own omission of those acts, by laying down (in which the Council of Trent agrees with her) that our Lord did not institute the Sacrament for that end. And doubtless she had in view any use made of the consecrated

---

[n] De Orat. c. 19. p. 313. O. T. and note b. ad. uxor. ii. 5. and note z. p. 439.   [o] Bingham, 15. 4. 9.

[p] Sess. 13. c. 5.   [q] Sess. 21. c. 1. and 3.

elements, altogether distinct from the object for which our Lord left His Body and Blood. The words "gazed upon" relate to an unconcerned and irreverent presence at the Mass without communicating; "carried about" evidently relates to the "processions" in which the Blessed Sacrament was carried about for veneration.

With regard to the third point, the Elevation, it is thought that, when in the eleventh or twelfth century, the custom began of holding up the Host to the people immediately after its consecration, it was not held up for worship. It is remarkable, at least, that S. Bonaventura, giving in detail nine reasons for the holding up of the Host, some of which, it has been observed [r], "relate to duty or disposition of the people on this occasion," to the commemorative sacrifices, and the whole act of Christian worship, does not speak as if It was held up, to be Itself adored. He says [s];

" The Body of our Lord Jesus Christ is, on many grounds elevated by the Priest in the Mass. Of these, the first and chief is, to obtain the grace of God the Father, which we have lost by our sins.—The second is, to obtain every good which we need in the present life and in that to come. The third, to claim our right, which we have in heaven now in hope, hereafter at length in substance; 4) to shew the power of God; 5) to declare His wisdom; 6) to shew His bounty; 7) to shew the goodness of Christ; 8) to gladden the Holy Church by the standard of the army; 9) that we may imitate and follow Christ."

It seems almost inconceivable then, if the Host

[r] Palmer on the Church, i. 11, p. 312.
[s] Expos. Miss. c. 4. Opp. vii. 78.

were at that time, "lifted up" for adoration, S. Bonaventura, mentioning so many and such reasons, should not mention it here.

The object of the removal of this rite may have been the same which pervades the Liturgy, viz. to concentrate the whole soul on the reception and Communion itself, doing away with all rites, which had had distinct objects. People had commonly stopped short in the Sacrifice, and the Adoration. The Elevation was removed. Yet it is remarkable that the Homily on the Sacrament, while excepting against the private Masses and the Communion in one kind, says nothing about the Elevation or the adoration connected with it.

But further, the Article says that " the *Sacrament* was not by Christ's ordinance, reserved, carried about, lifted up, or worshipped." It says nothing whatever about the adoration of *Christ* in the Sacrament. It excepts, at most, against a later custom, and adoration connected with it. By no honest interpretation can this be extended to a worship, *not* of the *Sacrament*, but of Christ present there.

Bishop Andrewes states the distinction so clearly, that no one can call it subtle or refined. He enunciates in devout words a broad principle, which I see not how any Christian can gainsay. " [t] *Christ Himself, the Substance of the Sacrament,* in and with the Sacrament ; out of and without the Sacrament wheresoever He is, is to be adored. But the king [u] laid down that *Christ, truly present in the Sacrament,*

[t] Ad Card. Bellarm. resp. p. 195. [266. Ang. Cath. Lib.]

[u] James, whom he was defending.

is also truly to be adored; He, the Substance of the Sacrament, but, *not the Sacrament,* i. e. the 'earthly part,' as Irenæus; the 'visible,' as Augustine. But we, in the Mysteries too, 'adore the Flesh of Christ' with Ambrose[x], and not *that thing,* but— *Him* Who is worshipped on the Altar.' For the Cardinal [Bellarmine] enquires amiss, *what* [Quid] is worshipped there? for he should have asked, *Who?* For Nazianzen says, 'Him,' not it. ["[y] She falls in faith before the Altar and calling upon Him who is honoured thereupon."] 'Nor do we eat the Flesh, unless we have worshipped,'[z] saith Augustine. And yet we in no wise worship the Sacrament."

Even Melanchthon makes this same distinction, and that, with reference to the practice of the Elevation.

"[a] He [Mr. George] asked also about the 'Elevation.' Many of our people have abrogated it; we, here, retain it, according to the old custom; nor do I think that you should change that custom hastily. Although many questions would be avoided if that one custom were avoided, yet, since the Body of Christ is given with the signs, that outward reverence cannot be condemned, if the mind judges rightly and does not adore the sign, but understands that something else is given there, besides the sign. At all periods of the Church, in what they call the Action of the Mystery, the Church casts itself to the earth. Therefore I do not see how thou canst remove the custom; but people must be

---

[x] "The Flesh of Christ, which now too we in the Mysteries, adore." See the whole passage in Doctrine of the Real Presence, p. 465.

[y] See Ib. p. 436. [z] Ib. p. 521.

[a] C. R. 2422. "Luther abrogated it A.D. 1542. This letter then was written before 1542." Bretschn. iv. p. 735, note 6.

taught aright. I, although I see that there is some inconvenience, yet would not advise thee to change, without the other communicants of your Churches."

Neither does the Declaration, at the end of the Communion Service, any way interfere with the Adoration of our Saviour, truly present there. That Declaration was inserted by our bishops in 1661, to satisfy those who leaned to the Non-conformists, after they themselves had declared it to be unnecessary [b].

They altered it from the form, in which it previously existed, substituting the Words, "any *Corporal* Presence of Christ's natural Flesh and Blood," for those unauthorized words, "any real or essential Presence of Christ's natural Flesh and Blood." The word "Corporal," then, is a very emphatic word, having been carefully selected to displace the words "real and essential."

The Declaration, then, is not a protest against any doctrine, but an explanation that no such worship is intended, as the Non-conformists feared. The Church of England therein declares, that by kneeling,

" no adoration is intended or ought to be done either unto the Sacramental Bread and Wine, there bodily received, or unto any Corporal Presence of Christ's natural Flesh and Blood."

Of the outward elements, there can, of course, be no question. All Christians, every where, would hold the worship of these to be idolatry. The

[b] Promp. 18. § 15. Cardwell, Hist. of Conf. p. 350.

other point denied, is that any worship is due to
" any *Corporal* Presence of Christ's *natural* Flesh
and Blood." Now over and above the important
fact, that the word "Corporal" was deliberately
substituted to displace "real and essential," the
use of the two words "corporal" and "natural" is
in itself significant. The Declaration itself proceeds to explain what it means by "natural," and
in so doing lays emphasis upon it.

" The *natural* Body and Blood of our Saviour Christ are
in Heaven, and not here; it being against the truth of
Christ's *natural* Body to be at one time in more places
than one."

The Declaration seems to be directed against the
heresy of " Ubiquitism," as though our Lord's " natural Body " had the properties, belonging to His
Divine Nature. But in so doing, care is taken to
guard against any imputation of a denial of the
Real Presence. The words, "any *corporal* Presence," in themselves convey a tacit contrast with
some other mode of Presence. Else it had been
enough to say "any Presence." A statement drawn
up so carefully would not contain words, which had
much seeming emphasis, but were really superfluous. Again, the word "natural" is three times
repeated; "Christ's *natural* Flesh and Blood,"
" the *natural* Body and Blood of our Saviour
Christ," "it being against the truth of Christ's
natural Body." The words " corporal Presence."
in themselves suggest the contrast of a Presence,
"not after the manner of a Body." The words
" natural Body " suggest the contrast of a Presence
" not after the way of nature." Our Articles state

that "the Body of Christ is given, taken, and eaten, only after an heavenly and spiritual manner." The Homily speaks of it as "spiritual food," a "heavenly refection," a "ghostly *substance*." The Declaration "denies any *corporal* Presence of Christ's natural Body and Blood." Plainly, it does not deny "any heavenly or spiritual Presence of Christ's natural Body and Blood." Yea rather, by markedly denying the "Corporal," it suggests the belief in that, which is the contrast with "Corporal," viz. "the spiritual Presence of that Body and Blood."

To this it is objected[c];

1.) "The substantial presence of Christ's *Body* is a *bodily* or *corporal* presence; for the word *corporal* is not more limited to the sense of something *material* than the word *body* is. And if a human body *can be* present in an immaterial form, there can be a *corporal* presence of an immaterial kind."

The argument, as I understand it, is this; that if, by His Divine omnipotency, our Lord and God caused His Flesh and Blood to be present in an immaterial form, still *that* Presence, in that it would be the presence of a *body*, would be a "*corporal* Presence," and so that this Declaration, by rejecting a "corporal Presence of Christ's natural Flesh and Blood," in fact, denies every sort of Presence of His Flesh and Blood, because every sort of presence of a body must be corporal.

Mr. Goode, in urging this, has overlooked the fact that the words are not merely "*corporal* Presence," but "any corporal Presence of Christ's na-

[c] Mr. Goode, p. 622, 3.

tural Flesh and Blood." The word "corporal," in
this context, describes the mode of existence of
the Body. "Corporal Presence," by itself, might
signify the "presence of a body," as the Corinthians
said of S. Paul, "his bodily presence is weak [d],"
and as in legal terms "[e] corporal oath," i. e. an oath
accompanied by an action of the body; "corporal
possession," and the like.

But in such a phrase as, "the corporal Presence
of Christ's natural Flesh and Blood," the Presence
of His Body is already expressed by the words
"Flesh and Blood;" so that, unless the word "corporal" expressed, not the fact of the Presence of
Christ's Body, but the mode of Its Presence, it
would be mere tautology. It is incorrect to say
"*corporal*" or "*bodily* Presence of a *body*," meaning
thereby simply the presence of that body. The
word "Corporal" is an adjéctive, expressing, as (ad-
jectives do) some quality of that with which it is
joined. The words, "*corporal* Presence of Christ's
natural Flesh and Blood," must then mean His
"Natural Flesh and Blood present after a corporal
manner or after the manner of a body." No one could
argue, that the "*corporal* Presence of Christ's natural Flesh and Blood" was one and the same with
the "*spiritual* Presence of Christ's natural Flesh and
Blood;" or "an *immaterial* Presence of Christ's
natural Flesh and Blood." The words "corporal,"
"spiritual," "immaterial," are plainly added in the
respective sentences, in order to express the *mode*
of the presence of that Body. Mr. Goode grants,
for the time, that "a human body [our Lord's

[d] 2 Cor. x. 20.   [e] Du Cange v. Corporalis.

Human Body] can be present in an immaterial form," i. e. that God's Omnipotency can effect this. He says, "if a human body can be present in an immaterial form, there can be a corporal presence [i. e. the presence of a body] of an immaterial kind." This is, in truth, only to say the same thing over again in other words. But then it is incorrect to transfer the word "corporal" to the other part of the sentence, where it defines the mode of the existence of that body; and having just conceded that a body *can* be present in an immaterial form, to infer, in fact, that because it is a *body* which is present, it can only be present in a *corporal* way, i. e. *not* in an immaterial form. The fallacy is, that Mr. Goode uses the words "corporal presence" in the sense of "the presence of a body" and then would transfer it to the rubric, where it is used of the *mode* of the Presence of that Body. The belief that our Lord's Body is "present in an immaterial form," would be expressed by the words, "the *immaterial* Presence of Christ's Natural Body and Blood;" not by the words, "the Corporal Presence of Christ's Natural Body and Blood." Since then this belief in "the *immaterial* or *spiritual* Presence of Christ's Body and Blood" would not be expressed by the term "the *Corporal* Presence of Christ's natural Flesh and Blood," neither can it be condemned under those terms.

Both, the original framers of the rubric, and those who reformed it, clearly saw the value and importance of the word, by which the phrase "the Presence of the Body and Blood of Christ" should be described and qualified. They who first framed the sentence, moulded it carefully to exclude the Real Presence altogether. Happily, what authority they had, came from the State, not from the Church; and so the early death of Edward VI. cut short their work. But they framed their words effectually for their purpose, to exclude any "real or essential Presence." "No adoration," they said, "is intended, or ought to be done, unto any *real and essential* Presence of Christ's natural Flesh and Blood." The reformers of the Rubric carefully expunged the words "real and essential," and substituted the word "corporal." It is a mere paradox to say, that the framers and reformers of the Rubric meant the same thing; and that while its reformers deliberately ejected what its framers deliberately inserted, it is all one as if they had not ejected it and substituted another word.

2. The other objection is, that "[f] the rubric was intended to oppose the doctrine of the Church of Rome;" and that

"the Church of Rome does not mean by 'corporal presence,' a gross material presence, but precisely that sort of presence which is imagined by the writers under review, namely a substantial presence of the body after a supernatural manner in a spiritual and immaterial form."

I have already shewn, that the rubric was not directed against the doctrine of the Church of Rome, but was brought in at the request of the non-Conformists, who objected to the act of kneeling at the Holy Communion. Further, Mr. Goode himself shews, that the words "corporal presence of Christ's

[f] Mr. Goode, p. 623.

natural Flesh and Blood" do not express the doctrine of the Roman Church. The Council of Trent has no such language. Bellarmine expressly disclaims it [g].

"Adverbs, which assert a corporal mode of existing are not used of Christ in the Eucharist, although they are said of Him, as He resides in heaven; other adverbs, nothing hinders from being used. The reason is, that (as we have often said) Christ in the Eucharist hath not the mode of existence, which bodies have, but rather that of spirits, since He is wholly in every part. So then we shall say, that Christ is in the Eucharist, 'truly, really, substantially,' (as the Council rightly speaks) but we shall not say 'corporally,' i. e. in that manner in which bodies exist of their own nature; nor 'sensibly, moveably,' &c. Yea, it might be said, on the contrary, that He is there spiritually, as Bernard saith in the sermon on S. Martin, where he affirms that 'the true substance of the Flesh is exhibited to us, yet spiritually, not carnally.' Yet it does not seem that this word is much to be used; for there would be danger, lest it should be drawn by the adversaries to denote, not so much the mode [of the existence of Christ's Body] as the Nature Itself [i. e. that what is given in the Holy Eucharist is not the Body of Christ, but His Spirit]; on account of which same peril it does not seem, that the saying, 'that He is not there corporally,' is much to be used, unless an explanation be forthwith added."

So far then from the phrase, "the *corporal* Presence of Christ's natural Flesh and Blood," being a phrase of the Roman Church, it would, according to Bellarmine, be an incorrect phrase. Bellarmine even pronounces the phrase, "Christ is present corporally," incorrect, and he only dissuades from the

g De Euch. ii. 2.

absolute negative, "Christ is *not* present corporally," for fear it should be understood in the meaning that "His Body is not present, really though spiritually." The Council of Trent (in a passage which I have already alleged[h] as agreeing with one of the Lutheran Gerhard in regard to the Real Presence of our Lord in the Holy Eucharist) uses only the words "really, truly, substantially," and "sacramentally;" and denies, as well as our rubric, that our Lord is present in the Holy Eucharist, "according to the *natural* mode of existing," in which it asserts that "He for ever sitteth at the Right Hand of the Father."

"For neither are these things mutually repugnant, that our Saviour Himself sitteth at the Right Hand of the Father in heaven, *according to the natural mode of existing,* and that, nevertheless, He be, in many other places, sacramentally present unto us in His own substance, by that manner of existing which, though we can scarcely express it in words, we yet can, by the understanding illuminated by faith, suppose, and ought most faithfully to believe, to be possible with God."

We have then no reason (but the contrary) to think that the statement in that Declaration is directed against a doctrine which it does not express.

There is only one way in which the words can be explained, according to the idiom of our language. The words, "the *supernatural* Presence of His Flesh and Blood," would signify, "His natural Flesh and Blood present after a *supernatural* way"; the words, "The *spiritual* Presence of His natural Flesh and

<hr>

[h] **Real Presence, p. 55.**

Blood," would signify that His Flesh and Blood are "present after a spiritual way;" the words, "the *sacramental* Presence of His natural Flesh and Blood," would express that His Body and Blood are "present in a *sacramental* way," i. e. in a manner proper to a Sacrament; the words, "The *ineffable* Presence of His natural Flesh and Blood," would denote that that Blessed Body and Blood are "present in an *ineffable* way," i. e. a way which we have no words to utter.   So, then, a "corporal Presence of His natural Flesh and Blood," must mean that that Body and Blood are "present in a corporal way," i. e. after the manner in which bodies ordinarily exist.

The principle so clearly stated by Bp. Andrewes, "Christ Himself, the substance of the Sacrament, in and with the Sacrament, out of and without the Sacrament, is, wherever He is, to be adored," would, in itself, recommend itself to any pious mind. Wherever our Lord and Saviour is, *there* He is to be adored.   For He is Very God.   God is set forth to us as "dwelling in the heavens" i. e. not on earth only, but in all imaginable created space, that we may not conceive of Him (as the Heathen did) as bounded by space or limited to this earth, where also we do not see Him, as He Is, in His Glory.   Still, at all times He has given to man special places on earth, where to worship Him.   When, in the time of Enos, grandson of Adam, "[1] men began to call on the Name of the Lord," they not only worshipped in public together (as the word implies), but they worshipped probably in some fixed place.   Abraham, Isaac and Jacob all worshipped in places where

----

[1] Gen. iv. 26.

God appeared to them, as specially present there. The Holy Ghost has authenticated the words of Jacob, "Surely the Lord is in this place, and I knew it not." Abraham "[j]fell on his face" "before God," when God appeared unto him. Jacob "[k]made supplication to God," in the Angel who appeared to him at Peniel. To Moses God appeared locally in the flame of fire in a bush and bade him shew signs of reverence; "put off thy shoes from off thy feet, for the place whereon thou standest is holy ground." In the Tabernacle "[l]the Glory of the Lord appeared unto all the people, and a fire came out from before the Lord, and consumed the sacrifice, and the people fell on their faces." In the times of Joshua and the Judges, as in those of the Patriarchs, God accustomed man to see and adore Him, in a created form. Whether it was the Father, or (as so many of the Fathers believed) the Son who appeared, it was the invisible God, Whom they, or the Prophets afterwards, worshipped, or offered sacrifice to, under the form of man, or of the Angel of the Lord, or of His created Glory[m]. Solomon knew, and spake by the Holy Ghost, that[n] "the heaven and heaven of heavens cannot contain" God, "how much less this house that I have builded!" Yet there, in that house, God appeared by His Glory; there He was worshipped: thitherward[o] did they pray; there did "He place His Name."

[j] Gen. xix. 3.   [k] Hos. xii. 4.   [l] Lev. ix. 23, 4.

[m] Jos. v. 14. Jud. ii. 1—5; vi. 11—23; xiii. 3—23. 1 Chr. xxi. 15, 16. Ezek. i. 28; iii. 23; xliii. 3; xliv. 4. Dan. viii. 17.

[n] 1 Kings viii. 27.   [o] Ib. 30, 35, 42, 44, 48.   Dan. vi. 10.

The pure worship then, of the Infinite God, in and beyond all the heavens and the heaven of heavens, not contained by them, but containing them, was perfectly compatible with a worship of Him on earth, wherever He made His presence certainly known, whether under the form of man or of an Angel or of created fire. Not the created fire, or any created form was worshipped, but the invisible God under them, and present with them.

Idolatry was for man 1) to worship any created thing or being, or any creature of his imagination, as God, besides the one true God. This was forbidden by the first commandment; "Thou shalt have no other gods besides Me." Or 2) it was, for man to invent forms for himself, whereby to symbolise the Invisible God, and to worship Him under any symbols which God had not ordained, and where, consequently, He is not present in any special way of His own appointment. This was forbidden in the second Commandment, "Thou shalt not make *to thyself* any graven image, nor the likeness of any thing in heaven above or in the earth beneath, or in the waters under the earth. Thou shalt not bow down to them nor worship them." But the presence of a material object, or of a creature, did not, in itself, interfere with the spiritual worship of God, present there. Nay, they were precisely the most spiritual persons of the Old Testament, those to whom, above others, God foreshowed the Day of Christ—Abraham, "the friend of God," and the Patriarchs, Isaac and Jacob; Moses, to whom He "spake face to face;" and Joshua and Ezekiel and Daniel—to these among the most eminent saints of the Old Testament, did God reveal Himself, and receive worship under some created form.

It is, then, in analogy with God's way under the older dispensation, that the Church has ever worshipped our Lord truly and spiritually present in the Sacrament, notwithstanding that, locally and after the natural manner of the existence of a body, His Human Nature is at the Right Hand of God in Heaven.

As it was no derogation to the spirituality of God's Being, or to the belief in His Presence everywhere, that, in the Old Testament, He willed to be worshipped in the Shechinah or created glory, whereby He Who is Omnipresent, marked out that He was present in that spot, so neither is it any derogation to our Lord's Divine Person, that the Church worshipped *Him* in the Sacrament of His Body and Blood, Who, as our Intercessor, and in His natural mode of being, is at the Right Hand of God. We are in danger of derogating from God, when we would do Him honour of ourselves, not when we receive simply what He tells us. When people, in order to represent to themselves God's Infinity, conceive of Him as diffused through unbounded space, they lower their belief in that Infinity, the more they aim at approaching some adequate conception of it. Although the whole of God is nowhere, it *is* true to conceive of God, as being wholly in one spot of this earth. For God is Indivisible. It is *not* true, to conceive of God, as diffused everywhere, if we attach to this thought any idea of extension or parts, or of the finest imaginable matter, or (as we think) spirit, or any other mode of conception, which interferes with His absolute simplicity of Being. Does it seem a strange thing that, in the language of the second century, "[p] Thou holdest Jesus Christ, the Son of God, the Saviour, in thy two hands?" How is it stranger, than that the Babe, bound in swaddling clothes and lying in a manger, motionless, speechless, helpless, was Almighty God? Nestorius scoffed and said, "[q] One, who is two or three months old, I will not call God." The wise men saw and worshipped; owning, too, by their presence, that He, Whom they reverenced as a King and worshipped as God, should, as Man, die.

The question, then, as to the Adoration of our Lord present in the Holy Eucharist, should be considered, apart from any notion of seeming unfitness. People have profanely spoken of " wafer-gods." They might as well have spoken of " fire-gods," of the manifestation of God in the flaming fire in the bush; or "light-gods," of His manifestation in the tabernacle and the temple; or " human-gods " or " angel-gods," of His appearance to the Patriarchs and Prophets. Much more, might they have used the title, " Infant God," as a term of reproach against the " Holy Child Jesus."

The simple question is, "Is our Lord and God present there ?" If, or rather since, He is present there, the outward appearance is no more hindrance to us, than the dress which He wore as Man. St. Thomas, when he fell down and cried "My Lord,

---

[p] Inscription at Autun. See Real Presence, p. 337, 8.

[q] Relat. Synod. Eph. ad Imp. P. ii. Act. 1. n. 7. T. iii. p. 1100. ed. Col.

and my God," regarded not what raiment his Lord wore after His Resurrection.

But "[r] in that Sacrament Christ is," as S. Ambrose saith, "because it is the Body of Christ." "[s] For Christ is not divided, but is One."

Inseparable both from His Body and His Soul was the Godhead of Christ. It indwelt His Body, when that Body lay lifeless in the tomb. It descended with His Soul into Hell, a terror to the powers of darkness. Inseparable is His Godhead from His Body, in any way of Being, Natural or Supernatural. This follows from the doctrine of the Incarnation, that God the Son "[t] took man's nature in the womb of the Blessed Virgin of her substance; so that two whole and perfect natures, that is to say, the Godhead and Manhood, were joined together in One Person, never to be divided." Where God's Almighty Word caused His Body to be, in whatever mode of being, *there* His Godhead is, because It is inseparable; *there* is Christ Himself, our Redeeming Lord, the Object of our thankfulness, and reverence, and love, and Adoration.

The Ancient Church then did not so much teach that He was to be adored there; but, rather, it in fact adored Him. "*That* earth," says S. Ambrose[u], "is to be adored, which the Lord Jesus, by assuming Flesh, took upon Him;"—"the Flesh of Christ, which now too we, in Mysteries, adore, and which the Apostles adore in the Lord Jesus." In like way, S. Gregory of Nazianzus says of his sister[v], " She falls in faith before the Altar, and calls upon

---

[r] Real Pres. p. 461.   [s] Ib. p. 465.   [t] Art. ii.
              [u] l. c.   [v] Real Pres. p. 436.

Him Who is *honoured* thereupon." And Theodoret asserts at once, that [w] "the mystic symbols do
not depart from their own nature; for they remain
in their former substance and figure and form, and
can be seen and touched as before; but," he adds,
"in thought they *are* conceived and believed and
adored, as being those things which are believed."
And S. Augustine[x], "Because He walked here in very
Flesh, and gave that very Flesh for us to eat, for
our salvation; and no one eateth that Flesh, unless
he hath first worshipped; we have found out in
what sense such a footstool of our Lord's [Ps. 99. 5]
may be worshipped, and not only we sin not in worshipping, but that we sin in not worshipping."

These, in different Churches, speak not their own
opinion, but of the existing worship. "She calls
upon Him who *is honoured* on the Altar;" "the Flesh
which *we*, in mysteries, *adore;*" "they *are believed
and adored.*" "No one *eateth* that Flesh, unless he
hath first worshipped." The structure of their words
in itself shows that they are speaking, not of what
they thought should be done, but of what was done.
They say, "is honoured," "we adore," "are adored;"
words which could only be used of actual practice.
Immediately, they attest the worship of Italy and
Africa, and the Patriarchate of Antioch. But what
they speak of without any limitation, as the existing
mode of worship, was, beyond all doubt, the worship
of the whole world. "What is the Altar," says S.
Optatus [y], "but the throne of the Body and Blood of
Christ?" "Here too," says S. Chrysostome [z], "will the
Lord's Body lie; not wrapped in swaddling clothes,

[w] Ib. p. 86.   [x] Ib. p. 521.   [y] Ib. p. 408.   [z] Ib. p. 548.

as then, but encircled all round by the Holy Ghost."
Nay, it had been seen in vision, how angels also
worshipped there. "I once heard one relate," says
S. Chrysostome[a], "that a certain wonderful old man,
accustomed to see visions, said that such a vision
was once vouchsafed him, and at that time [of the
consecration] he suddenly saw, as man might see, a
multitude of Angels clothed in white robes, and en-
circling the Altar, and bowing down, as one might
see soldiers standing in the presence of the King.
And," adds S. Chrysostome, "I believe it."

Some of those, indeed, who denied the doctrine
of the Real Presence, saw clearly that the Adoration of our Lord, thus present, is the legitimate
consequence of the belief in that Presence. Calvin
and the Zurich Zwinglians used it as an argument
ad invidiam against Luther and the Lutherans.

"In vain," says Calvin[b], "does he reject the inference;
'The Body is in the bread, therefore the bread is to be
adored.' *For so have we ever reasoned,* 'if Christ is in the
bread, He is, with the bread, to be adored.'"

Calvin was far too acute, not to have been con-
scious, that he was arguing sophistically in both
these instances. He knew too well the process of
reasoning, not to know that both inferences were
palpable fallacies. Had it been a valid inference,
"The Body is in the bread, therefore the bread is
to be adored," then it would have been a valid inference as to our Blessed Lord's raiment when He was
on earth, "His Body is beneath that raiment, there-

[a] Ib. p. 547.   [b] Opp. viii. 727.

fore the raiment is to be adored."   Had that other argument been valid, "If Christ is in the bread, He is, *with the bread*, to be adored," then it would have been valid to say, "If God was in the flaming fire in the bush, then God was, with the flaming fire, to be adored;" or, "If God, when He spake in the Angel to Manoah and accepted his sacrifice, was present in that Angel, then God was, with the Angel, to be adored."

It is the known test of a correct form of reasoning, that the same form of reasoning must be applicable to every other subject.   But Calvin's fallacy rested on the acknowledgment of the truth, "where Christ is, *there* He is to be adored."   His fallacy was, that he threw in the words, "with the bread," as if, because God was present with or amid His creature, therefore the creature was to be worshipped with God.

In like way, the Ministers of Zurich taunted Luther with inconsistency, for inveighing against the festival of Corpus Christi.

" ᶜHe inveighs terribly and heavily against his Papist friends on account of this festival, and does not avow openly with them that the Sacrament ought to be adored.   What then?   The bread is the true and natural Body of Christ: and in the Supper Christ is present, truly and corporally (as the Pope and Luther teach).   *Why then ought not the Lord to be adored there, where you say that He is present?*   Why should we be prohibited to adore that, which not sacramentally only, but corporally also, is the Body of Christ?   Thomas feeleth the true Body of Christ, risen from the dead, and falling on his knees, adores, saying, ' My Lord and my God.'   The disciples adore the Lord, both before and

ᶜ Tractat. A. 1545. p. 98, 9.

after the Resurrection (Matt. xxviii. Acts i.). And the Lord, in John (c. ix.), says to the blind man; 'Believest thou in the Son of God?' 'And he said, Lord, I believe; and he worshipped Him.' If we taught that the bread of the Lord was the natural Body of Christ, we should also certainly, with the Papists, faithfully worship Him."

On the other hand, Chemnitz, even while criticising the Council of Trent, vindicates clearly the principles on which we adore our Lord present in the Sacrament [d].

" First, it must be shewn, what, in this fifth chapter and sixth Canon, is the matter of controversy. For some things, I readily admit, are uncontroverted. For that Christ, God and Man, is to be adored, no one but an Arian denies. And that His Human Nature also, on account of Its union with His Godhead, is to be adored, no one but a Nestorian questions. For when the Eternal Father brought the Only Begotten Son into world, He saith, 'Let all the Angels worship Him.' As Matthew also plainly beareth witness (c. xxviii.) that the Apostles in Galilee worshipped Christ. It is certain moreover, that the adoration of God is not tied to place or time. (John iv. 1 Tim. ii.) Christ then, at all times and in all places, is to be adored. If then we believe, that Christ, God and Man, is, in a peculiar mode of presence and of grace, present at the celebration of His Supper, so that He there, truly and substantially, exhibits to communicants His own Body and Blood, whereby He willeth so to unite Himself with us, that to each who receives with faith, He, by this most precious pledge, applies and seals the gifts of the New Testament, which, through the giving up of His Body and the shedding of His Blood, He obtained for His Church;—if, I say, we believe these things truly, from our heart, it neither can nor ought to be but that faith should venerate and adore Christ, present in

[d] Exam. Conc. Trid. P. 2. Sess. 13. c. 5.

that action.   So Jacob (Gen. xviii.), Moses (Exod. xxxiv.), Elijah (1 Kings xix.) had no special command to worship God in those places; but, since they had a general command to worship God everywhere, and were certain, that God was truly present under outward and visible symbols, and that He was revealing Himself there in a special and gracious manner, they assuredly worshipped God Himself there, Whom they believed to be present there.   Nor would their faith have been true, if invocation or adoration, i. e. the honour due to God, had not followed."

Why should we think it a strange thing, to worship our Redeeming Lord, wherever He says that He is to be found.   We do not think that we are localising the Infinite God, if we conceive of Him in space, and adore Him *in* the highest heavens. Yet He comprehendeth the heavens, not they Him, the Infinite.   We do not think that we are tying down our Lord's Divine Nature, if we believe, that He, our Lord and God, is, as He promised, specially present where two or three are gathered together in His Name, in our Churches, or in the mountains and caves and dens of the earth, in the prison-house or the Catacombs.   We think it no degradation to Him, the Infinite God, that He did not abhor the Virgin's womb, or that He lay in the manger amid the brute cattle, or was bound in swaddling clothes. Believing, as we believe, we should, with the Magi, have fallen down and worshipped the speechless Infant, knowing Him to be God, the Word.   We should have thought His raiment, as man, no hindrance to our adoring Him.   Why then should we think it too strange a thing for His marvellous condescension, that He should now give us "His blessed Body and Blood under the form of bread and wine?"

Or how should His Body which He gives us, not be His living, life-giving Body? Or how should His life-giving Body be apart from His Godhead, which makes It life-giving? Or how, since His Godhead is present there, should we not adore? We do not adore the Sacrament; as, when He was upon the earth, we should not have adored His raiment, even although the touch of it conveyed the hidden virtue from Him, the Source of life and healing. But Himself, wheresoever or howsoever He is present, we are bound to adore. Our duty to Him as His creatures, our love to Him as our Redeemer, our hopes in Him as our Deliverer from the wrath to come, constrain us to worship Him, to plead to Him, with our whole heart, and mind, and soul, and strength.

And while we adore Him, we would own to Him, "*That* is not the deep condescension of Thy love, O Lord, that Thou vouchsafed to come to us, under these forms of Thy creatures. Senseless and inanimate though they be, *they* never sinned against Thy love. *The* miracle of Thy mercy is it, that Thou thus vouchsafest to come to *me* the utter sinner, Thy poor sinner. Out of the abyss of my nothingness, I adore the abyss of Thine All-Mercifulness, my Saviour and my God. Lord, make me to love Thee, as Thy love deserveth; make me to humble myself before Thy humility; fit me, all unworthy as I am, O Lord, to receive Thee, my God and my All."

Thanks be to God.

APPENDIX TO CHAPTER I.

In the above argument, I have dwelt as little as possible upon the statements of Mr. Goode, both, because I wish to avoid, as much as may be, personal controversy, and because I did not wish to interrupt the argument by personal details. It may be useful, however, while that history is fresh in the memory, briefly to examine the passage of Hospinian, upon which Mr. Goode has grounded a charge of, at least, very culpable carelessness against me. It will shew how unsafe it is, to rest such charges on the statements of party writers, such as was Hospinian.

Hospinian wrote his book against the Formula Concordiæ, which established, for Lutheranism, the original Confessions of Augsburg, and disavowed the change made in the Latin in 1540. He wished to make out that Luther and Zwingli taught the same doctrine as to the Presence of Christ in the Holy Eucharist. The 10th Article, especially in the German copy, stood in his way. So he has two theories to account for it; 1) that it was dishonestly framed by the Lutherans, in order to avoid irritating the Emperor; that it expressed belief in Transubstantiation, which the Reformers who composed it, and the Princes who presented it, did not hold; that when it came out against their knowledge, they [*he* does not *say*, " falsely "] falsely and most dishonestly disavowed it and substituted for it the Latin form. 2) That the words, not perversely interpreted, do not contradict Zwinglianism. These solutions contradict one another, and are alike unfounded. It would indeed be a strange power of language, that the same words

should express Transubstantiation, or the belief that the
natural substances do not remain, and fit in with Zwinglianism, or the belief that nothing is present save those substances.   I will give first his assertion that the statement is
compatible with Zwinglianism; then, his so-called proof
that it is identical with the Roman doctrine. He winds up
thus [a];

"But even by these very words of the Confession, if taken, not
according to the absurd glosses of contentious men, but according
to the subsequent interpretations of the Confession itself, the
harmony of the Churches who follow the doctrine of Zwingli,
with the Confession of Augsburg, is not removed, as is learnedly
indicated in the 'Neustadt monition.'"

Hospinian's other theory is grounded on the supposition
that the Princes at Augsburg withdrew the *German* Confession which they there subscribed. How it happened
that Hospinian, although a Swiss, living close upon the
times of the Confession, having large access to documents
then unprinted, professing to give a history of it, could fail to
have learned that the German Confession which he quoted,
had been recognized and was of authority among the Lutherans from the time when it was presented until then, I
know not.   For myself I became acquainted with the
Lutheran Confessions in their Latin form; and so, I suppose, did Mr. Goode; and we were, so far, alike misled by
Hospinian.

Hospinian's account of the German Confession is,

" In the exceeding fear of present perils, which the adversaries,
the Papists, were creating to those who professed the Gospel, with
the Emperor and other princes, by atrocious calumnies and cruel
counsels and incitements, the Confession of Augsburg was written,
most softly, and more languidly than ought to have been, out of
the desire of adapting themselves to the opinions and language of
the Papists, as Philip openly attests in his letter to Luther, and
Luther himself professes, that he could not have used such moderation and mildness."

[a] Hist. Sacr. ii. 156.

It is one thing to speak mildly of the belief of an opponent; another to suppress what one believes, when professing to declare that belief, or to declare, either in false or ambiguous terms, what one believes or teaches. The Lutherans were now formally stating their belief in order to obtain toleration, and, as they thought, bearing witness to the truth. To set forth what was taught among them, untruly or ambiguously, while professing to declare the whole truth, would not have been "mildness," but cowardice, faithlessness, lying, and hypocrisy.

Hospinian proceeds;

"*Hence* [i. e. to avoid offending the Emperor by avowing the truth] the 10th Article in the first German Wittenberg edition stands thus: 'Of the Lord's Supper it is thus taught, that the true Body and Blood of Christ are truly present under the species of bread and wine, and in it are distributed and received: wherefore also the contrary doctrine is rejected.'"

What Hospinian here quotes, as "the *first* German Wittenberg edition," is the authorised German edition, which Melanchthon put forth, which he never altered, which he appealed to as authentic.

"[b] These words indicate that *not the substance, but only the form* of bread and wine is present, and covers the Body of Christ, lying hidden under each form through the concomitance of the flesh and blood. Moreover *these words are accepted by the Papists as agreeing with their own views*, as the Confutation opposed by the Papist to the Confession shews."

Mr. Goode adds in explanation;

"That Confutation expressly says 'Decimus Articulus in *verbis nihil offendit*.'"

1) Charles V. gave to the authors of the "Confutation" to refute, not the *German* form of the Confession in which the words "under the form of bread and wine" occur, but the *Latin*[c] form of the Article, in which they do *not* occur.

[b] Hospinian quoted by Mr. Goode, p. 42.
[c] See above, p. 29.

2) Of this *Latin* form, the authors of the Confutation say, that "it did not *offend in words*," i. e. in what it expressed, *provided only* that those doctrines which it did not contain, were *added*, Concomitance and Transubstantiation [d]. The Roman Controversialists declare that those doctrines were wanting to the Confession of Augsburg, which Hospinian declares that it contains. And plainly they were right in this.

"And he says that Lindymus whom the rest of the Jesuits follow, asserts that, at first, the doctrine and *the very words* of the Confession of Augsburg were the same with the doctrine and words of the Papists concerning the change of the mystical bread into the Body of the Lord."

I have not access to one of the works here quoted by Hospinian. The other does not contain these words. Lindanus was writing to the Wittenburg divines, who had abandoned Luther's doctrine, and he urged against them the inconsistency of their position, as being themselves Lutherans, but abandoning, in a great article of faith, what Luther taught. It is a very common thing, with Roman Controversialists, to infer belief of Transubstantiation, from belief in the Real Presence. But when it was the question of making a formal theological statement, they ever added the doctrine of Transubstantiation, thereby confessing that it did not lie in these words.

"And in proof he [Lindanus] alleges copies of the Confession of Augsburg first published in German, and the Apology in which mention is made of the kind of bread, under which the true Body and Blood of Christ are present, and the change of the bread into the Body of Christ is asserted."

So then Lindanus quotes the Apology, in which the elements are twice spoken of, as remaining in their natural substances, in proof that the Lutherans taught Transubstantiation, as much as he quotes this German copy.

Hospinian proceeds ;

"For this cause, not all even among the Princes who had given

d Above, p. 49.

their names to the Confession of Augsburg, assented to the words of the tenth Article, in which the substantial presence and distribution of the true Body and Blood of Christ under the species of bread and wine is asserted, and the contrary doctrine is disapproved. For Philip Landgrave of Hesse, as his letters attest, contradicted this article early, even at the very Diet of Augsburg, as Chytræus attests most plainly in the history of the Confession of Augsburg."

1) The Landgrave as a politician, wished to strengthen, as he thought, the Protestant cause by alliance with the Swiss. Melanchthon, before his arrival at Augsburg, rather describes his belief, as shaken by letters from the Swiss, and as needing to be strengthened. No opposition of his is recorded; he hesitated, but signed the Confession [e].

But, 2) of what moment, had he been a Zwinglian alto-

---

[e] Melanchthon, in the letter quoted by Chytræus, is speaking of the Landgrave before he arrived at Augsburg, and then too, as vacillating; "the Chancellor of the Hessian came yesterday, and said that his Prince was on the road. With him came Schnepf, a good man, who loves you very greatly, who held out some hope that his Prince could be retained in his duty, although he does not conceal that there is great peril. He relates what a contest he had with him on the Lord's Supper. He says that he is marvellously pressed by constant letters of the Swiss, and that Surio Strum returns to him almost every month, to spur him on, eager already. This tortures me greatly. Perhaps it is of use, that you should write to him, or at least to our younger prince, *to confirm the mind* of the Macedonian [Philip] in *sound doctrine*. He seems often to be impelled by slight pushes." (Mel. Luth. May 4. C. R. 679.) May 11, the Landgrave was expected "on that day or the next." (Mel. Vit. Ib. 686.) Eleven days afterwards, when the Confession was not yet finished, he was on the point of signing it. " Now the Macedonian is contriving to sign our Confession, and it seems that he may be brought back to ours'. I pray thee then most earnestly to write to him, and exhort him, not to load his conscience with the defence of any impious doctrine." (Mel. Luth. May 22. Ib. 698.)

gether? He was altogether and openly [f] an immoral man. He himself, in writing [g] drawn up for Bucer to shew to Luther and Melanchthon, alleges as a ground why they should sanction his bigamy, that he was habitually guilty of adultery, and that especially at Diets [such was that at Augsburg], and so could neither check sin in his subjects (as his preachers wished), nor himself communicate, since it would be to his damnation. He even threatened to leave Lutheranism [h], unless a dispensation were given him by Luther and the others to have a second wife.

3) The Landgrave, according to the statement of John

[f] "For the Emperor and the world tolerate me and every one who ' Huren offentlich haben.' " C. R. iii. p. 855.

[g] Memorial, was D. H. M. Bucerus bei D. M. Luthero und M. Ph. Mel. ausrichten soll. C. R. 1888. A.

[h] Melanchthon writes confidentially to his friend Veit Dietrich. "Know that we were deceived, not by Aretius Felinus [Bucer] but by Jason himself, [the Landgrave] under pretence of piety, who desired that, for necessary causes, his conscience might be consulted for, affirming too by oath, that he had need of this remedy. We answered, that the law must be retained as to that saying 'they two shall be one flesh:' but if there be such necessity, he should use it secretly and without public scandal. He threatened defection too, if we would not provide for him. He is altogether a crafty nature. I loved him for certain virtues. For I have heard him too discussing learnedly and eloquently on our controversies, as few could, and I thought him an enemy to idolatry, and thought that 'the leader of the people was to be honoured.' But he has the nature of Alcibiades, not of Achilles. For what this brave man [Achilles in Homer] says, ' I hate that man like the gates of hell, who hideth one thing in his breast, uttereth another,' that [Prince] of ours cares not for. Nor did he follow our counsel, mastered by passion. I could mention much more. But let us pray God, to heal this scandal. He himself says that he will make no public declaration. But in this very matter he has often held out one thing, done another. And I fear the beginning of insanity, which is in his family." (Vit. C. R. 1998.) Melanchthon's dread of the scandal from the publication nearly killed him. (See Ratzeberg in C. R. iii. p. xvii.)

Casimir, Elector Palatine, owned himself guilty of dishonesty, and charged the other Lutheran princes with the like. He is a credible witness against himself; no one would believe him against the Elector of Saxony. The El. Pal. writes to his father-in-law the Elector Augustus;

"[i] We have often heard from our beloved Cousin the Landgrave Philip (of blessed memory) that the Confession of Augsburg was framed according to the circumstances of that time, and so that the Elector and Princes could comfortably slip out at the door; but that afterwards since in it and the Apology what was at first obscure and doubtful was explained and amended, yet so that the foundation was retained, and such amendment was approved by common consent, which took place at Naumburg and Frankfort with the knowledge of your loved self, and notwithstanding such changes, and divers other Confessions which issued, the Papists when they have upbraided the States of the Confession of Augsburg therewith, have been solidly answered, that we should not look at the various forms, but at the foundation thereof, in which, God be praised, we are at one."

In "the *Frankfort* Recess," A. 1558, the Protestant Princes, and among them the Landgrave of Hesse, protested, in the most solemn way, to the Emperor, that they held exactly the same belief which was contained in their Confession of Augsburg, *presented to the Emperor in* 1530. In the convention of Naumburg, A. D. 1561, those Protestant Princes who owned the altered Latin Confession, owned it only as expressing more fully " the belief and trust in our Lord's Satisfaction and merits," not at all as to the Eucharist. The declaration of the Protestant Princes at Frankfort was made, to meet the imputation of varying their doctrine, " that it may not be given out that they are disposed to any innovation or divisions in doctrine."

"[k] Their Electoral and Princely Graces herewith, and in virtue of this Recess, do, knowingly, considerately, and freely, renew, repeat, attest, and confess, their oft-made and individual Confession—that they adhere to, follow, and conform to, the pure true, doctrine contained in the Divine, Prophetic, and Apostolic

[i] June 22, 1578, in Hosp. ii. p. 307.   [k] C. R. 6483. ix. 493.

writings of the O. and N. T. and also in the three great Creeds, and also of the Confession of Augsburg with its Apology, drawn from the aforesaid Prophetic and Apostolic doctrine, as a summary and body of doctrine, and agreeing therewith, and truly founded thereon, as the irrefragable main foundation, literally and in its right, true, uncorrupted meaning, *which in* 1530, *was at Augsburg, delivered to H. Imp. Maj.* our most gracious Lord, by the Electoral, Princely and other States. They purpose also, by the help of God, to provide, that the teaching, preaching, acting, in their Churches, be conformable to the aforementioned, well-known, doctrine, and not willingly and knowingly to tolerate or allow any room or place to, any contrary, seducing, erroneous opinions or sects, but steadfastly to abide and persevere to our lives' end, in the true only rule of the Divine, Prophetic, and Apostolic writings and also in the above-mentioned Confession and Apology of Augsburg."

If the Landgrave of Hesse, in presenting this, did not abide by the Confession presented in 1530, he plainly called God to witness to a lie.

" And that consequently, in the first authorised edition of the Confession, which appeared in 1531 in Latin, these words were altered, and great complaints were made of the German edition of 1530 as having been surreptitiously put forth, ab avaro aliquo typographo, without authority."

This whole statement is a mis-statement. 1) "The first authorised edition of the Confession in 1531," was not "in Latin " only, but in German also. 2) Neither the Latin nor the German was altered, but remained as the Princes and states had signed them, and with their signature. 3) The complaints were specially made of the Latin copy, not of the German. 4) They did not relate at all to the Article on the Holy Eucharist, which had been given accurately in both. The words which Hospinian supposed to have been suppressed, and to have been altered into the Latin form, are the exact words which Melanchthon then published authentically in the German, as being, together with the Latin, the words of the genuine Confession of Augsburg.

Mr. Goode sums up in his own words ;

" That which appears in the German edition was evidently, from the historical account given of the matter, a sketch drawn up by more timid hands, under the fear of the strongly expressed views of the Emperor on the subject."

The fact is, the " German Edition " was drawn up by the same hands of the same German Reformers, Luther, Melanchthon, &c. ; submitted to and accepted by the same authorities ; signed by the same Princes and States ; presented at the same time to the Emperor ; read, in preference to the Latin, at the express desire of the Elector of Saxony ; laid up, exclusively, in the State Archives ; reprinted by Melanchthon himself ; cited by him in explanation of the Latin ; laid as the foundation of conference with Roman Catholics ; unaltered in this article to the end ; embodied in the permanent symbolical books of the Lutherans, so long as they valued those books, and until they parted with faith altogether.

APPENDIX B.

Mr. Jenkins' statement as to the Synod of Petrikow of 1551, which he supposes to have occasioned the clause on the opus operatum to have been removed from the Articles in 1562, is as follows;

"[a] The National Synod of Piotrkow representing the whole Church of Poland had set forth only ten years before, the true definition on this subject and established the fact, which every reader of the schoolmen well knows, that the doctrine in question is never advanced against the qualification of the recipient, but against the supposition that the moral disqualification of the celebrant affects the validity of the Sacraments; in other words that the effect of the rite was *ex opus operante* instead of *ex opere operato.*"

To this Mr. Jenkins adds the note; "the Synod was held in 1551, and its acts (drawn up by the Archbishop of Gnesen) were published in Posen in 1557, i. e. between the publication of the Articles of 1552 and 1562."

The facts as to the Synod, as far as relates to this Confession of faith, are these;

The Bishops of Poland were suspected of inclining to the opinions, afloat at the time of the Reformation [b]. Mea-

[a] Strictures, p. 4.

[b] Neugebauer Hist. Rer. Pol. L. 8. A. 1551. p. 578. "At the same time a Synod was held at Petricow, in which Nicolas Dziergow, Archbishop of Gnesna, was carried on by great zeal against heretics, so that he added a new oath to the accustomed oath, since among the Bishops themselves, not a few were suspected of heresy."

sures were adopted in consequence, which Hosius Bp. of Warmerlaa, afterwards Cardinal, thus relates [c],

" This is now the eleventh year, since, in the provincial Synod of Petricow, at which Nicholas Dziergowski, Archbishop of Gnesna, presided, certain heads of doctrine were proposed, that the Bishops might deliver on oath their opinion respecting them. But since these statements were nakedly put forth, I was asked briefly to explain them and make them clearer, and commit to writing the matters demanded of the fathers, that they might better understand what that was, on which they were to deliver their opinion upon oath. This I set to work at diligently, as far as the shortness of time permitted, and after I had reduced to order those heads of doctrine, I endeavoured to confirm them by testimonies of Scripture and of the Fathers, and by probable reasons as well, that the fathers [Bishops] might be more easily induced to approve them. This my labour was not in vain. For as soon as the heads of doctrine had been read, which I had framed, all the Bishops who were then present, forthwith sware to them, and subscribed with their hands to the little book, which I had produced; nay, they decided also, that it should be printed. But since only four days had been allowed me for writing it, and the matter treated of was weighty and difficult, I begged the fathers not to decide hastily as to that writing, undertaking, at the same time, that within a few months, I would weigh more accurately, and polish up, enlarge and enrich what I had written. They assented without difficulty. But since the Archbishop was very pressing, and called upon me to hasten the publication, I, amid the varied cares with which I was then distracted, in two months, completed the first part only, which treated of faith and hope. This was printed at Cracow."

This first sketch, as he himself stated in his preface, was

[c] In his Preface to the Vienna edition of his work, Confessio Catholicæ Fidei Christianæ; vel potius explicatio quædam confessionis in Synodo Petricoviensi, &c.

twice reprinted at Dillingen. It appeared anonymously. Bishop Hosius enlarged it, at the request of the Archbishop of Gnesna. It became a very popular controversial work. It was printed very faultily at Maintz; reprinted, with its errors of press, at once at Antwerp and Paris; and then, under the care of the author, at Vienna, who again enlarged his work in what he called the third edition, which he published at Vienna in 1561. These manifold alterations and enlargements of his work shew how entirely Bishop Hosius regarded it as his own.

In this work, the term "opus operatum" is vindicated[d], yet not as to Sacraments generally, but as to the Eucharistic Sacrifice. The original statements, which the Bishops subscribed at Petrikow, are nowhere preserved. The first edition at Cracow had been *enlarged* from that original sketch, as the author himself tells us.

What Mr. Jenkins has mistaken for "Acts drawn up by the Archbishop of Gnesna, and published at Posen in 1557," is, I imagine, the Maintz edition of 1557, which bears in its title-page, that it was published chiefly at the expense of a Posen bookseller[e]. Certainly, Hosius himself knew of no "Acts" of the Synod; and the Bishops only accepted what he required them to swear. Bp. Hosius' work bears the title "Christian Confession of the Catholic Faith, or, rather, a sort of explanation of a Confession made in the Synod of Petricow by the fathers of the Provinces of Gnesna and Lemberg in the kingdom of Poland A. D. 1551."

It contains no fresh definition of the "opus operatum," but vindicates it, and, in proof that "the Mass has its value ex opere operato, not on account of the holiness or act of the priest, but on account of the saving Victim, of whose immolation a representation is then made[f]," cites the authors referred to by Mr. Jenkins.

---

[d] De cærem. a rebus sumptis. f. 277. ed. Vienna.

[e] The name of Maintz is, at the end of the volume.

[f] Hosius treats of the opus operatum, and with the same reference to the Mass only, de Sacram. Euch. fol. 93.